TENEBRAE

TENEBRAE

Holy Week after the Holocaust

THERESA SANDERS

ORBIS BOOKS

Maryknoll, New York 10545

Founded in 1970, Orbis Books endeavors to publish works that enlighten the mind, nourish the spirit, and challenge the conscience. The publishing arm of the Maryknoll Fathers and Brothers, Orbis seeks to explore the global dimensions of the Christian faith and mission, to invite dialogue with diverse cultures and religious traditions, and to serve the cause of reconciliation and peace. The books published reflect the views of their authors and do not represent the official position of the Maryknoll Society. To learn more about Maryknoll and Orbis Books, please visit our website at www.maryknoll.org.

Copyright © 2006 by Theresa Sanders.

Published by Orbis Books, Maryknoll, NY 10545-0308.

Manufactured in the United States of America.

Library of Congress Cataloging-in-Publication Data

Sanders, Theresa, 1963–
    Tenebrae : Holy week after the Holocaust / Theresa Sanders.
        p. cm.
    Includes bibliographical references and index.
    ISBN-13: 978-1-57075-685-6 (pbk.)
    ISBN-10: 1-57075-685-6
    1. Catholic Church—Relations—Judaism. 2. Judaism—
Relations—Catholic Church. 3. Holy Week services.
4. Christianity and antisemitism. 5. Holocaust, Jewish
(1939–1945) I. Title.
    BM535.S2145 2006
    261.2'6—dc22
                                                    2006013623

Contents

Preface   vii

Acknowledgments   xvii

1. The Convent and the Cross   1
   The Convent   1
   The Cross   13

2. Ash Wednesday   21
   Ash Wednesday: A History   24
   Celebrating Ash Wednesday   25
   Dust: Genesis and Return   31
   Dust and Ashes: The Book of Job   36
   Ashes to Ashes: Man-Made Mass Death   44

3. Palm Sunday   50
   The Passion of Jesus: Scripture   51
   The Passion of Jesus: Liturgy   52
   The Passion of Jesus: Music, Drama, and Film   55
   The Passion of Jesus: History   65

4. Holy Thursday, the Chrism Mass   78
   The Chrism Mass   80

5. Holy Thursday, the Mass of the Last Supper   87
   Evening Mass of the Lord's Supper   92

6. Good Friday   117
   You Judas!   118
   Good Friday: The Celebration of the
     Lord's Passion   127

7. Tenebrae   **141**
   "One Hesitates to Call Their Death Death"   147
   Tenebrae   151

8. **Easter and Beyond**   155
   The Easter Liturgy   158
   The Liturgy of the Word   161
   Jesus, Who Has Been Taken from You   166

9. **Conclusion**   174
   Notes for the Future   175

Notes   *180*

Works Cited   *203*

Index   *215*

   Biblical Passages   215
   Subjects   217

Preface

In the summer of 2003, I found myself traveling to Poland with the Holocaust Educational Foundation's East European study tour to visit the remains of the concentration and extermination camps that dot the Polish countryside. My fellow seminar participants, all educators in Holocaust studies, came from a variety of backgrounds and disciplines. I was the only theologian in the bunch, however, and I found myself paying particular attention to the role that Catholics and Catholicism played in the destruction of Europe's Jews.

It was particularly meaningful to me that twice—once while viewing the mass execution site at Majdanek, and once while standing outside the notorious Block 11 at Auschwitz—I had the strange experience of hearing church bells ringing out the hour. The contrast was appalling: churches proclaiming the good news of Christ, as around me lay the bones and ashes of millions of Jews who had been murdered in the heart of Christian Europe.

It was clear to me at that point that there is an urgent need within Catholicism to take seriously the challenges posed by the Holocaust. It is not simply a matter of sorting out what responsibility Catholics and their leaders had for the ghettos and for the death camps. That work is being done by several eminent historians and will no doubt take many years to complete. The more difficult task, however, is to make contemporary Catholicism the focus of serious, sustained scrutiny to see how it might still be contributing to hatred against Jews or, at the very least, benefiting from such hatred. In the contemporary world a tremendous amount of energy is focused on vilifying Jews and Judaism, despite the fact that Jews constitute only a very tiny minority of the world's population. There is a pressing need to investigate Catholicism to see if somehow it might in some way be bound up with what has come to be called "the longest hatred."

To put the issue in more concrete terms: In the past several years, several careful scholarly works, as well as some works less careful and less scholarly, have been published regarding the activities of the Vatican and its churches during the Second World War. One particularly thorny issue concerns Rome's willingness to sign a Concordat with the Nazi government. That agreement guaranteed the Church freedom to operate within German lands, but at the same time it prohibited the Church from meddling in politics. Thus, when the Nazis began to implement their plan to destroy Jews, the Vatican's ability to protest had already been considerably weakened. Defenders of Rome's decision to sign the pact point out that if such a compromise had not been reached, the Church would simply have been expelled from Germany altogether. In that case, defenders say, the pope would have lost even what little authority he had. Signing the Concordat, they insist, guaranteed the Church its survival.

However, the question that must be asked is this: Survival towards what end? With what voice does the Church now speak, now that it has witnessed the slaughter of nearly all of Europe's Jews? What now is its identity? What, with hindsight, would it have done differently in the face of the massacre, and what action will it take in the future should an attempt be made to destroy the remnant that Hitler left behind?

These are questions not of history but of mission. They cut to the very heart of the Church's ongoing life and self-understanding. As Pope John Paul II has put the matter, "The fact that the *Shoah* took place in Europe, that is, in countries of long-standing Christian civilization, raises the question of the relation between the Nazi persecution and the attitudes down the centuries of Christians towards the Jews."[1] It is a question with potentially devastating consequences. Elie Wiesel has said that the Holocaust is not a Jewish problem but rather a Christian problem. Catholicism must face deeply frightening questions about its place among the ashes of so many millions of Jewish children, women, and men. How can its festivals be celebrated and its symbols venerated after six million were murdered within earshot of its churches? Trying to find an answer to that question is the purpose of this book.

In truth, the book is intended as an experiment. It is an attempt to rethink both the symbol of the cross and the cycle of liturgies that, year in and year out, give the cross context and meaning. One of the most important periods in this respect is Holy Week, and it is to these days that I have turned my attention. These seven days precede Easter and mark the end of the Lenten season. By looking at the liturgies, scriptural portions, rituals, and themes that characterize this period (as well as at Ash Wednesday, which begins the season of Lent, and at Easter and the Feast of the Ascension, which follow it), I hope to find where they provide resources for a future in which another Holocaust would become unthinkable.

In choosing which elements of Holy Week to focus on, I have of necessity been somewhat inconsistent. Some chapters attend closely to a particular reading or psalm, for example, while others give the scriptural texts only cursory attention in order to consider broader themes or cultural implications. No doubt other authors would make different choices. The overall thesis of the book is that Holy Week is best understood as, in the words of Catholic theologian Karl Rahner, a festival of holy pain.[2] It is a week that marks the human longing for God, even as it directs our attention to the spaces where the causes of God, the causes of justice and healing and dignity, might be served.

These questions were not always at the forefront of my thinking. I remember very clearly the day in 1982 when a Jewish historian came to speak to my college classmates and me about antisemitism. The course we were taking, an introduction to the study of religion, was required of all students, and most of us were less than enthusiastic about it. But a guest speaker was a novel distraction, so I listened with interest as he began his presentation. His opening question took me by surprise: "What, historically, has been the reason Christians have used to justify persecution of Jews?" None of us answered. In truth, it had never occurred to me that Christians *had* persecuted Jews.

I had grown up in Youngstown, Ohio, a once-booming steel town that voted Democrat and prayed Catholic. There were a few Jewish students in the parochial schools I attended, but their presence didn't attract any particular attention that I knew of. On my block lived one Jewish family, and at the top of our street was a temple, the parking lot of which served as a gathering place for the neighborhood children. There we were allowed to play hopscotch and freeze-tag and Double Dutch, and we were even permitted to hit tennis balls against the windowless side of the temple's social hall. My experience with Jews and Judaism was thus both pleasant and limited. It had truly never occurred to me that Christians and Jews had ever had anything but a cordial, if distant, relationship with one another.

I knew, of course, about the Holocaust, and as a high school student I had watched the famous television miniseries by that name when it aired in 1978. But the events I saw on the screen seemed far away and could be attributed, as nearly as I could make out, to some strange mania that had swept through Germany, a foreign sickness that had inexplicably spread like a plague and then died out. Or, alternatively, I attributed the Holocaust to the mesmerizing powers of one small man with a small mustache who somehow kept an entire nation under his hypnotic spell. I read novels about the heroic actions of priests and nuns who had sheltered Jews, and I took pride in belonging to a religion that had, so far as I knew, resisted Nazism with nothing but courage and determination.

Thus when the visiting historian, getting no help from his audience, answered his own question by saying, "Christians persecuted Jews because they believed Jews killed Jesus," I was stunned. I remember shyly approaching him afterwards and explaining earnestly that the idea that Jews were Christ-killers had never occurred to me, that I had gone to Catholic schools all my life and had never once been told to hate Jews, and so on. I don't remember how he responded, but I imagine that it was with weariness and with a shake of his head at how little I knew of my own history.

I began to learn of that history as a graduate student when I spent a year as a teaching assistant to a professor who specialized in contemporary Jewish literature. During the course of those two semesters, I read several books about Jewish history and culture, as well as texts dealing with theological issues raised by the Holocaust. One of these was Simon Wiesenthal's *The Sunflower*, in which Wiesenthal tells the story of a Jewish prisoner in a concentration camp who is called to the bedside of a wounded Nazi soldier. When the prisoner arrives, the dying SS man, whose face is completely wrapped in bandages, confesses that he participated in horrible crimes against Jews and begs for forgiveness. The prisoner, for his part, responds only with silence. At the end of the story, however, he turns to his audience and addresses them: "You, who have just read this sad and tragic episode in my life, can mentally change places with me and ask yourself the crucial question, 'What would I have done?'"[3]

What follows Wiesenthal's tale is a series of essays written by prominent historians, theologians, jurists, novelists and philosophers in response to the prisoner's question. Included are the reflections of short-story writer Cynthia Ozick, and I remember the shock and wounded outrage I felt as I read her words: "The SS man had a Catholic education . . . Does the habit, inculcated in infancy, of worshiping a Master—a Master depicted in human form yet seen to be omnipotent—make it easy to accept a Führer?"[4] Here was someone suggesting that being Catholic might make one more, rather than less, inclined to follow Adolf Hitler. The suggestion was too appalling for me to absorb fully at the time, but it stayed with me and nagged at my conscience.

Of course, antisemitism in the United States these days is nowhere near as overt as it was in Nazi Germany, but relations between Christians and Jews remain troubled. Following the release of Mel Gibson's *The Passion of the Christ* (2004), a poll taken by the Pew Research Center in Washington found that thirty-six percent of those who had seen the movie held Jews responsible for the crucifixion. An earlier poll done by ABC news found that eight percent of Americans felt that "all Jews today" still bear responsibility for Jesus's death.[5] Nor is the matter confined to statistics. A few years ago I was sought out by a Jewish university student who was distraught because she had been told by her Catholic roommate that she was going to hell; the reason for her damnation was that her people had killed God.

During my trip to Eastern Europe, I had the opportunity to visit the church featured in Claude Lanzmann's 1985 documentary film *Shoah*. In the film, Lanzmann asks a group of parishioners who are milling around the church yard why the Jews were killed in the Holocaust. One man responds with a story that he says he heard from a friend. According to the story, when the Jews of a town outside of Warsaw had been gathered by Nazis into the town square, their rabbi turned to his people and told them that two thousand years ago Jews had condemned an innocent Christ to death and had cried out, "Let his blood fall on our heads and on our sons' heads." The rabbi (according to the parishioner) then said, "Perhaps the time has come for that, so let us do nothing, let us go, let us do as we're asked." When pressed by Lanzmann to say if he agrees that Jews in the Holocaust were paying for the death of Christ, the parishioner replies that he doesn't think Christ would have sought such revenge and that he is only repeating what the rabbi had said. Another parishioner is not so retiring, however. She exclaims, "It was God's will, that's all!," pointing out that Pilate had wanted to crucify Barabbas, but that the Jews had insisted on killing Jesus instead, willingly taking his blood onto their own heads. In Lanzmann's film, the parishioners say these things as a Holocaust survivor, one of only three Jews known to have escaped from Chelmno, stands in their midst and stares impassively at the camera.

It was not difficult to find traces of hatred for Jews on the journey through Poland. In Lodz, my fellow travelers and I saw coarse Stars of David spray-painted on several of the town's buildings. A guidebook explained, "The Anti-Semitic iconography which can be seen painted on the walls in certain cities, particularly Lodz, is chiefly the work of the local football fans and as such is not, paradoxically, directed against Jews." In other words, accusing a rival soccer team of being Jewish is considered to be a generic insult rather than a slight against actual Jews. The same book, however, advised that "it would be wise for those [Jews] maintaining a traditional appearance not to stray too far from groups or the main streets, particularly in the provinces."[6] In two major cities, our traveling group was told that even now Jews are reluctant to subscribe to mailing lists having anything to do with ongoing Jewish life. It seemed that their fears were justified; one of the few active synagogues we ran across had swastikas gouged into the walls outside its door.

That this can happen in the twenty-first century is an indication that there is still much work to be done to ensure that "Never Again" is something more than an empty slogan. What I hope to do in this book is to engage in a conversation with both the events of history and the themes of the Catholic Holy Week to see what we might learn from each.

Chapter One examines the controversy that surrounded the placing of a large cross outside of Auschwitz by Roman Catholics, and the establishment of a Catholic convent just outside of

Auschwitz's gates. The arguments and angers that swirled around these events touched on several of the painful and ongoing issues that trouble Jewish-Catholic relations. The chapter asks what the cross of Jesus can mean after Auschwitz.

Chapter Two begins with a consideration of the Catholic Ash Wednesday liturgy, focusing especially on its scriptural portions. It shows how the Ash Wednesday readings might be illuminated by two other texts featuring dust and ashes, namely, the expulsion story in Genesis 3 and Job's last speech in the Book of Job. Using the insights of philosopher Edith Wyschogrod, the chapter explores how the meaning of death changed with the twentieth century's capacity for inflicting mass annihilation. It concludes that Ash Wednesday should remind Catholics not simply of their own mortality, but also of the power humans now have for murder on a massive scale. The day issues a call to repent of how that power was used in the Holocaust, and to be vigilant that it not be used in such a way again.

Chapter Three shows the interconnections among history, scripture, liturgy, art, film, and drama as they relate to the death of Jesus, on the one hand, and to the history of antisemitism on the other. At the center of this complex set of interrelations lies Palm Sunday, the celebration that inaugurates Holy Week. The Palm Sunday liturgy has come under increasing scrutiny as historians have revised their assessments of how Jesus died and as the Church has revised its positions regarding Judaism and Jews. Much of the chapter centers on the debate among scholars regarding the historical reliability of the Passion accounts.

Chapter Four examines the Chrism Mass of Holy Thursday. It shows how theologies of ministry have taken on a supersessionist tone in which the Jewish priesthood has been replaced by the priesthood of Jesus. It also looks at alternative ways of thinking about priesthood, in which ministry is conceived as solidarity with and service to the community of faith.

Chapter Five looks at how the story of Passover has been incorporated by Christians into their telling of the Passion and death of Jesus. The last meal that Jesus shared with his followers is commemorated each year on what is known as Holy Thursday. This chapter shows that the Holy Thursday liturgies have appropriated the language and images of Passover in ways that are problematic for two reasons: first, because by adopting elements of Jewish

tradition, Catholicism has also understood itself as having superseded Judaism; and second, because Judaism itself has undergone
significant transformations since the time of Jesus. Not to take
account of this evolution is to freeze Judaism in the past and to
view contemporary Judaism as merely a fossil religion that by all
rights should have died out with the advent of Christianity. One
point of particular interest in the chapter is how Jewish and Catholic
traditions vary in their assessment of martyrdom.

Chapter Six begins with a consideration of Judas and why he
continues to play such a prominent role in the Christian imagination. First, he represents all of sinful humanity. Second, however, he allows those who worship Jesus to differentiate themselves from those who betrayed him. Since Judas is in tradition
consistently associated with Jews, this dual dynamic is particularly troubling.

Chapter Seven looks at the liturgy known as Tenebrae (Latin
for "darkness"). Pope Benedict XIV in the eighteenth century
wrote, "On the three days before Easter, Lauds follow immediately on Matins, which in this occasion terminate with the close
of day, in order to signify the setting of the Sun of Justice and
the darkness of the Jewish people [*tenebrae Judaici populi*] who
knew not our Lord and condemned Him to the gibbet of the
cross." The "darkness" of Tenebrae thus refers not only to the
darkness of night and the darkness of death but also to the supposed moral and spiritual darkness of Jews. The focal point of
this chapter is Jewish writer Paul Celan's haunting post-Holocaust
poem called "Tenebrae." It emphasizes the empty dark waiting
of Holy Saturday and considers the deeply frightening, deeply
troubling possibility that meaningless death is the final word and
that it is foolish to think otherwise.

Chapter Eight considers the liturgies and meaning of the
Catholic festival of Easter. It interprets Easter faith not as the
assurance of things unseen but rather as the unhinged, unjustifiable claim that the panhandler, the prisoner, and the homeless
on the street corner are somehow honored guests in the Kingdom
of God. Easter faith is the conviction that life is not merely a tale
told by an idiot, full of sound and fury and signifying nothing.
It is the decision to live as though God appears in the poor, the
lame, the sick, and the dying, and the belief that if one can't see
God there, then one shouldn't expect to see God anywhere else.

What is too often lost in the celebration of Easter is precisely this sense of risk. In the hermeneutics of salvation, Easter is often seen as the happy ending to a well-worn tale that is enjoyable precisely and only because it all happened far away and long ago, and no one need be too concerned about it anymore. Suffering here and now, in other words, is insignificant because it has already been overcome by the glory of the resurrection.

As this chapter will show, such an interpretation not only minimizes the claims that Jewish suffering might make against Catholicism, but leads Catholic tradition to a kind of unthinking triumphalism. Properly understood, however, such an interpretation should be undercut by one more festival in the Catholic cycle, a feast so strange that no one seems to know quite what to do with it. It is the Feast of the Ascension, the day in the liturgical year that celebrates the departure of Jesus from the earth to his throne in heaven. It is a feast that, this chapter suggests, should mitigate any tendency towards hubris. The ascension story ends with the loss of Jesus and with a hope that someday Jesus will return to set all things in order. That sense of loss and longing can serve as a point of connection between Catholicism and Judaism, as both traditions acknowledge a world in fundamental disorder, and wait with hope for a time when justice and mercy will flourish.

A few things to note:

The word "Holocaust" is used here to refer to the murders of six million Jews by the Nazis. Many millions of other people were killed in the concentration camps or died as a result of the war that engulfed much of the world. This book concerns itself, however, with the six million who were slaughtered as part of the Nazi plan to annihilate every single living Jew regardless of nationality or political belief or, indeed, religious belief or affiliation. What Jews believed did not matter to Hitler. All that mattered was that they had inherited "Jewish blood" and were therefore to be wiped from the face of the earth. Similarly, the word *Shoah* (Hebrew for "devastation") is used to refer to the same Nazi plan of destruction.

Unless otherwise specified, the term "Catholic" should be understood as referring to the Roman Catholic Church and its traditions, liturgies, and theologies.

Regarding scriptural quotations, unless otherwise noted, all references to the Tanakh (or what Christians often call the Old

Testament) are taken from the Jewish Publication Society version (1999). Unless otherwise noted, all references to the Christian New Testament are taken from the New Revised Standard Version (HarperCollins, 1993). When liturgical readings from scripture are cited, they are taken from the liturgical texts themselves rather than from the Bible. All references to the Talmud are taken from the translation published by Soncino Press in London and edited by I. Epstein.

References to the Catholic *Sacramentary* are from *The Roman Missal (Sacramentary), Second Typical Edition, Approved for Use in the Dioceses of the United States of America*, trans. International Committee on English in the Liturgy, Inc. (New York: Catholic Book Publishing, 1985).

Many of the events discussed in the book took place in Poland or were recorded originally in Polish. Rather than reproduce the characters of the Polish alphabet, I have substituted English spellings.

And, finally, a caveat: I do not write this book on behalf of or as a representative of the Catholic Church. I write simply as someone interested in the ways in which Catholicism and Judaism interact in the post-Holocaust world.

Acknowledgments

A condensed version of Chapter 2 appeared in the *Journal of Ecumenical Studies* 41 (no. 1), 2006: 39–54, and is used here with permission.

A condensed version of Chapter 5 appeared in *Horizons: The Journal of the College Theology Society* 32 (no. 2), 2005: 235–54, and is used here with permission.

Excerpts from the *Lectionary for Mass for Use in the Dioceses of the United States of America*, Second Typical Edition © 1998, 1997, 1970, Confraternity of Christian Doctrine, Inc., Washington, DC, are used with permission. All rights reserved. No portion of this text may be reproduced by any means without permission in writing from the copyright owner.

English translation of the *Catechism of the Catholic Church* for the United States of America, Copyright © 1994, United States Catholic Conference, Inc.—Libreria Editrice Vaticana. English translation of the *Catechism of the Catholic Church Modifications from the Editio Typica*, Copyright © 1997, United States Catholic Conference, Inc.—Libreria Editrice Vaticana. Used with permission.

Excerpts from the English translation of Rite of Holy Week © 1970, International Committee on English in the Liturgy, Inc. (ICEL); excerpts from the English translation of The Roman Missal © 1973, ICEL; the English translation of an excerpt from an ancient homily on Holy Saturday from The Liturgy of the Hours © 1974, ICEL. All rights reserved.

John Felstiner's English translation of Paul Celan's poem "Tenebrae" is used here with permission. The translation is taken from *Paul Celan: Poet, Survivor, Jew* (New Haven: Yale University Press, 1995), 101.

Thanks must go first to Theodore Zev Weiss, President of the Holocaust Educational Foundation, who organized the 2003 East

European Study Tour, and to Geoffrey Giles, who conducted the trip. Thanks also to Jane McAuliffe, Dean of the College of Arts and Sciences at Georgetown University, who sponsored the Royden B. Davis Symposium on the Cross at Auschwitz at Georgetown University in 2003, and to the participants in that program, most especially Prof. Alan L. Berger.

Stephen Okey, Kevin Spicer, Gerard Sloyan, and Mary Catherine Sanders read early drafts of the work and offered helpful feedback. Avi Patt and Jason McFarland were extremely generous in sharing their expertise. Ori Soltes, Liora Gubkin, Ariel Glucklich, Joe Murphy, Tod Linafelt, Beth McKeown, Bud Ruf, and Kathleen Hughes also contributed insights. David Goicoechea organized a symposium at Brock University on the thought of John Caputo in 2003, and the paper that I delivered there was the seed from which this book grew. Thanks finally to Susan Karp for her assistance in the Woodstock Library.

CHAPTER 1

The Convent and the Cross

In 1984, a group of Catholic nuns of the Carmelite order established a convent just outside of what was once the Auschwitz concentration camp in Poland. Five years later, a large[1] cross was erected on the convent grounds in memory of Polish Catholics who had been murdered at the site in 1941. These actions, neither one of which was accompanied by much fanfare, eventually became so controversial that they caused an international uproar.

I wish to begin this book with an exploration of the convent and the cross, because the arguments and anger that swirled around them touched on several of the painful and ongoing issues that trouble Jewish-Catholic relations. Certainly I do not expect to resolve these issues in one chapter or even in one book. My aim is rather to help explain the controversies' several origins and to show how a careful and honest consideration of them might point the way towards a new understanding of Catholicism. Literature professor Harry James Cargas, who did much to foster interreligious dialogue, once defined himself as a "post-Auschwitz Christian."[2] This book hopes to be a post-Auschwitz interpretation of some of the central feasts of the Catholic faith, especially Holy Week. There is no better place to begin such a project than with Auschwitz and with its convent and its cross.

THE CONVENT

When the Carmelite nuns established a convent just outside the perimeter of Auschwitz, they did not foresee the furor that would ensue. Their intent seemed simple enough: to pray for all of those who had lived and died in the camp. Who could possibly object to such a plan?

1

Plenty of people, as it turned out.

First, the building that the nuns had chosen for their convent, though it was located outside the gates of Auschwitz itself, was nonetheless considered by many to be a part of the camp. Its location appears on maps distributed by the Auschwitz museum, and it lies within the bounds of what had been designated in 1979 as a cultural heritage site by the United Nations Educational, Scientific and Cultural Organization (UNESCO).[3] Its renovation and use by the Carmelites was thus legally questionable, as well as troubling to those who felt that the camp should not be altered in any way lest its historical significance be lost.

Along these same lines, not just the building's location but also the way it had been used by the Nazis gave some pause. The structure had been erected before World War I and had been originally designed as a theater for the entertainment of army troops stationed nearby. During the Second World War, however, it was taken over by the Nazis to store canisters of Zyklon B, the pesticide used in the gas chambers.[4] Those chambers, of course, have become symbols of and shorthand for the Holocaust itself. Renovating the site where the gas was stored seemed to some a trivializing of, or, worse, an attempt to cover over, the Nazis' systematic, technologically advanced mass murder.

The building itself is a large brick structure clearly visible from the doorway of Block 11, Auschwitz's notorious Death Block. It was in Block 11 that prisoners awaiting execution at the nearby Wall of Death were held. It was in Block 11 that unspeakable tortures were carried out. And it was in Block 11 that one of the first experiments using Zyklon B as a means of mass murder was carried out. On September 3, 1941, approximately six hundred Soviet prisoners and more than two hundred other people were gassed to death in that building's basement.[5] To some, placing a convent so close to a site that had witnessed such horror was an outrage.

A few of the objections to the convent's establishment were, perhaps, based on misunderstanding or misinformation. For example, at one point a controversy arose over how money had been raised to renovate the convent building. In 1985, a Belgian Catholic charity named Aide à l'Eglise en Détresse had initiated a fund-raising campaign to help the Carmelites begin their foundation at Auschwitz. The organization had issued a newsletter appealing for donations that included this statement:

After the Pope's visit [in 1985], we wish to present him as a gift from our benefactors in the Benelux countries [i.e. Belgium, the Netherlands and Luxemburg] the sum of money necessary to found the convent, which will become a spiritual fortress and a guarantee of the conversion of strayed brothers from our countries as well as proof of our desire to erase the outrages so often done to the Vicar of Christ.[6]

Some Jews assumed (with considerable justification, given the Church's long history of anti-Jewish teaching) that they were the "strayed brothers" to whom the letter referred. The statement about "outrages done to the Vicar of Christ" was thought to be a veiled reference to the frequently repeated charge that Pope Pius XII had done little to save Jews during the Holocaust.

It is possible that the language about strayed brethren did not refer to Jews at all, but rather to those who had given Pope John Paul II a less-than-warm welcome when he had visited Holland. Many Dutch Catholics had protested the pope's visit there, and many had openly disagreed with papal teachings on abortion, homosexual practice, and the status of women in the Church. It was perhaps in reparation for these challenges to the pope's authority that the agency had initiated its fund-raising efforts.[7] It is also possible that the language was directed at Poles who had drifted from the Church under the influence of Communism.[8] However, given the context of the Church's historical attitudes towards Jews, it is not surprising that the letter became a source of anger and contention.

Another controversy arose when the nuns stated that they intended to pray for the victims of Auschwitz. The Mother Superior of the convent explained, "Let the Jews understand that the prayers of the Carmelite nuns are also offered for the souls of those victims who were also of the Jewish persuasion."[9] Some interpreted their mission as a campaign to convert posthumously the souls of Jews who had been murdered at the site.

The history of Catholic teachings regarding the conversion of Jews is enormously complex, and each pronouncement, whether dogmatic or theological, deserves close examination in its own right. It would not be inaccurate, however, to say that for most of its history, the Catholic Church has thought of itself as having inherited Israel's covenant with God and thus as having in some sense superseded Judaism. Catholics have traditionally sought to convert Jews and thus to bring them to salvation through faith in Jesus.

Recently, however, significant changes have occurred within the Church and consequently in the way the Church thinks of itself in relation to the world. These changes came to fruition in the Second Vatican Council in the 1960s, most notably in the document known as *Nostra Aetate*, or the "Declaration on the Relationship of the Church to Non-Christian Religions." Admittedly, this declaration affirms a supersessionist position, stating that "Jerusalem did not recognize the time of her visitation," and expressing regret that only a few Jews accepted the Gospel. The document refers to the Church as "the new people of God," and it "awaits that day, known to God alone, on which all peoples will address the Lord in a single voice and 'serve him with one accord.'" Nevertheless, *Nostra Aetate* affirms the validity of the original covenant between God and Israel and, citing the apostle Paul, asserts that "the Jews still remain most dear to God because of their fathers, for He does not repent of the gifts He makes nor of the calls He issues."[10]

Even more recently, in 2002 a committee of American Catholic bishops released a document stating that Catholics should recognize the salvific nature of the Jewish covenant, and that the Church's task of evangelization "no longer includes the wish to absorb the Jewish faith into Christianity and so end the distinctive witness of Jews to God in human history." The Church now recognizes, said the document, that the witness of Jews to the Kingdom of God "must not be curtailed by seeking the conversion of the Jewish people to Christianity."[11]

Likewise, numerous contemporary Catholic theologians affirm the will of God to bring all people, regardless of religion, into heavenly life. For example, in the twentieth century, the renowned German theologian Karl Rahner pointed to the universality of God's salvific will by invoking the all-encompassing grace of God. He observed,

> However little we can say with certitude about the final lot of an individual inside or outside the officially constituted Christian religion, we have every reason to think optimistically—i.e. truly hopefully and confidently in a Christian

sense—of God who has certainly the last word and who has revealed to us that he has spoken his powerful word of reconciliation and forgiveness into the world . . . In Christ God not only gives the *possibility* of salvation, which in that case would still have to be effected by man himself, but the actual salvation itself, however much this includes also the right decision of human freedom which is itself a gift from God.[12]

For Rahner, as for much contemporary Catholic theology, God became incarnate in history for the salvation of all, and only an outright rejection of divine love (which is not at all the same thing as a rejection of baptism) could annul the gift of salvation. While not all Catholics would agree with him, and while his ideas cannot be considered dogmatic, many contemporary theologians take for granted the notions that God wills the salvation of all people regardless of religion and that baptism cannot be considered the only criterion for entrance into life in heaven.

Thus it is somewhat misleading to say, as Daniel Jonah Goldhagen does in his book *A Moral Reckoning: The Role of the Catholic Church in the Holocaust and Its Unfulfilled Duty of Repair*, that "The Church's official doctrine, faithful to Christian Scripture and now in existence for almost two millennia, is unbending and unequivocal: Jews cannot attain salvation through Judaism."[13] Goldhagen is correct to point out in hard-hitting fashion how the *Catechism of the Catholic Church* (which, it should be noted, does not carry the weight of an infallible pronouncement) perpetuates the idea that salvation comes only to those who profess faith in Jesus Christ. Unfortunately, he dismisses voices such as Rahner's as "hair-splitting formulations clergy and theologians think up in order to try to soften the Church's positions regarding the Jews."[14] Those hair-splitting formulations can sometimes make all the difference in the world. They are in fact responsible for the admittedly glacial changes that have come to the Church in the past half-century and that Goldhagen otherwise applauds as at least minor steps in the right direction.

In any case, Catholic efforts to convert Jews have never been aimed at the dead. There is no tradition at all in Catholicism of posthumous conversion. Canon law actually forbids baptism (and thus initiation into the Christian faith) of those who have already died. The Catholic practice of praying for the dead stems rather from two sources: first, a belief that God's judgment on those who have died might be influenced by the prayers of the living, and second, that even those whom God has chosen for salvation must undergo a period of trial that might be lessened by prayerful intercession.

Since ancient times, Christians have prayed that their beloved dead might receive the mercy of God and thus be admitted into everlasting life, and the practice continues today. At a contemporary Catholic funeral, for example, the following prayer might be said: "Merciful Lord, turn toward us and listen to our prayers: open the gates of paradise to your servant and help us who remain to comfort one another with assurances of faith, until we all meet in Christ and are with you and with our sister for ever."[15] The purpose of the prayers is to intercede on behalf of the dead, but also to seek comfort and healing for the living.

The second reason why Catholics pray for the dead stems from a belief that even those whom God has destined for salvation might need to undergo a period of preparation before being admitted. In medieval times, this interval between death and eternal life was given the name of purgatory, and any number of colorful descriptions of it were developed, most notably, of course, by the poet Dante. Teachings about purgatory were bound up with the practice of granting indulgences, whereby the living believed they could reduce the agonies of the dead by saying prayers, going on pilgrimages, or, of course, donating money to the Church. In the wake of the Protestant Reformation, the sale of indulgences was banned by the Church. However, the practice of granting them for prayer and good works continues. There is a basic and enduring sense in Catholic tradition that the dead must be cleansed and refined before gaining access to heaven. Likewise, there is a basic and enduring belief that the prayers of the living might help speed along the purgatorial trials of the deceased. Thus, it is quite common for Catholics to pray that the souls of their beloved might come more quickly into paradise.

Thus when the Carmelite nuns expressed their intention to pray for the dead, posthumous conversion was not what they had in mind. Given the contentious atmosphere in which the convent was built, however, their statement aroused both suspicion and anger.

If some of the furor over the convent had roots in misinformation, miscommunication, or misunderstanding, other controversies were based on serious, authentic, and fundamental differences in world view. One of these stemmed from the Carmelite sisters' original desire to name the convent in memory of a deceased nun named Edith Stein.[16] Stein, born into a Jewish family in 1891, had converted to Catholicism as an adult and at the age of forty-two had entered the Carmelite order. As hostilities against Jews rose in Germany, Stein had fled to Holland and joined the community of Carmelite nuns in Echt. It turned out that Holland was no safer than Germany had been, though. In 1942, Dutch bishops issued a letter of protest against Nazi policies, and the Nazis retaliated by rounding up Dutch Jews who had converted to Catholicism. Stein was arrested at her convent, deported, and murdered at Auschwitz. In 1998, Pope John Paul II canonized her as a martyr for the Catholic faith.

Explaining why Stein was to be honored among the Church's saints, the pope proclaimed, "From now on, as we celebrate the memory of this new saint from year to year, we must also remember the Shoah, that cruel plan to exterminate a people—a plan to which millions of our Jewish brothers and sisters fell victim."[17] In his eyes, Stein was a symbol for all innocent victims of persecution: "*May such criminal deeds never be repeated* against any ethnic group, against any race, in any corner of this world!"[18] In the eyes of many Jews, however, canonizing Stein was an affront to those who had gone to their deaths holding fast to their Jewish faith. Two leaders of the Anti-Defamation League wrote, "We as Jews feel that we have lost Edith Stein twice. The first time was at her conversion to Catholicism. The second time is with her canonization, by which some groups appropriate her as a Christian martyr even though her death relates to the Jewish focus of the Holocaust."[19]

Much of the anger that Jews felt towards Stein's canonization stemmed from the fact that Stein herself had written a testimonial in which she had offered her life and death "for the expiation of the unbelief of the Jewish people and so that the Lord may be welcomed by his own people and his kingdom come in majesty."[20] Naming the convent after a converted Jew who had prayed for the conversion of all Jews appeared to some as an unbearable insult. When the Carmelites at Auschwitz were informed of this, they agreed to change the name.

Another issue concerned the specifically contemplative nature of the Carmelite order. The Carmelites trace their origins back to the twelfth century, to a group of hermits living on Mount Carmel in what is now Israel. Spiritually, however, they consider the prophet Elijah to be their inspiration. According to the biblical story, Elijah was told by God to go out to the top of a mountain to wait for the Lord to pass by. Elijah did as he was told, and as he waited a great wind split the mountain, "but the Lord was not in the wind." Then an earthquake shook the ground, and a fire raged, but God was not present in either of those terrors. After the fire came "a soft murmuring sound," and according to the biblical account, "When Elijah heard it, he wrapped his mantle about his face," because in the quiet he recognized the presence of God (I Kings 19:9–13).

The Carmelites have undergone numerous changes since the twelfth century, most notably the split that resulted in two different orders, the Discalced Carmelites and the Carmelites of the Ancient Observance. What both groups hold in common, though, is a sense that God can be found in silence and in the quiet of a contemplative heart. The Carmelite nuns living at Auschwitz surely shared this conviction.

Since the Holocaust, however, "silence" has become a freighted term. On the one hand, in the work of some post-Holocaust writers, silence is seen as the only appropriate response to the horrors of the *Shoah*. Elie Wiesel, for example, observes that the Holocaust has become "a fashionable subject: good to impress or shock." He continues, "One reaches the point of longing for the days when only a few people dared speak of it; now everybody does. Too much. And too lightly."[21]

On the other hand, silence is equated with complicity. It raises the ghosts of all those who saw evil and did nothing about it, whether through fear or apathy or tacit approval. David Patterson makes this point forcefully when he writes, "From the standpoint of the victims, the silence of the cloister's walls is the silence of indifference, the silence that profanes the Name [of the divine] and robs the world of its face." This is not to suggest, he says, that the Carmelites are to be equated with Nazis: "But it is to suggest that their view of the world and of the ideal life could play into the hands of the Nazis. For it could play into the hands of an indifference toward the condition of this world—and toward the plight of Jews in this world—as one turns away from this world to prepare to enter the next."[22]

This brings us to another objection to the presence of a Carmelite convent at the death camp, an objection that has to do with differences between Christian and Jewish notions of prayer. In many strands of Christian tradition, especially Christian mystical tradition, prayer is understood as a form of communication between the individual soul and the divine. For example, the sixteenth-century Carmelite mystic Teresa of Avila spoke of prayer as "taking time frequently to be alone with Him who we know loves us."[23] Likewise, her fellow Carmelite John of the Cross described the ideal prayer as "the Divine union of the soul with God."[24] The emphasis in these Catholic mystical texts is on the interior personal journey that individuals make towards God.

Of course, Catholics do gather together to pray and to worship in communion with one another. The liturgy of the Mass is precisely a collective prayer offered by the faithful gathered in the name of Jesus. And yet, there is in the history of Catholicism, particularly Catholic mysticism, something of a bias towards the individual: towards his or her relationship with God and towards the salvation of his or her soul. Until recently, this could be seen even in the Mass, as up until the liturgical reforms of the Second Vatican Council in the 1960s, it was not unusual for each member of a congregation to spend the hour of the liturgy engaged in more or less private worship. Moreover, Mass could be celebrated by an individual priest alone with no congregation present at all.

This "vertical" understanding of prayer is very different from that found in much of Jewish tradition. David Patterson explains that "Jews do not retreat to the cloister to pray; rather, they pray in a *minyan*, standing as a community before the Holy One."[25] This is, of course, something of a generalization, since according to Jewish tradition some prayers may be recited even if a quorum of ten is not present. Moreover, Judaism recognizes the importance of an individual's relationship with and response to the divine. Still, just as in Christian tradition there is a tendency to think of prayer as the action of an individual, so in Judaism prayer is more often thought of as a communal activity.

This distinction leads to diverging conceptions of the relation between prayer and action. Writes Patterson, "The Christian encounters God as love; the Jew responds to God as the *commandment* to love and therefore to *act* in a certain manner."[26] Again, Patterson's remark is a generalization. After all, according to the New Testament, Jesus taught that those who love God must also love their neighbors. And yet if Patterson's statement is a generalization, it is nonetheless a useful one.

Consider, for example, this passage from the Spanish Carmelite mystic John of the Cross: "The Christian, then, if he will direct his rejoicing to God with regard to moral good, must realize that the value of his good works, fasts, alms, penances, etc., is based, not upon the number or the quality of them, but upon the love of God which inspires him to do them."[27]

In John's view, loving God comes first, and good deeds on behalf of the neighbor not only come second, but have value only insofar as they are rooted in a desire for union with God. Though John believes that it is the duty of a Christian to perform works of charity, these works are subordinate to considerations of the soul and its ascent towards God. Indeed, charitable works are worthless if not done with an eye towards that union. John identifies two reasons why a person might rejoice in good deeds: "for that which they are in themselves, or for the good which they imply and bring with them as a means and instrument."[28] The Christian, he says, "must rejoice principally and solely in the possession and employment of this moral good after the second manner—namely, in that by doing these works for the love of God he will gain eternal life."[29] Loving good works only for their own sake is the product of an earthly mentality. It is to act as the heathen act and is to risk the flames of hell.

John illustrates this point with his interpretation of Jesus's parable of the ten virgins, in which five bridesmaids bring extra oil for their lamps when they go out to meet the bridegroom, and five do not. When the bridegroom arrives, the foolish virgins ask the wise ones for help in lighting their lamps. The wise refuse to comply, and as a result the foolish bridesmaids are refused entrance to the wedding banquet (Matt. 25:1–13). John interprets the parable by commenting that the ten virgins "had all kept their virginity and done good works; and yet, because the joy of five of them was not of the second kind (that is, because they had not directed their joy to God), but was rather after the first and vain kind, for they rejoiced in the possession of their good works, they were cast out from Heaven with no acknowledgement or reward from the Bridegroom."[30] John concludes, "The Christian, then, must rejoice, not in the performing of good works and the following of good customs, but in doing them for the love of God alone, without respect to aught else soever."[31] Good works done for the sake of doing good profit nothing. The only truly acceptable reason to do good, from John's point of view, is to give pleasure to God.

John's fellow Carmelite Teresa of Avila had a similar understanding of the relation between spiritual ascent and good deeds, though she put far more emphasis on performing charitable works than John did. In her mystical treatise *The Interior Castle*, Teresa stressed the importance of caring for others: "This is the reason for prayer, my daughters, the purpose of this spiritual marriage: the birth always of good works, good works. This is the true sign of a thing, or favor, being from God, as I have already told you. It benefits me little to be alone making acts of devotion to our Lord, proposing and promising to do wonders in His service, if I then go away and when the occasion offers itself do everything the opposite." Immediately, however, Teresa retracted her own statement: "I was wrong in saying it profits little, for everything having to do with God profits a great deal."[32] She went on to explain that acts of charity derive their importance not from their inherent value but from the spirit in which they are performed: "The Lord doesn't look so much at the greatness of our works as at the love with which they are done."[33]

This tendency within Christian mysticism to value love for and union with God over performing acts of charity has occasionally led practitioners to claim that good works are utterly irrelevant to religious life and that the only thing that matters is the individual's relation with the divine. In the early fourteenth century, for example, a Christian mystic named Marguerite Porete described six stages through which a soul passes before it reaches its final destination in heaven. The third of these stages, a stage which must be surpassed if the soul wishes to progress, is reached "when the Soul considers herself in the affection of the love of the work of perfection, by which her spirit is sharpened through a boiling desire of love in multiplying in herself such works."

This stage, according to the mystic, is actually dangerous, because while in it the soul may be tempted to love the works themselves rather than God: "For no death would be martyrdom to her except abstaining from the work she loves, which is the delight of her pleasure and the life of her will which is nourished by this." In order to overcome this temptation, the soul must detach herself from the pleasure of doing good: "And thus she relinquishes such works from which she has such delight, and she puts the will to death which had life from this."[34] The soul does this in order that she may see that "there is nothing except God Himself Who is, from whom all things are."[35] Good works must be sacrificed if God is to be found.

Marguerite Porete was burned at the stake as a heretic.[36] Heresy, though, is often simply orthodoxy *in extremis*. A tradition's heresies reveal much about its inner workings—the tensions and unresolvable oppositions that give it life. The heretical ideas of Marguerite Porete show a basic tendency within Christian mystical thought to diminish the value of good works in favor of the union of the soul with God.

On the other hand, consider a work of fiction, first published in 1946, entitled *Yosl Rakover Talks to God*. Written as if it were the diary of one of the last fighters of the Warsaw Ghetto Uprising, the book gives voice to the agonies of faith and doubt that arose during the Holocaust and in its aftermath. It begins by telling readers, "In one of the ruins of the Warsaw Ghetto, preserved in a little bottle and concealed amongst heaps of charred stone and human bones, the following testament was found, written in the last hours of the ghetto by a Jew named Yosl Rakover." It then offers the text of the fictional diary, dated "Warsaw, 28 April 1943."[37]

The diary describes what happened that day in the ghetto: the raging artillery fire and the flames that swept through the streets. Its real purpose, though, is to offer testimony both to God and about God. As he looks back at his own life and at the whole of Jewish history, the diary's fictional author, Yosl Rakover, reflects, "I am happy to belong to the unhappiest of all peoples in the world, whose Torah embodies the highest law and the most beautiful morality." Yosl believes in God, he says: "For if You are not my God—whose God are You? The God of the murderers?" And yet, there is something even higher than God to which he professes his fidelity: "I believe in the God of

Israel, even when He has done everything to make me cease to believe in Him. I believe in His laws even when I cannot justify His deeds . . . I love Him. But I love His Torah more. Even if I were disappointed in Him, I would still cherish His Torah."[38] Reflecting on Yosl's extraordinary profession of faith, twentieth-century philosopher Emmanuel Levinas remarks that for Judaism, God is made manifest in the Word of God that is the Torah. Unlike in Christianity, he says, in Judaism "the connection between God and man is not a sentimental communion within the love of a God made flesh [l'amour d'un Dieu incarné], but a relation of minds [entre esprits] mediated by instruction, through the Torah."[39] Christian tradition, particularly its mystical tradition, tends to prize the silence of contemplation that fosters spiritual ascent and union of the soul with God. Jewish tradition, on the other hand, tends to prize the righteousness found in fidelity to the Torah. It is not surprising that when Jews were informed of cloistered Carmelite nuns praying at Auschwitz, some suspected that such prayers would do little to bring about palpable change in Christians' treatment of or attitudes towards them.

It is also not surprising that most Christians could not foresee the furor that the convent would cause. Polish Archbishop Henryk Muszynski, for example, confessed, "I would never have expected that the Jews would react in such a way. We thought that first of all, it's the same God. I expected that believing Jews would have more or less the same feelings. I was very much surprised that the Jews had something against the nuns who were engaged in silent prayer in this place." Tellingly, he concluded, "We didn't know each other, we didn't have any contact with each other."[40]

In 1993, the convent was closed, and the nuns left the town of Oswiecim.[41] They left behind them the painful memories and angry words of both Catholics and Jews. They left behind something else as well: the large cross that had been raised at the site in 1989. That cross continues to be a source of controversy and debate.

THE CROSS

In the eyes of many Jews, the presence of both the convent and the cross at Auschwitz seemed to diminish the Jewish focus of the Holocaust. Roughly one hundred forty thousand non-

Jewish Poles were imprisoned at the infamous concentration camp, and more than half of those died there.[42] By contrast, nearly one million Jews died at Auschwitz, most of them murdered at Auschwitz-Birkenau, the killing center a mile or two from the main camp. Jews accounted for about eighty-seven percent of the total number of Auschwitz's victims.[43]

Nonetheless, after the defeat of Hitler's army, many Poles felt that their suffering under Nazi occupation had been forgotten by the rest of the world. They wished to establish a memorial to their fallen heroes in the form of the cross, and they felt that the presence of the convent would sanctify the ground where so many had been murdered.

However, the fact that the memorial was not simply a plaque or a sculpture, but was rather a Christian cross, caused significant consternation. At various times in history, Christians have justified persecution of Jews by charging them with crucifying Jesus. In the fourth century, Saint John Chrysostom wrote regarding Jews, "You did slay Christ, you did lift violent hands against the Master, you did spill his precious blood. This is why you have no chance for atonement, excuse, or defense."[44] Innumerable Christian commentators have echoed his sentiments. Given this history, placing a cross within sight of the place where a million Jews were murdered was read by some as a gesture of Christian triumphalism.

On the other hand, Catholic teachings about Judaism have changed significantly in recent years. In the 1960s, the Church officially proclaimed that Jews were not to be held responsible for the death of Jesus. Moreover, throughout his reign, Pope John Paul II issued statements expressing regret for Christian involvement in the Holocaust, most notably the 1998 pronouncement, "We Remember: A Reflection on the *Shoah*." Continuing to hold the Church responsible for past errors was, in the eyes of some, a failure to recognize that much Catholic teaching had changed.

The controversies surrounding the cross and the convent were not limited to academic debate. In 1989, an American rabbi named Avraham Weiss led six students over the convent's fence during a protest demonstration. They were beaten by

Polish workers on the site and removed from the grounds.[45] Years later, in the summer of 1998, a Polish Catholic layman named Kazimierz Switon urged his followers to place hundreds of small crosses around the convent grounds.[46] The following spring, when authorities attempted to remove the crosses, Switon installed explosive devices to protect them. The small crosses and the explosives were removed under police supervision, but debate continued.[47]

The Catholics who built the memorial outside of Auschwitz to honor Polish martyrs did not choose just any cross for the site. Rather, they chose the one that had been used for the Mass celebrated by Pope John Paul II during his visit to Auschwitz-Birkenau in 1979. The cross was large—large enough to have been seen by the crowds who had gathered for that solemn occasion years earlier. When it was erected in the gravel pit outside of Auschwitz, its upper reaches could be seen from inside the camp by anyone standing across from Block 11.

It was not the only cross erected. As has been noted, several hundred smaller ones were placed at the site by Kazimierz Switon and his followers. Still others were planted along with small Stars of David by a group of Boy Scouts who, with apparently good intentions, wished to memorialize Auschwitz's dead. These were all removed. The large cross, however, still stands.

In one way, it is surprising that such a furor erupted over the cross at Auschwitz. After all, a cross stands at the entrance to the memorial at Chelmno, but that one has generated little controversy. What accounts for the difference?

The answer seems to lie in the symbolic value that has accrued to Auschwitz over the past sixty years. Ironically, the camp plays such a powerful role in the memory of the Holocaust precisely because so many of its prisoners actually survived. At Chelmno at least one hundred fifty-two thousand people were gassed; three Jews survived. At Belzec at least four hundred thousand were gassed; two survived. At Treblinka at least eight hundred thousand were gassed; fewer than forty survived.[48] By contrast, an estimated 1.1 million Jews were deported to Auschwitz, and one hundred and forty thousand of them survived.[49] Their testimonies constitute a large portion of the documentation available about the Holocaust, and their memories have contributed greatly to the collective memory of the *Shoah*. It is only natural then that the name of Auschwitz has come to be synonymous with the Nazi plan to exterminate the Jews. Thus when Catholics erected a cross at the concentration camp, the action appeared to some as an attempt to erase the specifically Jewish nature of the Holocaust. (One can only imagine what the reaction might have been had the cross been erected at Auschwitz-Birkenau, the extermination site where, beginning in 1942, most of the Jewish victims were actually murdered.)[50]

What does the cross—not just the cross at Auschwitz, but "The Cross," any cross, if one can speak of a symbol devoid of its context—*mean*? Henryk Muszynski says that the cross is "a mark of power and victory over weakness, sin, hatred, and all those things that are the negation of full love and true Christianity."[51] On the other hand, Jewish scholar and camp survivor Elie Wiesel observes, "The cross was a symbol of compassion and love and mercy for the Christian. It was a symbol of persecution for the Jew."[52] Jacob Neusner puts the point more strongly: "The cross stands to humiliate, to express hatred, to serve God by acts of hatred and contempt."[53]

One doesn't have to look too deeply into Catholic history to find numerous examples of the cross being used as a source of contempt for Jews. Catholics have frequently pointed to the crucifixion of Jesus and charged Jews with deicide. At times, that charge has turned deadly; in 1096 the Jews of Mainz were slaughtered at the hands of Christians who wore crosses on their vestments and who accused the Jews of killing God by charging that "You are the children of those who killed our object of veneration, hanging him on a tree; and he himself had said: 'There will yet come a day when my children will come and avenge my blood.'"[54] Moreover, the symbol of the cross accompanied the crusaders as they made their bloody way towards the Holy Land.

Even in the twentieth century, Christians who would never have thought of harming Jews themselves were able to justify the Holocaust as God's punishment by pointing to Jesus's crucifixion. One Polish Christian who hid many of his Jewish neighbors from the Nazis during the war nonetheless went to a nearby town to watch a group of Jews being led to their deaths. When asked by some of those under his protection why he wanted to witness such a thing, he explained that because Jews had handed Jesus over to his death two thousand years ago, he would now watch Jews being taken to slaughter.[55] The sentiment seems to have been widespread. Describing a pogrom that took place in 1941 in the Polish village of Radzilow, Menachem Finkelsztajn testified that the mobs were spurred on by propaganda "stating that it was time to settle scores with those who had crucified Jesus Christ . . . the Jews."[56] Helena Szereszewska, a Jew who spent part of the war hiding in a convent, recalled, "Every Sunday I listened to the priest's sermon. He often referred to the events which had so recently and so tragically taken place. He talked about the annihilation of the Jews. 'Everything that has happened to the Jews is atonement for the terrible sins they committed. It was God's punishment. The Germans are only the instruments of God's punishment.'"[57] Even as late as 1948, a meeting of the German Evangelical Church described the Holocaust as divine punishment and called on Jews to stop their rejection and ongoing crucifixion of Jesus Christ.[58]

Against this history, it must be pointed out that Jesus was executed under Roman authority for the crime of insurrection against the Roman empire. He was not killed by Jews, nor was he killed for the crime of blasphemy. The statement issued by the Second Vatican Council of the Catholic Church did not go far enough when it proclaimed that Jesus's death "cannot be blamed upon all the Jews then living, without distinction, nor upon the Jews of today."[59] What it should have added was that Jesus was crucified by the Romans, just as thousands of other Jews had been crucified before him, including two thousand of the followers of Judas son of Hezekiah in the year 4 BCE, not far from Jesus's home in Nazareth.

Can the cross continue to serve Christians as a symbol of their faith, or has it become too freighted by centuries of antisemitism for it to stand as anything other than an incitement to hatred and violence? Even the best intentions are sometimes thwarted by unavoidable confrontations with history. In an essay urging that the controversial cross be removed from Auschwitz, Polish Jesuit priest Stanislaw Musial notes that one need not be a psychologist to understand why Jews would be disturbed by the symbol: "It is enough to be kindhearted."[60] He points out that for a century and a half after the death of Jesus, Christians did not use crosses in their services, and he calls for contemporary Christians to renounce their need for monuments. Those who wish to venerate a cross at Auschwitz, he says, already have a place where they can do so: the death cell of a Polish priest named Maximilian Kolbe.

The story of Saint Maximilian Kolbe (canonized as a martyr by Pope John Paul II in 1981) is as follows: Kolbe was taken prisoner by the Nazis in 1941 and was sent to the Auschwitz camp. In reprisal for an escape, the guards chose ten men at random and sentenced them to death by starvation. One of those ten, a Polish army sergeant, begged for mercy, pleading that he had a wife and children. Hearing the man's cries, Kolbe stepped forward and offered himself in the man's place. His offer was accepted, and Kolbe was sentenced to slow starvation along with his fellow victims, until he was finally injected with poison two weeks later. Regarding this sacrifice, Musial asks,

> Do we Christians, and with us—I dare humbly say— people of good will, need a different monument at the Oswiecim [Auschwitz] camp? Those who have need of material religious symbols will find plenty of them in Father Kolbe's cell (block X, [sic][61] the so-called death block). Father Kolbe's cell points the way for all of us. It tells us to build a world without death cells, without hatred, in the spirit of love and dialogue, in the spirit of humility, in the face of the prodigious task of interpretation of the world . . . in the face of suffering that oppresses mankind, and of the oft rampant evil.[62]

There is no need for a cross at Auschwitz, argues Musial, other than the one commemorating the selfless act of Maximilian Kolbe. And yet Saint Maximilian's life was not so simple. To be sure, no one doubts his courage in offering his life for another prisoner. Moreover, before his arrest, he and his monastery cared for thousands of refugees, including fifteen hundred Jews. On the other hand, though, that same monastery published a daily newspaper that routinely contained vicious attacks against Jews. The newspaper defended the Nuremberg laws passed in Germany that, among other things, restricted marriage between Jews and non-Jews. It contended that the laws were a justifiable bulwark against Jewish domination of Germany. Likewise, it supported Italy's enactment of such laws, calling the legislation an "act of self-defense by Italians against Jews."[63] The newspaper urged Poles not to buy goods from Jewish merchants or manufacturers, and it published statements to the effect that Poland had been "too hospitable" to Jews for too long.[64]

Was Kolbe himself an antisemite? Assessments differ. What is undeniable, though, is that even the veneration of this martyr, even the honoring of this priest who sacrificed himself for a man he did not know, is bound up with centuries of Christian teachings of contempt for Jews. Praying at the cell of Maximilian Kolbe is tied to a chain of historical events and associations that are impossible to ignore and devastating to consider.

The pivotal question, then, is what the cross can say to the world after Auschwitz. I do not know the answer. This book, in truth, is intended as an experiment. It is an experiment in rethinking both the symbol of the cross and the cycle of liturgies that, year in and year out, give it context and meaning. I hope to find a new way of thinking about the cross, one that situates it in a long line of prayers and tears for a time when every bruised reed will be made whole, every life will be redeemed, and justice will be established on the earth.

What works against such an interpretation is Christianity's propensity for seeing the cross as merely a bit of high drama in a story that has already ended, and ended happily at that. In the Christian calendar, the weeping of Good Friday gives way to Easter Sunday's proclamation that what the world longs for has already in fact been accomplished. Not here on earth, to be sure: it has not been accomplished in time as we reckon it, but it is truly and finally finished. Everything that has followed since that day on that hillside near Jerusalem, in this view, is just the restlessness an audience feels after the final curtain has fallen but before the ushers open the exit doors.

What I am hoping to find is a new way of thinking about the Catholic liturgical cycle to see if there is not some other way of reading it, some other way of living it. I would like to make sense of Good Friday, as well as of the feasts that lead up to it and that follow in its wake, in such a way that neither the horror of the cross nor the horrors that have followed, one after another, century after century, are lost. My thesis is that these feasts are best understood as, in the words of Catholic theologian Karl Rahner, festivals of holy pain. They are festivals that mark the human longing for God, even as they direct our attention to the spaces where the causes of God, the causes of justice and healing and dignity, might be served.

CHAPTER 2

Ash Wednesday

In the spring of 2003, I helped to organize a symposium on the Holocaust to be held at the Catholic university where I teach. As the proposed speakers and I were attempting to find an agreeable date for the conference, I glanced at my calendar and immediately ruled out one of the days under discussion: Ash Wednesday. The thought of a largely Christian audience showing up with ashes on their foreheads as the panel discussed the extermination and cremation of millions of Jews in the Holocaust was just too gruesome to contemplate.

The Nazis' determination to reduce their victims to ashes is one of the most nefarious aspects of the Holocaust. Cremation was an attempt to erase every trace of both the murders and the murdered: both crimes and victims. And yet, of course, such evidence does not disappear quite so easily. Journalist Gitta Sereny wrote after observing the gray, sandy soil at Sobibor in 1972 that "one is jolted out of any effort at detachment by the sickening shock at realizing that—even these three decades later—one must be walking on ashes."[1] Martin Gilbert wrote regarding the end of his journey to Treblinka via horse-drawn wagon in 1959, "I stepped down from the cart on to the sandy soil: a soil that was grey rather than brown. Driven by I know not what impulse, I ran my hand through that soil, again and again. The earth beneath my feet was coarse and sharp: filled with the fragments of human bone."[2] Today at Majdanek, just outside of the Polish city of Lublin, one can visit an open-air mausoleum filled with the ashes of victims. At Birkenau one can view the pond into which some of the ashes from the crematoria were dumped. Bodies, it turns out, are not as easy to dispose of as the Nazis would have liked. Nonetheless, great effort was made to eliminate every bit of evidence of the genocide.

The process by which the Nazis murdered and then disposed of six million Jews developed only in fits and starts. In 1941, the feared *Einsatzgruppen* or "Operational Units" were dispatched to exterminate whole communities of Jews that had formerly been under Russian control.[3] Their method, though, was inefficient and expensive. Lining villagers up and shooting them so that their bodies fell into mass graves taxed increasingly scarce supplies of bullets. Moreover, the mass killings took a psychic and physical toll on Nazi personnel. Officers suffered nightmares as well as stomach and intestinal difficulties. At one point, SS chief Heinrich Himmler had to encourage his troops by telling them that though their duty was repulsive, it was ultimately necessary just as the extermination of vermin was necessary.[4]

The Nazis soon realized that another plan had to be devised if their dream of a Jew-free Reich was to come true. To solve the problem, they set up new installations capable of using poison gas to murder more quickly and efficiently. At Auschwitz, the first experiments with the pesticide Zyklon B (prussic acid) took place in the summer of 1941. Soon gas chambers (or, in some instances, specially constructed vans that fed fumes directly into the cargo hold) were set up in Chelmno, Belzec, Sobibor, Treblinka, Majdanek, and Auschwitz-Birkenau.

Early on, most of those who were gassed at these sites were buried in mass graves, a process that led to numerous complications. Franz Stangl, *Kommandant* of two Nazi killing centers, remembered his first impressions of Belzec in April 1942: "The man I was talking to said that one of the pits had overflowed. They had put too many corpses in it and putrefaction had progressed too fast, so that the liquid underneath had pushed the bodies on top up and over and the corpses had rolled down the hill. I saw some of them—oh God, it was awful."[5] When Himmler became concerned about leaving such evidence of the massacres behind, bodies were dug up and burned on huge pyres.[6] The intent was to burn the bodies so thoroughly that, as Rudolf Höss put it, "it would be impossible at some future time to calculate the number of corpses burnt."[7]

At Auschwitz itself, the first crematorium began operation in September 1940 to dispose of the bodies of inmates who had died from disease, execution, or starvation. It proved inefficient, however, and at various times thousands of corpses were buried in mass graves instead. In 1942 those bodies were unearthed and burned on pyres stoked with benzine. At some point the Nazis figured out that they could save on money and supplies if they stoked the flames with human fat instead.[8]

As the killings increased, the need to dispose of evidence became acute. Four larger crematoria were completed at Auschwitz in 1943. The plan was that these four would be able to accommodate over four thousand bodies each day. However, by increasing the number of bodies in the ovens and reducing the time given to each incineration, the Nazis doubled the capacity of these crematoria.[9] If bodies did not burn completely due to decreased incineration time, they were swept into an ash pit below the furnaces and pulverized with wooden mortars. The resulting ashes were then poured into nearby rivers and ponds or, sometimes, used as fertilizer for the camp's farms.[10]

As the war dragged on and supplies ran low, murder by gas was deemed a luxury that the Nazis could not always afford. Thus, at times, victims were simply burned alive.[11] In the summer of 1944, according to a Polish woman testifying at the Nuremberg trials, many of these victims were children; babies were torn from their mothers' arms and thrown straight into the crematoria fires without being gassed first.[12] Reflecting on this fact, Jewish theologian Irving Greenberg issued what he calls a working principle: "No statement, theological or otherwise, should be made that would not be credible in the presence of the burning children."[13]

What is there to say in the presence of burning children?

And how can Christians keep putting those ashes on their foreheads? What can ashes possibly mean after infants have been tossed onto pyres alive?

To explore this issue, cautiously, tentatively, keeping Greenberg's dictum in mind, we will begin with a consideration of the Ash Wednesday liturgy, focusing especially on its scriptural readings. Second, we will show how these might be illuminated by two other texts featuring dust and ashes, namely, the expulsion story in Genesis 3 and Job's last speech in the Book of Job. Finally, we will explore how the meaning of death changed with the twentieth century's capacity for inflicting mass annihilation. What this chapter hopes to show is that Ash Wednesday should remind Catholics not simply of their own mortality but also of the power humans now have for murder on a massive scale. The day issues a call to repent of how that power was used in the Holocaust, and to be vigilant that it not be used in such a way again.

ASH WEDNESDAY: A HISTORY

Ash Wednesday begins the season of Lent. On this day each year, Catholics as well as other Christians around the world gather to inaugurate forty days of fasting, prayer, and almsgiving. Ash Wednesday is not a Holy Day of Obligation; in other words, attendance at Mass on this day is not incumbent upon the faithful. And yet, at least in the United States, churches draw large congregations on Ash Wednesday, and pews are filled with Catholics wishing to offer gestures of repentance for their sins.

Ash Wednesday is a day designated for fasting and abstinence. The meaning of these terms varies from country to country, but in the United States, anyone between the ages of eighteen and fifty-nine is asked to eat only one full meal during the day, and, in addition, those fourteen and older are asked to abstain from eating meat.[14] All of the faithful are urged to use the period of Lent which begins with Ash Wednesday to increase their efforts in prayer, self-denial, and works of mercy.

The Christian practice of placing ashes on the heads of the faithful on Ash Wednesday goes back over a thousand years. By the tenth century, an English monk named Aelfric described the ritual as already widespread: "On the Wednesday, throughout the whole world, the priests bless, even as it is appointed, clean ashes in church, and afterward lay them upon men's heads, that they may have in mind that they came from earth, and shall again return to dust . . . We read in the books, both in the old Law and in the new, that the men who repented of their sins bestrewed themselves with ashes, and clothed their bodies with sackcloth."[15] At the Synod of Benevento in 1091, Pope Urban II urged that all churches adopt the custom.[16]

Rituals involving dust and/or ashes can be traced much further back, to ancient Near-Eastern stories and rites. At times, dust and ashes were associated with mourning. For example, the Tanakh says that Tamar put dust on her head after she was raped by her half-brother and then sent away (2 Sam. 13:19). Job, after losing his children and goods at the hands of the Accuser, went and sat on an ash heap (Job 2:8). The prophet Ezekiel foretold mourning on behalf of the city of Tyre by predicting, "They shall cast dust on their heads / And strew ashes on themselves" (27:30). In the Book of Esther, when Mordecai heard of the sentence of death that had been passed on all the Jews, he put on sackcloth and ashes (4:1).

At other times, dust and ashes are connected more explicitly with repentance. For example, Daniel fasted in sackcloth and ashes, crying to God, "We have sinned; we have gone astray; we have acted wickedly; we have been rebellious and have deviated from Your commandments and Your rules . . ." (Dan. 9:3–5). In the Book of Jonah, when the king of Nineveh heard of God's displeasure, he put on sackcloth and sat in ashes, demanding that his people turn from their evil ways. He even ordered Nineveh's livestock to repent, directing that they don sackcloth and cry mightily to God (3:6–9).

In his famous work *The Elementary Forms of the Religious Life*, anthropologist Emile Durkheim noted a relation between rituals of mourning and rituals of expiation, both of which he designated as "piacular" rites. The term derives from the Latin word *piaculum* which, though it usually refers to means of appeasing a deity through sacrifice, also calls to mind anything that inspires fear or sorrow. Durkheim observed, "At bottom, the sentiment which is at the root of the real expiatory rites does not differ in nature from that which we have found at the basis of the other piacular rites: it is a sort of irritated sorrow which tends to manifest itself by acts of destruction."[17] We should not be surprised that in the ritual of Ash Wednesday we encounter a mixture of dread, penitence, and a keen sense of mortality.

CELEBRATING ASH WEDNESDAY

In Catholic practice, there is no requirement that the celebration of Ash Wednesday take place during a Mass. The liturgical norms stipulate that ashes can be given apart from a eucharistic celebration (that is, apart from a service in which the faithful receive the sacrament of communion), though they should not be imposed apart from a service in which the day's scriptural portions are read. Those scriptural readings, which do not vary from year to year, include Joel 2:12–18, 2 Corinthians 5:20–6:2, and Matthew 6:1–6, 16–18. Several themes bind these texts together, the most important of which is the need for hearers to be reconciled to God. Underlying each of the readings one also finds a common assumption about history: that events have a meaning determined by God, and that things will go well for those who do what God has commanded.

In the first reading, the Book of Joel urges hearers to repent and to return to God with fasting, weeping, and mourning. If the hearers do so, the text promises, God might remove the scourge (whether it is locusts or invading armies is unclear) that has befallen them. Repentance must come first:

> Even now, says the LORD,
>   return to me with your whole heart,
>   with fasting, and weeping, and mourning;
> Rend your hearts, not your garments,
>   and return to the LORD, your God.

Then comes the possibility of reward:

> Perhaps he [God] will again relent
>   and leave behind him a blessing . . .

Apparently the people's efforts are successful, as the reading concludes,

> Then the LORD was stirred to concern for his land
>   and took pity on his people. (*Lectionary* n. 219)[18]

In the second reading, Paul appeals to the Corinthians for repentance. He does not prescribe particular rituals of remorse; instead, he simply urges his readers:

> We implore you on behalf of Christ,
>   be reconciled to God.

It is clear that in the short run, those who work for Christ will face hardship. In a part of the letter not included in the Ash Wednesday reading, Paul recounts how he has suffered beatings, imprisonment, sleepless nights, and hunger, as well as many other afflictions (6:4–5). Such suffering is a small matter, though, "For this slight momentary affliction is preparing us for an eternal weight of glory beyond all measure, because we look not at what can be seen but at what cannot be seen; for what can be seen is temporary, but what cannot be seen is eternal" (4:17–18). In this text, the reward for doing what God commands is not immediate. It is postponed until another day, but it will come just as surely as day follows night. Thus the portion read during the liturgy concludes:

> Behold, now is a very acceptable time;
> behold, now is the day of salvation.

The Ash Wednesday Gospel reading (Matt. 6:1–6, 16–18) is a speech in which Jesus urges his followers to be discreet in performing religious acts. First, says Jesus, the disciples should not give charitable donations publicly, but should do so as privately as possible:

> "But when you give alms,
>   do not let your left hand know what your right is
>   doing,
>   so that your almsgiving may be secret.
> And your Father who sees in secret will repay you."

Second, they should not pray in the synagogues to be noticed but should pray in their rooms with the doors closed: "And your Father who sees in secret will repay you." Third, when they fast they should not look glum or let others know that they are fasting, but they should wash their faces and comb their hair: "And your Father who sees what is hidden will repay you."

As Jacques Derrida has pointed out, on the surface of this passage is a renunciation of reward: the disciples are told not to look for the pleasures of public recognition or esteem. However, at the same time, the disciples are promised that if they sacrifice social rewards they will gain other (and presumably better) profits from God. Derrida observes that "an infinite calculation supersedes the finite calculating that has been renounced. God the Father, who sees in secret, will pay back your salary, and on an infinitely greater scale."[19] The disciples are not asked to give for the sheer joy of giving or for the good of others. Rather, they are promised that their good deeds will be noticed by God and that they will receive compensation for them.

The conviction that there is a moral order to the universe, that the good will be rewarded and the wicked punished, and, further, that those rewards and punishments can be discerned in the events of history, is very old. It has a home in ancient Judaism as well as in Christian tradition from its inception. After Auschwitz, however, it is a conviction that many find troubling. Richard Rubenstein, famous for his "death of God" theology, says that the turning point of his theological career came during an interview he had with a German Protestant clergyman regarding the meaning of the Holocaust. The clergyman had worked heroically against the Nazis and had testified at the Eichmann trial. And yet when it came to the murder of six million Jews, the pastor felt very strongly that what had happened in the camps was the will of God. Rubenstein recalls: "He looked at recent events from a thoroughly biblical perspective. In the past, the Jews had been smitten by Nebuchadnezzar and other 'rods of God's anger' [see Jeremiah 27:6 as well as Isaiah 10:5]. Hitler was simply another such rod . . . Of course, he granted that what Hitler had done was immoral, and he insisted that Hitler's followers were now being punished by God."[20] For the pastor, history was the stage on which God's will was continually enacted. He was not alone in his views. Franz Stangl, *Kommandant* of the Treblinka death camp, also seems to have believed in the sovereignty of God over world events. Shortly before his death Stangl was asked by an interviewer, "Was God in Treblinka?" His answer: "Yes. Otherwise, how could it have happened?"[21]

And yet such confidence in an overarching plan of God working itself out in history can seem too monstrous to contemplate. Philosopher Emil Fackenheim rejects in particular the notion that the Holocaust was punishment for sin. He points to the fact that the Nazis killed regardless of their victims' religious beliefs or actions; under German law, anyone who simply had three or, in many cases, two Jewish grandparents was subject to extermination.[22] Fackenheim asserts that "not a single one of the six million died because they had failed to keep the divine-Jewish covenant: they all died because their grandparents *had* kept it, if only to the minimum extent of raising Jewish children." He concludes, "Here is the rock on which the 'for our sins are we punished' suffers total shipwreck."[23] Richard Rubenstein summarizes his own position by stating, "I have elected to accept what Camus has rightly called the courage of the absurd, the courage to live in a meaningless, purposeless Cosmos rather than believe in a God who inflicts Auschwitz on his people."[24]

And yet the Ash Wednesday liturgy is filled with prayers that a faithful heart will merit divine reward and be spared divine punishment. During the blessing of the ashes, the presider prays, "Pardon our sins and keep us faithful to the discipline of Lent, for you do not want sinners to die but to live with the risen Christ, who reigns with you for ever and ever." During the imposition of ashes, the following antiphon may be sung (though there are two other options as well): "Let the priests and ministers of the Lord lament before his altar, and say: Spare us, Lord; spare your people! Do not let us die for we are crying out to you." After the faithful receive the Eucharist, the priest prays, "Lord, through this communion may our lenten penance give you glory and bring us your protection."[25] The economy is clear: pay in repentance what you hope to gain in security.

In some strands of Christian tradition, this economy has been taken with deadly seriousness. The tenth-century English monk Aelfric tells of a certain man who refused to receive ashes on Ash Wednesday. The man (or, as Aelfric calls him, "the heretic") went riding later in the week and was attacked by hounds. In the process of defending himself, he was impaled on his own spear: "He was then buried, and there lay upon him many loads of earth within seven nights, because he had refused those few ashes." Another man who broke the lenten fast nearly died as the result of consuming a single morsel. Still another failed to observe the lenten regulations regarding abstaining from drink and was gored by a wild boar, "and so paid for the untimely draught."[26] Christians such as Aelfric could see the hand of God quite clearly in the events of history.

But then there is the Holocaust. The Holocaust can be thought of as part of a divine plan or as punishment for sin only if one is willing to tell one million burning children that their murders are part of God's will. The position seems untenable.

Nor can one simply relocate the question of reward and punishment, looking for satisfaction only in a world to come. It would be quite easy to disregard the events of history entirely and to say simply that in the end, at a Final Judgment, the good will be saved and the evil lost, and that up until then we should not attempt to discern the hand of God. This would have the effect, however, of obliterating any notion of salvation history. It would remove God entirely from the sphere of human events except in the capacity of onlooker and scorekeeper. But the *Shoah* is a problem precisely because Judaism has consistently looked to history to discern the will of God. Philosopher Eliezer Berkovits explains, "For the person who does not recognize the presence of God in the Exodus, at Sinai, in the words of the prophets, in innumerable events of Jewish history, Auschwitz presents no problem of faith. For him God is forever absent. Only the Jew who has known of the presence of God is baffled and confounded by Auschwitz."[27] If God were not understood as having a role in world events, the Holocaust would remain a terrible human question, to be sure, but it would be devoid of theological significance.

Likewise, a Catholic theology cannot afford to turn the events of this world into mere shadows of a more "real" world to come. To do so would be to deny the significance not only of Jewish history, but also of the life of Jesus and of all that has happened in Christian life since. And so Catholic theology is, like Judaism, caught between a view of history in which every twist and turn of events can be read as an expression of the will of God, on the one hand, and a vision in which history occurs either outside of or merely as a prelude to divine will, on the other. If it chooses the former, it turns mass murder into the will of God. If it chooses the latter, it abandons the very foundation on which it is based.

It seems there is no way out of the dilemma.

Perhaps we will fare better if we take a cue from Elie Wiesel, who, in the context of precisely this problem, writes, "Therefore, I never speak of God now. I rather speak of men who believed in God or men who denied God."[28] Perhaps we will find surer footing if we construct a theology based not on speculation about what God has done or will do, but rather on what has in recent years become known as the "turn to the subject." If we take as our starting point the human experience of faith and the texts which that experience has generated, we might find new insights into problems that are ancient and yet at the same time terribly new.

In this light, the scriptural portions read on Ash Wednesday, as well as the accompanying prayers and antiphons, can be read, not as descriptions of the world as it is, but rather as expressions of the writers' outrage at injustice. They can be understood, not as rules explaining a divine economy of repentance and reward, but as cries against a situation in which might makes right and evil is allowed to flourish. The meaning of history is mysterious and elusive. We cannot point with confidence to events as definitive examples of divine reward or punishment. What remains constant, however, is the responsibility that believers take upon themselves for obeying the precepts of God. The fact that we cannot conclusively discern the meaning of events does not excuse us from acting in accordance with what the scriptures prescribe for those who seek to serve the Lord.

This point is illuminated by two other biblical texts in which dust and ashes play a crucial role. The Book of Job, unlike the readings from the Ash Wednesday liturgy, does not provide a clear vision of what an ideal world would look like. It does provide insights, though, into the meaning of our mortality, and it points us in directions that may prove helpful in constructing a post-Auschwitz theology. Before examining the story of Job, however, we should look more closely at the story in Genesis 3 of the expulsion of the first man and woman from the Garden of Eden. Interpretations of that story underlie much Catholic thinking on the nature of sin and the need for repentance.

DUST: GENESIS AND RETURN

During the Ash Wednesday service, those in the congregation are asked to come forward to have their foreheads marked with the sign of ashes. As the priest or other minister imposes the ashes, he or she can choose either of two exhortations, one of which is "Remember, man, you are dust and to dust you will return."[29] Humans are dust. The reminder hearkens back to the Genesis story of creation, in which the Lord God formed the first human being ('ādām) out of the earth ('ādāmāh). Further, it evokes the expulsion of the first man and woman from the Garden of Eden, as God says, "By the sweat of your brow / Shall you get bread to eat, / Until you return to the ground ['ădāmāh]—

/ For from it you were taken. For dust you are, / And to dust you shall return" (Gen. 3:19).

In Hebrew there is a clear linguistic connection between being human and being made of the earth. In English, much the same connection is expressed by a constellation of words that includes human, humus, humility, and homage. Because we are human and made from humus, we are humble before the Lord and give the Lord homage. We make ourselves like dirt before the living God because the living God made us from dirt into the divine image. We are dirt. We will be dirt. Remember that, we are told, and give homage to the Lord in fasting and prayer and humility.

The story of the expulsion of Adam and Eve from the garden has come to signify far more, though, than a simple reminder of the humble origins of human beings. Since at least the fifth century, Christians have interpreted the events recounted in the story as having cosmic significance. They are not understood simply as things that happened long ago and far away, but rather as events of the most pressing urgency here and now.

Throughout Christian history, there have been a number of interpretations of the Genesis story. Early on, followers of Jesus tended to read the Genesis text in the same way most Jewish interpreters did: as a cautionary tale about the perils of disobedience. Rabbinic commentators accepted the notion that Adam and Eve were cast out of paradise because they ate the fruit of the forbidden tree. This expulsion had consequences not only for them, but for their children as well. According to the Apocalypse of Moses (a pseudepigraphical text with roots in the first century C.E.), as Adam lay dying, he sent Eve and their son Seth to the gates of paradise to ask for oil from the tree of divine mercy; the oil would ease his pain and allow him to rest. Unfortunately, the archangel Michael refused the request, at which point Adam cried out to Eve, "Why have you wrought destruction among us and brought upon us great wrath, which is death gaining rule over all our race?"[30]

In texts such as this one, not only human beings were affected by the couple's disobedience, but the natural world as well. The earth, because it did not take proper notice of the sin and inform God of it, was sentenced by God to be watered only from above, and to have its fruits fail from time to time. It would bring forth sickly grain, barren trees, and thorns and thistles, and its surface would be broken up into valleys and mountains.[31] One tradition says that the moon, because it did not hide but shone after the sin of Adam, angered God, who "lay bare its days to affliction." For this reason the moon waxes and wanes rather than shining continually.[32]

And yet Jewish commentary mitigated somewhat the punishments meted out as a consequence of Adam and Eve's disobedience. One tradition reports that God had originally sentenced Adam to eat the same food as his animals and thus had said, "Cursed be the ground because of you; / By toil shall you eat of it / All the days of your life: / Thorns and thistles shall it sprout for you" (Gen. 3:17–18). However, when Adam broke out in a sweat and protested that the sentence was too harsh, God relented and said, "Since your face broke out in a sweat, 'You shall eat bread.'"[33] Moreover, as a substitute for the tree of life, God gave the Torah to Adam.[34] God also permitted Adam to bring spices such as cinnamon from the garden, so that even in exile he would be able to offer acceptable sacrifices to God.[35]

Nor was the exile of Adam necessarily for all time. According to the Apocalypse of Moses, upon Adam's death God called out to the man's body and told it, "I told you that *you are dust and to dust you shall return.* Now I promise to you the resurrection; I shall raise you on the last day in the resurrection with every man of your seed."[36] At Adam's death, angels took his body to paradise, where they anointed it and clothed it. Adam was then "buried according to the command of God in the regions of Paradise in the place from which God had found the dust."[37] Thus, though disobedience had dire consequences, these could be mitigated, and were, in the end, revocable.

Early Christian commentators focused considerable attention on the sin of Adam and Eve, understanding it along with Jewish interpreters as the cause of much human suffering. Sickness, pain in childbearing, and the need to support oneself by tilling the earth were all seen as consequences of sin. And yet interpreters differed when it came to the question of death: Was death a result of sin? Would Adam and Eve have been mortal, even if they hadn't been expelled from the garden?

According to two fifth-century theologians, Julian of Eclanum and Theodore of Mopsuestia, the answer was yes: Adam and Eve would have died even if they had not sinned. Julian and

Theodore, both bishops and both learned scholars, held that death was a natural part of human existence and could not be attributed to the actions of Adam. Argued Julian,

> Our mortality is not the result of sin, but of nature! Why does Genesis not say, "because you sinned and transgressed my precepts"? This should have been said, if bodily dissolution were connected with a crime. But recall, what does it say? "because you are earth." Surely this is the reason why one returns to earth, "because you were taken out of it." If this, then, is the reason God gives, that one was from earth, I think it can be assumed that one cannot blame sin. Without doubt it is not because of sin, but because of our mortal nature . . . that the body dissolves back into the elements.[38]

For Julian, as for his colleague Theodore, mortality was a natural and hence God-given component of human nature, and what God had made could not be evil.

The most vociferous opponent of the ideas of Julian and Theodore (both of whom are associated with the heresy known as Pelagianism) was Augustine of Hippo. Augustine argued that death was indeed a punishment handed down by God because of the sin of Adam. Augustine won the day, and his ideas were later enshrined at the Council of Trent, which in 1546 declared,

> If anyone does not profess that the first man Adam immediately lost the justice and holiness in which he was constituted when he disobeyed the command of God in the Garden of Paradise . . . and consequently incurred the death with which God had previously threatened him and, together with death, bondage in the power of him who from that time had the empire of death . . . that is, of the devil; "and that it was the whole Adam, both body and soul, who was changed for the worse through the offense of this sin" . . . let him be anathema.[39]

And yet, of course, Trent did not have the last word. The recent *Catechism of the Catholic Church* (2003), while affirming that death entered the world on account of sin, admits nonetheless that "man's nature is mortal," and that "in a sense bodily death is natural."[40] As the *Catechism* sees the matter, humans are naturally mortal but had been destined by God to be immortal. As a consequence of sin, humans were reduced back to their original state. Thus death *per se* is not a punishment, but the loss of immortality is.

Twentieth-century Catholic theologian Karl Rahner has given the relation between sin and death careful and subtle nuance. Rahner, while agreeing that death as we know it is a consequence of sin, maintains that death itself, that is, death as the natural end of human beings, is neither evil nor the result of Adam and Eve's disobedience. (Rahner, well schooled in evolutionary science, does not maintain that Adam and Eve are to be understood as literal historical beings, but uses "Adam" to mean "humanity in that form in which it existed at the beginning of its own history.")[41] According to Rahner, death is the "definitive consummation" of our existence. Death does not merely befall us, but is rather "the elevation of the history of freedom into its finality."[42] In dying, we gather ourselves into one final act of freedom, choosing for or against the grace of God that Rahner believes permeates all of our lives. Thus death is actually an opportunity for us to finalize our relationship to God in a definitive way.

What is unnatural about death, as Rahner sees it, and what can be identified as penalty for sin, is what he calls the "hiddenness" of death. Death comes to us in this post-Eden world as something fearful and unknown: as a rupture rather than as a gift. Writes Rahner, "Emptiness, hopelessness, surcease, insubstantiality, the indissoluble conjunction of supreme deed and sheer instinctive submission, of utter clarity and fundamental dubiousness: all these peculiarities of the death that we actually die are nothing but manifestations of sin."[43] Dying as transformation into a final life with God is a good; dying with fear, frustration, regret, ignorance regarding our future, or anger at our finitude (in other words, dying as we all do, to a greater or lesser extent) is a result of sin.

It is possible, then, to read the pronouncement in Genesis that we are dust and will return to dust not as a condemnation but simply as a statement of how things stand. We are mortal and come to an end in death. What we should make of that fact is another question, one we will take up in examining another biblical text in which dust and ashes figure prominently: the Book of Job.

DUST AND ASHES: THE BOOK OF JOB

The physical reminder of our humble human status as Lent begins is ashes, while the linguistic reminder is the word "dust." In the Tanakh, the term for dust (*'āpar*) is three times paired with the term for ashes (*'ēper*).[44] In the first of these instances, the pairing of *'āpar* and *'ēper* seems to designate the vulnerability and lowliness of human beings. It occurs in the Book of Genesis, as Abraham is pleading with God to spare the cities of Sodom and Gomorrah. Abraham prefaces his request to God by saying, "Here I venture to speak to my Lord, I who am but dust and ashes" (18:27). His remark is a self-humbling gesture recalling his origins and acknowledging himself to be of little worth. Notably, however, though he comes from dust and will one day be nothing but ashes, Abraham is still bold enough to argue his case before the Lord. His smallness in the face of what might easily become divine wrath does not deter him from urging God to treat the cities with fairness. This is a point we will return to shortly.

The other two pairings of "dust and ashes" appear in the Book of Job, and both of these are spoken by Job himself. The first occurs in an address Job makes to his friends. Having lost his livestock, servants, and children as the result of a wager between God and the Accusing Angel (*ha-satan*), and having been afflicted with sores on his body from head to foot due to that same wager, Job vents his frustration and decries his situation. Angry at his sudden turn of fortune, Job compares his status before his troubles began to his status as he speaks to his friends. In the past, he says, he took care of the needy and offered counsel to the many who sought his advice. Now, however, people laugh at him and keep their distance. What happened to change his situation? Says Job, "He [God] regarded me as clay, I have become like dust and ashes" (30:19). An alternative translation reads, "He has flung me to the muck, and I'm a cliché, like dust and ashes."[45] Here, as in Abraham's speech, the phrase "dust and ashes" signifies "of little worth." The fragility of humankind is understood not simply as a fact but also as a judgment; Job has no more value than does muck or clay or an empty cliché.

The next instance of the two terms appearing together occurs in Job's final speech to God (42:6). Throughout the text, Job has demanded that God appear so that he might press his case against what he perceives to be divine injustice: "Indeed, I would speak to the Almighty; I insist on arguing with God" (13:3). Finally, God appears, or at least God speaks. Addressing Job as a voice from a whirlwind, God demands, "Who is this who darkens counsel, / Speaking without knowledge? / Gird your loins like a man; / I will ask and you will inform Me" (38:2–3). God then recites a long litany of divine accomplishments and offers several mocking reminders that Job himself is poor and puny and would never be able to accomplish anything nearly so wonderful as God has. God asks, "Where were you when I laid the earth's foundations? / Speak if you have understanding. / Do you know who fixed its dimensions / Or who measured it with a line?" (38:4–5). God continues: "Do you give the horse his strength? / Do you clothe his neck with a mane?" (39:19). And again: "Is it by your wisdom that the hawk grows pinions, / Spreads his wings to the south?" (39:26). Job, in other words, is being told by God to remember that he is merely dust, and that unto dust he will return.

In response, Job acknowledges his vulnerability before the greatness of God: "See, I am of small worth; what can I answer You?" (40:4). God, however, does not seem satisfied with this answer and continues to goad Job: "Have you an arm like God's? / Can you thunder with a voice like His?" (40:9). In verse after verse, God recalls divine achievements and shows the impotence of Job. Finally, God finishes speaking, and Job is allowed one more opportunity to make his voice heard. What he says, however, is enigmatic. At first Job simply repeats a theme he has returned to again and again: the overwhelming power of God. He says to God, "I know that You can do everything, / That nothing you propose is impossible for You." He then acknowledges his own limitations: "Indeed, I spoke without understanding / Of things beyond me, which I did not know" (42:2–3). His final verse, though, is both difficult to translate and difficult to interpret. It is not surprising that renderings of Job 42:6 vary widely. However, how one interprets this small sentence affects how one understands the meaning of the entire book.

In Hebrew, the text of 42:6 reads, *'al-kēn 'emě'as wěnikhamtî 'al-'āpār wā'ēper.*[46] The first term, *'al-kēn*, simply means "therefore," or "upon such conditions." The second term, *'emě'as*, is a verb that means to reject or to refuse or to despise. It is the term Job uses to describe how children react to his maggot-ridden body (19:18). The third term begins with the prefix that means "and" and is a verb meaning to be sorry, to suffer grief, or to console oneself. The last two terms are preceded by a preposition and, as we have seen, refer to dust and ashes. A literal translation thus might read, "Therefore I despise and I am sorry upon dust and ash."[47] Consider, though, how various translators have rendered the passage:

> "Therefore I despise myself and repent in dust and ashes." (New Revised Standard Version)

> "Therefore I recant and relent, being but dust and ashes." (Jewish Publication Society)

> "Therefore I feel loathing contempt and revulsion (toward you, O God); and I am sorry for frail man." (John Briggs Curtis)[48]

> "I shudder with sorrow for mortal clay." (Jack Miles)[49]

> "Therefore I despise and repent of dust and ashes." (Edwin M. Good)[50]

The first two translations assume that the target of Job's negative feelings is himself. The New Revised Standard Version (NRSV) makes this clear, inserting the object "myself" into the text, even though the word does not appear in the Hebrew. Though the translation of the Jewish Publication Society (JPS) is not as explicit as that of the NRSV, it nonetheless portrays Job as dissatisfied with his words, if not with his very self, and thus as willing to "recant and relent."

The next translation, that offered by John Briggs Curtis, also hypothesizes that there is a missing object in the sentence. As Curtis reads the text, however, the implied object of Job's scorn is not himself but rather God. Curtis considers two other verses within the story (7:16 and 34:33) in which Job expresses revulsion, and he concludes that at least in 42:6, if not also in these other two, "there can be little doubt that the unexpressed object of the loathing is God."[51] Indeed, the JPS version of the Tanakh translates 34:33, in which Elihu reproaches Job, as, "Should He requite as you see fit? But you have despised (Him)!"[52] Here the translation apparently has no qualms about inserting the missing object, God, into the sentence. It is only later, when it comes to Job's final speech, that the JPS seems unwilling to insert "God" as the object. Curtis speculates that in 42:6, if not also in 7:16 and 34:33, an editor may have removed the name of God from the text in order to spare the sensibilities of more pious readers.

The translation of Jack Miles differs from that of Curtis in that Miles assumes that the object of both of the two verbs is not missing but is rather present in the sentence. Miles understands the pair of verbs to be a hendiadys—two words expressing a single action. Hence, he renders the verbs as one movement; Job "shudders with sorrow." As Miles sees the passage, though, the cause of Job's shuddering is neither Job himself nor God, but rather humanity as the frail creature of God: humanity as dust and ashes. According to Miles, when Job looks at the pathetic being whom God has created, he feels both disgust and pity. Miles explains, "Revulsion and compassion are not mutually exclusive. Who, seeing photographs from the Nazi concentration camps, has not felt both?"[53] Job's encounter with the living God, in Miles's view, does nothing to change his mind about the wretched state of humanity. Rather, upon hearing the divine voice, Job comes to know even more clearly that he is in the right and that God is in the wrong. God really has acted unjustly, and Job is correct to call him to account.

Miles's translation has an advantage over the previous three in that it does not supply words not present in the text itself. Edwin M. Good's translation enjoys this same advantage. Like Miles, Good assumes that the object of the verbs is present in the sentence: namely, "dust and ashes." Where he differs, however, is in his interpretation of what that dust and those ashes mean. As Good sees it, what Job rejects in the verse is repentance itself. Good explains, "Insofar as 'dust and ashes' stands for the abjection of rituals of repentance for sin and of mourning for the dead, to 'repent of dust and ashes' is to give up the religious structure that construes the world in terms of guilt and innocence. It is to repent of repentance."[54] The point of the text, as Good sees it, is that evaluating the world in terms of guilt and innocence is useless. Worse, it is a misconstrual of reality. Good concludes, "The world's events are not responses to human moral activity and inward disposition . . . [T]he world spins on its own kind of order, of which Job had very little sense."[55]

All of these interpretations are complicated by the fact that after Job finishes his speech, God has one last scene. In the last few verses of the book, God tells one of Job's companions, "I am incensed at you and your two friends, for you have not spoken the truth about Me as did My servant Job" (42:7). God then commands Job's three friends to sacrifice bulls and rams in the presence of Job, and God indicates that things will go very badly for them unless Job prays on their behalf. When Job does pray, God increases his holdings twofold. God gives him twice what he had before, as well as ten new children.

We must wonder, though, what exactly Job said that gained him such favor from God. The friends, we are told, did not speak the truth about God *as Job did*. What truth did Job speak? And where did the friends go wrong?

The first two translations of 42:6, those that see the passage as expressing repentance on Job's part, seem unable to provide satisfactory answers to these questions. For if we assume that Job was speaking the truth during his long complaints against God, then why should Job despise himself, recant, or relent in 42:6? If he had been speaking the truth in his tirades against God, then recanting would be duplicitous. Alternatively, if we assume that Job spoke the truth in repenting in 42:6, then why are the friends taken to task by God? They, after all, were the ones who had urged Job to repent all along. Zophar the Naamathite, for example, had advised Job, "[I]f you direct your mind, / and spread forth your hands toward Him—If there is iniquity with you, remove it, and do not let injustice reside in your tent— / Then, free of blemish, you will hold your head high" (11:13–15). Why should Zophar or the other two friends be blamed by God for telling Job to repent, if it was in his repentance that Job spoke the truth?

Of course, we might translate the text in accordance with the NRSV and the JPS, but *interpret* it quite differently. Elie Wiesel, who so often identifies himself with Job in his own writings, does precisely this in an essay called "Job: Our Contemporary." In this essay, Wiesel at first expresses outrage at the cravenness of Job's final speech. He imagines Job as saying to God, "Yes, I am indeed small, insignificant; I had no right to speak, I am unworthy of Your words and thoughts. I didn't know, I didn't understand. I couldn't know. From now on I shall live with remorse, in dust and ashes."[56] Such cowardice on Job's part is a betrayal, as Wiesel sees it, of the millions who suffered unjustly, the millions who "could be seen on every road of Europe. Wounded, robbed, mutilated. Certainly not happy. Nor resigned."[57]

However, Wiesel also offers an alternative assessment of Job's words. Perhaps, he suggests, Job's quick abdication is really a gesture of defiance against and an indictment of God. Writes Wiesel, "He did not hesitate or procrastinate, nor did he point out the slightest contradiction. Therefore we know that in spite or perhaps because of appearances, Job continued to interrogate God. By repenting sins he did not commit, by justifying a sorrow he did not deserve, he communicates to us that he did not believe in his own confessions; they were nothing but decoys."[58] In this reading of the text, Job does not surrender his dignity or his right to question God's justice, just as Wiesel himself continues to ask God about the murders of six million.

Wiesel's interpretation actually takes us closer to the translations of Job 42:6 offered by Curtis and Miles. Those renderings, it should be pointed out, seem better able than the first two translations to handle the Book of Job's conclusion. If in 42:6 Job expresses not repentance but rather contempt for God and/or sorrow for human beings, then perhaps what follows is God's recognition of just how badly Job was treated. The fact that God gives back twice what Job had before his trials occurred might be read as evidence that it is God who repents rather than Job. After all, the Torah stipulates, "In all charges of misappropriation . . . the case of both parties shall come before God: he whom God declares guilty shall pay double to the other" (Exodus 22:8).[59] By restoring Job's fortunes, perhaps God is acknowledging divine wrongdoing and recognizing Job's uprightness. Moreover, God's anger at Job's friends would then be due to their willingness to speak well of God even when God did not deserve such praise. They would be told to offer sacrifices for acting as yes-men, rather than as servants with the dignity and self-respect that Job exhibited.

Before pursuing this idea further, let us turn to Edwin Good's translation to see how it might make sense in light of the last scene of the Book of Job. Recall that Good's translation has Job rejecting paradigms of guilt and debt altogether. What Job repents of is not sin, but rather religion itself. However, as we have seen, in the text's final episode Job agrees to pray on behalf of his friends, and as a result God gives him double what he had before. The irony of this is not lost on Good. He comments, "That makes no unitary sense."[60] By the end of the book, Good points out, the friends seem to have been right all along in saying that God rewards pious behaviors, even though God says that they were wrong. Job, who according to God spoke the truth in rejecting religion, nonetheless is rewarded for enacting religious rituals. And God, who (as Good understands the matter) praised Job for speaking rightly when he rejected religion, seems to renege on that insight and reward religious behavior instead. Good's explanation of this is simply that the book is fraught with ambiguities and uncertainties and that no unitary interpretation of it is possible. He concludes, "The world is full of jokes. Religion is only one of them."[61] For all of its insights into human weakness and suffering, the Book of Job, in Good's view, leaves us with as many questions as we had when we began.

Which, as it happens, brings us back to where we began: Ash Wednesday. What can the Book of Job tell us about Ash Wednesday?

During that solemn day's ceremony, the faithful are marked with ashes, and one of the two exhortations they might hear is "Remember that you are dust and to dust you shall return." The ritual is a stark reminder of mortality, but it is also, at the same time, a theological statement. The question we have been trying to address is precisely *what kind* of theological statement the ritual makes. What do we learn by being told that we are mortal?

It seems that Good is correct and that no single interpretation of the Book of Job is able to accommodate all of the text's twists and turns. The best we can hope for, then, is tentative interpretations and partial insights. In that spirit I offer the following:

First, the Book of Job should not be read as endorsing repentance on Job's part for sins he did not commit. The NRSV's translation, in which Job despises himself and repents in dust and ashes, seems insupportable, both because of its questionable insertion of the reflexive pronoun and because of its inability to explain the text's final outcome. Moreover, unless interpreted in the sense indicated by Wiesel, the JPS translation, in which Job recants and relents because he is dust and ashes, suffers from the same weaknesses.

Second, we can then say with confidence that the book does not use the fact that humans are "dust and ashes" as an excuse for them to abdicate moral responsibility. If in 42:6 Job were to have repented for sins that both he and God knew he did not commit, then our very status as moral agents would have been undercut. The message of the book would have been something like, "Yes, God is arbitrary and capricious, but your job is to accede to divine whims at all costs." Human beings would then be relieved of any and all questions regarding justice or righteousness, and our role would simply be to cower in the face of divine command. That this translation/interpretation is less than persuasive indicates that craven obedience is not what the text seeks to endorse. Just as Abraham pleaded his case before God even though he was but dust and ashes, Job refused to surrender himself to something that he believed to be wrong.

Third, the text can at the least be read as a critique of a God who demands righteous behavior of humans but who does not always exhibit such righteousness. Whether one translates 42:6 as expressing "loathing, contempt and revulsion" towards God, as John Briggs Curtis does, or simply as a sorrowful shuddering for the mortal clay shaped by God's hands, the book allows for human beings to question God and to press for a more just universe.

Fourth, even if Good is correct that Job in 42:6 abjures any paradigm of sin and guilt, the same does not hold true for the friends. The text, in other words, does not appear as a wholesale rejection of rituals of repentance. Job's friends are still asked to make recompense for their failure to speak the truth. They are also told, at least implicitly, to ask forgiveness for their actions from Job, as the sacrifice they offer must take place in Job's presence, and Job must agree to pray for them lest God treat them vilely (42:8). The friends are not told to grovel before God, nor does the text report that they offer the sacrifices simply out of fear or with a false sense of repentance. They are, however, called to account for their actions and to make right what they had done wrong.

Finally, the Book of Job muddies any effort to discern a clear correspondence between being righteous and being rewarded. At the beginning of the text, Job is a faithful servant of God and a wealthy man. Then his wealth is taken from him, though he is no less faithful a servant. At the end of the text, Job does what God tells him to do and is rewarded for it. Good is correct that "this makes no unitary sense." We cannot say on the basis of the Book of Job that God always rewards the faithful or that God always punishes the wicked. Nor, though, can we say that there is never a reason for the miseries that befall humans or the good things that come their way. All we can say is that neither disaster nor good fortune can be interpreted unambiguously as the plan of God.

In sum, what we learn from the Book of Job about being dust and ashes is that we are creatures who stand before a world that we do not understand, creatures who must take responsibility for our actions even when God does not seem so inclined. Moreover, we learn that meaningful repentance can take place only in the presence of those whom we have wronged. Finally, we learn that when God chooses to listen to the cries of human beings, it is to the voices of victims that God listens first.

It is those victims who challenge the meaning of Ash Wednesday in a post-Auschwitz world. The victims of the Nazis did not simply "return to dust." They were murdered (by people who had virtually all been raised as Christians) and they were burned, deliberately and purposefully. Technology and ideology combined to do on a massive scale what nature could not have done so efficiently. How that development has changed the very meaning of mortality is the final consideration of this chapter.

ASHES TO ASHES: MAN-MADE MASS DEATH

In her book *Spirit in Ashes: Hegel, Heidegger, and Man-Made Mass Death*, Edith Wyschogrod presents a history of how Western philosophers have thought of the meaning of death and its relation to life. She explains that for the most part, death has been viewed according to what she calls the "authenticity paradigm." This paradigm is governed by "the assumption that a good death, even if not free of pain, is the measure of a good life."[62] The ultimate test of one's life, according to this model, is whether one meets the inevitability of death with unflinching acceptance or with terror before the unknown.

Wyschogrod offers two examples of the authenticity paradigm, one ancient and one more modern. The first comes from Plato's *Phaedo*, which records the death of Socrates. According to the *Phaedo*, Socrates met his death not only with calm but with positive good cheer, taking time to instruct his disciples and to offer them words of encouragement even as the hemlock neared his lips. Because he had so thoroughly examined the nature of death while still alive, for him death held neither surprise nor sting. Socrates was able to accept the possibility that death would mean sinking into non-existence, even as he hoped that it might lead him to the freedom of the unimpaired soul, and the truth that is the goal of all philosophers. He underwent a "good death" because of the thoughtful and courageous quality of his life.

Wyschogrod's second example comes from the poetry of Rainer Maria Rilke. For Rilke, she says, death is not so much a future event as it is a dimension of the present. She explains that for the poet, "Only by integrating death into the texture of life is an authentic living and dying possible."[63] In this view, life can only be experienced in its depths if death is not only accepted but is allowed to illuminate each moment. And yet death does not thereby become the victor over life. Instead, death is the very condition of life; it is what makes the intensity of each moment possible and what makes each moment worth living.

This point is crucial to Wyschogrod's argument, as she believes that it is what differentiates Rilke's situation from our own. For Rilke, she explains, there is a continuity that binds the present and the future together. She cites the first of Rilke's *Duino Elegies:* "True it is strange to inhabit the earth no longer, / to use no longer customs scarcely acquired, / not to interpret roses, and other things / that promise so much, in terms of a human future . . . and to lay aside / even one's proper name like a broken toy."[64] Even as the poem contemplates the disruption between the cares of the living and the concerns of the dead, it asserts a continuity between them. Explains Wyschogrod, "For this reason the fundamental assumption, the hidden premise, which undergirds this verse is the indestructability of an accustomed field of reference—'the things that promise so much,' 'customs scarcely acquired,' 'roses,' 'the name laid aside'—since these are the stuff through which any meaningful grasp of the future comes about."[65]

However, says Wyschogrod, the possibility of anticipation, of "looking forward to," is precisely what has been called into question by the twentieth century and the advent of mass death. The threat of annihilation made possible by nuclear holocaust overwhelms any poetic holding-in-balance of life and death. We face, she observes, the prospect of wiping not only ourselves but all earthly being out of existence. This possibility of pure annihilation opens up a breach between our present and our future. In contemplation of mass destruction, we can no longer imagine, as Rilke did, the dead gently laying aside their customs, their roses, and their names like so many broken toys. We do not have the luxury of imagining individual souls parting reluctantly from those whom they leave behind. In the event of mass death, there is no one to leave behind, and thus no one to weight the meaning of death with a counterbalancing intensity of life. Concludes Wyschogrod, "By destroying the system of meanings which rendered death-accepting behavior possible, the effect of man-made mass death has undercut the power of the authenticity paradigm which permitted mastery over death."[66]

What can we say, then, about the Catholic admonition to remember that we are dust and that we will return to dust? Let us begin with what we cannot say. We cannot simply comfort ourselves with the idea that death is a part of life, that it always has been and always will be, and that our deaths will clear the way for the generation of new life. Not only has any projection towards "always" been called into question, but the notion that death contributes to life has been overshadowed by the possibility of the complete annihilation of all life. Moreover, death as the origin of life has been given sinister meaning by the calculations of Nazism: the use of human remains as fertilizer and stuffing for mattresses, among other things.[67] Such economics turn imagery of the "cycle of life" into mockery.

What we can say, however, is that we find ourselves at this point in history with extraordinary capabilities for inflicting death, and that reminders of that fact are more urgent than ever. Abraham and Job stood before a God who appeared capricious and who could return them to dust at any moment. Our capacity to inflict mass death is no less capricious and is, one might say, far more cunning. In *Spirit and Ashes*, Wyschogrod writes that what is unprecedented in our time is not so much the scale of annihilation as it is "that the *means* of annihilation are the result of systematic rational calculation, and scale is reckoned in terms of the compression of time in which destruction is delivered."[68]

Underlying the calculations of modern manufactured death is what Wyschogrod calls a "sorting myth," or a division of the cosmos into categories such as the righteous and the unrighteous, the pure and the impure, and the children of light and the children of darkness.[69] Such sorting myths have their roots in ancient religious thought, as Wyschogrod points out. The apocalypticism that marked the Jewish intertestamental period gave rise to Christian apocalypticism, and predictions of cosmic catastrophe have arisen periodically throughout the world ever since.

Ash Wednesday itself is a day of sorting, of distinguishing between the unrepentant and the repentant, the unsaved and the saved, and the believer and the hypocrite. However, what is new is our capacity to enact the apocalypse ourselves, to bring about apocalypse now. We have become the gods that we feared, and so our sorting myths are no longer simply hopes for a better world to come, but also blueprints for destruction. We have the power to wage upon all those whom we have "sorted out" the dire consequences that biblical writers could only threaten. They could devise sorting myths; we can enact them. Perhaps it is no coincidence that it was on Ash Wednesday that Dr. Joseph Goebbels, Hitler's Minister of Propaganda, wrote regarding Jews, "This riffraff must be eliminated and destroyed. Otherwise it won't be possible to bring peace to the world."[70]

As Wyschogrod points out, a sorting myth is able to feed on itself because those in its grip experience an ever more urgent need to clarify the categories that govern them. Purity becomes an obsession, as it did in Nazi Germany: "Yet the unconscious underlying assumption is that the null point—at which not a single individual in the group to be eliminated is left—functions as a *regulative ideal* which cannot be attained."[71] Sorting becomes ever more selective so that its logical end is annihilation. The spectre of nuclear warfare illustrates this possibility of sorting gone awry, as the very ones who initiated destruction would in the end succumb to the power that they unleashed.

If we take upon ourselves the powers of gods, our sorting will be disastrous. On the other hand, the ritual of ashes, understood as an expression of human longing for a more righteous world, can be a powerful call for self-scrutiny and reform. Seen in light of the twentieth century's experiments with mass death, the day can be a horrific reminder of what not God, but rather we, have wrought. Perhaps the admonition of Ash Wednesday should not be simply "Remember you are dust and to dust you shall return," but also, "Remember all those reduced to dust by the point of a sword, by clouds of poisonous gas, by bullets or bombs or slow starvation. Remember them and let their ashes turn you away from paths that lead only to death and destruction." It is not enough to remember that we ourselves are dust. We need to remember too that we have unprecedented powers for murder on a massive scale. If we are able to remember that we are dust, then, though we have the powers of gods, we might think twice before using those powers.

On September 6, 1944, Salmen Gradowski wrote a letter and then buried it in an aluminum canteen. He did not have the luxury of sending it to its addressee because Gradowski was a prisoner at Auschwitz. He was a member of the *Sonderkommando*, a group of Jews charged by the Nazis with disposing of the bodies of victims. His letter was discovered six months later during excavations of the site by the Special Investigating Commission of the Soviet Army. It was a long testimony, written in Yiddish, that detailed the author's deportation from Luna in 1942, his arrival at Auschwitz, and the horrors he witnessed during his time there. In his letter, Gradowski explains why he took the risk of recording his experiences:

> I have buried this under the ashes deeming it the safest place, where people will certainly dig to find the traces of millions of men who were exterminated.
>
> But lately they have begun obliterating the traces and everywhere, where there was much ash, they ordered to have it ground fine and to cart it away to the Vistula [River] and to let it flow with the current . . . Several graves are still full of ashes. Perhaps they had forgotten about them

or they themselves had maybe concealed it from the higher
authorities, why the order was: to obliterate all traces as
quickly as possible; so, by not carrying out that order, they
desisted from it . . .

Dear finder, search everywhere, in every inch of soil.
Tens of documents are buried under it, mine and those of
other persons, which will throw light on everything that
was happening here . . .[72]

In those ashes was buried a terrible choice, exactly the choice
that Ash Wednesday places in our hands each year. As humans
we are dust. As humans we have unprecedented powers to reduce
other humans to dust. What shall we do with our powers?

The choice the Nazis made did not spring from nowhere. Its
causes could be traced very clearly for those who had eyes to see.
One of those causes, it must be said, was nearly two thousand
years of Christian teaching of contempt for Jews, teaching that
had been reinforced by liturgy. As it happens, the ashes that are
distributed on Ash Wednesday are made from palm fronds
blessed at the previous year's Palm Sunday celebration. (This custom arose in the twelfth century and continues today.)[73] As we
will see in the next chapter, that celebration has a troubling history of its own, as its ritual reading of the Passion narratives
strengthened the notion that Jews were responsible for the death
of Jesus. Thus the ashes that call Christians to repentance each
year originate in a ceremony that has its own disturbing relation
to the Holocaust.

CHAPTER 3

Palm Sunday

In 1930, Adolph Hitler traveled to the Bavarian village of Oberammergau to watch the townspeople there enact their famous Passion play. Four years later, in celebration of the *Passionsspiel*'s three hundredth anniversary, he attended the performance again. This time he was greeted with great fanfare, and went on stage afterwards to congratulate the performers. The event must have made an impression on him, as in 1942 Hitler remarked that "it is vital that the Passion Play be continued at Oberammergau; for never has the menace of Jewry been so convincingly portrayed as in this presentation of what happened in the times of the Romans. There one sees in Pontius Pilate a Roman racially and intellectually so superior, that he stands out like a firm, clean rock in the middle of the whole muck and mire of Jewry."[1]

It may be shocking that a dramatic reenactment of the death of Jesus would have anything in common with Hitler's virulent hatred of Jews, but it should not be surprising. As we saw in Chapter 1, there is a long history of Christian accusations that Jews killed Jesus. This charge of deicide was used to incite the slaughter of the Jewish community in Mainz in 1096; in 1215, the Fourth Lateran Council forbade Jews to appear on public streets during Holy Week, presumably for their own protection.[2] In various countries and eras, local Church councils have had to issue laws against Passion dramas because of the violence against Jews that ensued.[3] If the virtue of drama is that it makes audiences feel as though they are active participants in the events unfolding on stage, this is also its danger.

What this chapter hopes to do is to show the interconnections among Passion plays, liturgy, history, and scripture as they relate to the death of Jesus, on the one hand, and to the history of anti-semitism on the other. At the center of this complex set of inter-relations lies Palm Sunday, the celebration that inaugurates Holy Week. As we will see, the Palm Sunday liturgy has come under increasing scrutiny as historians have revised their assessments of how Jesus died, and as the Church has revised its positions regarding Judaism and Jews.

THE PASSION OF JESUS: SCRIPTURE

There are basic similarities in the ways that the four canonical gospels portray the capture, sentencing, and death of Jesus. In the three synoptic gospels, for example, Jesus's disciple Judas meets secretly with Jewish leaders to make arrangements to betray Jesus (Matt. 26:14–16, Mark 14:10–11, Luke 22:3–6). According to all four of the gospels, Jesus arranges and holds a final meal with his disciples (Matt. 26:17–30, Mark 14:12–25, Luke 22:7–38, John 13:1–17:26). He then goes to a garden to pray (Matt. 26:36–46, Mark 14:32–42, Luke 22:39–46, John 18:1), and at that point, Judas brings a crowd to arrest Jesus (Matt. 26:47–56, Mark 14:43–50, Luke 22:47–53, John 18:2–12). Jesus is then taken before Jewish authorities (Matt. 26:57–68, Mark 14:53–65, Luke 22:54–71, John 18:13–27) and then to Pilate, where he is sentenced to die (Matt. 27:1–26, Mark 15:1–15, Luke 23:1–25, John 18:28–19:16). He is crucified, and after uttering a few final words, he succumbs to death (Matt. 27:32–56, Mark 15:21–40, Luke 23:26–49, John 19:17–37).

There are also, however, significant differences in the ways that the gospels tell the story. For example, according to John, the meal that Jesus holds with his friends takes place on the evening before Passover. The synoptics, on the other hand, portray the meal as a Passover celebration. Likewise, in their description of what happens at that meal, the synoptics include Jesus breaking bread and blessing a cup, actions not found in John.

Moreover, John's gospel contains details not found in the synoptics. According to John, Jesus washes his disciples' feet at the meal; later, the crowd that has arrested him takes Jesus to the house of Annas, father-in-law of the High Priest, before going to the house of Caiaphas. Neither of these events is recorded by the synoptics.

Luke's gospel differs from the other three in important ways as well. Luke has Pilate send Jesus to Herod, who then returns him to Pilate. And while Mark, Matthew, and John have Jesus brought before the Jewish authorities at night, Luke moves the interrogation to daybreak. The point is that different writers frame Jesus's story differently, often for dramatic effect or to express theological insights. However, what were written as theological narratives very soon came to be understood by Christians as literal accounts of what had happened. Explains Gerard Sloyan, "By the second century in the Greco-Roman world these believers were interpreting symbolic narrative as history. They had lost the Semitic skill of spotting a story crafted in biblical style. Christians have been misreading their own holy books ever since, often making Jews pay the price of their incomprehension."[4] This misunderstanding has been furthered by the Palm Sunday liturgy, which takes the gospel narratives and presents them in such a way that congregants feel as if they are actually reliving events that took place long ago. How this happens is the subject of the next section.

THE PASSION OF JESUS: LITURGY

The Palm Sunday liturgy, when celebrated in its fullest form, begins with a procession. After the presider dons red vestments and gathers with the congregation outside of the church, he begins the ceremony by praying, using what the *Sacramentary* calls "these or similar words":

> Today we come together to begin this solemn celebration in union with the whole Church throughout the world. Christ entered in triumph into his own city, to complete his work as our Messiah: to suffer, to die, and to rise again. Let us remember with devotion this entry which began his saving work and follow him with a lively faith. United with him in his suffering on the cross, may we share his resurrection and new life.[5]

There are four things to note immediately about this prayer. First, it utilizes verbs that heighten the sense that the liturgy is a re-enactment of what really took place in the time of Jesus.

Christians are asked to remember what happened then, to follow in Jesus's footsteps, and thus to share in Jesus's resurrection. The liturgy invokes memory and uses memory as a way of participating now in what happened then. Living as a Christian now means re-living the death of Jesus as it took place long ago.

Second, the prayer interprets the "saving work" of Jesus solely in terms of his death and resurrection. The saving work is not described in relation to Jesus's ministry as teacher, preacher or healer, as it is said to begin only with his entrance into Jerusalem.

Third, there is an emphasis in the prayer not simply on Jesus's death, but more specifically on his painful death. Jesus's work as messiah seems primarily to be found in his suffering, a suffering with which the faithful have been joined. Both of these points are reinforced by the opening prayer of the Mass itself, one version of which says, "Almighty, ever-living God, you have given the human race Jesus Christ our Savior as a model of humility. He fulfilled your will by becoming man and giving his life on the cross. Help us to bear witness to you by following his example of suffering and make us worthy to share in his resurrection."[6] Again, in this presentation, Jesus fulfills God's will not by preaching good news or by healing the sick. God's will is rather that Jesus should die a painful death, the example of which the faithful are encouraged to follow. As I will argue in Chapter Five, these details lead to a one-sided interpretation of the meaning of Jesus's death. They emphasize his suffering without presenting the context for it: that Jesus challenged the oppressive structures of his time and hence was executed by a brutal regime.

The final thing to note about the prayer is that Jesus, according to the text, entered Jerusalem "to suffer, to die, and *to rise* again." In this prayer, Jesus is not raised by God; rather, he *rises*, apparently of his own power. It is true that the idea of Jesus resurrecting himself does appear in the New Testament (e.g., John 10:17–18). However, the thrust of most early Christian preaching was not that Jesus had risen, but that Jesus had been raised up by God. Indeed, the earliest kerygma was the proclamation that God had raised Jesus from the dead. Only in the late first century did Christians begin to preach that Jesus rose due to his own power.[7] This point will be developed more fully in Chapter Seven, but it is well to note here how the Palm Sunday liturgy understands the resurrection.

What follows the procession's introductory prayer is the blessing of the palm branches that have been distributed to the congregation. The priest then offers a prayer and sprinkles the branches with holy water. Next, a gospel account of Jesus's entry into Jerusalem is read, and then the faithful process into the church. During this procession, the congregation sings appropriate songs or antiphons. The following are suggested: "The children of Jerusalem welcomed Christ the King. They carried olive branches and loudly praised the Lord: Hosanna in the highest." Or: "The children of Jerusalem welcomed Christ the King. They spread their cloaks before him and loudly praised the Lord: Hosanna to the Son of David! Blessed is he who comes in the name of the Lord!"[8]

What is notable about these antiphons is that in singing them, the congregation identifies itself with the biblical children of Jerusalem. Like those Israelites of old, the congregation waves olive branches in praise of Jesus the messiah. Unlike them, however, they now see themselves as part of the new people of God, joined to the old through the ritual reenactment of memory, but at the same time set apart from them. They have inherited the promise given to Abraham, but also understand themselves as the recipients of a new covenant sealed with the blood of Jesus. Thus identity is both established and denied, a dynamic that we will have occasion to note several times throughout this book.

What follows the procession is the Liturgy of the Word, during which the celebrant may omit both the first reading (Isa. 50:4–7) and the second reading (Phil. 2:6–11).[9] He may not, however, omit the Gospel reading, in which an account of the Passion is read. This reading may be proclaimed by a single person, or different parts may be performed by different readers, though the voice of Jesus is reserved for the priest. The *Saint Joseph's Sunday Missal*, for example, divides the text into four parts: a narrator, Jesus, a Voice (who may represent such characters as Peter, Judas, and Pilate), and the Crowd, whose parts are read by the assembled congregation. It is the Crowd who is charged with such lines as "Away with this man!"and "Let him be crucified!" and "His blood be upon us and upon our children!"[10]

Regarding troubling lines such as these, which have caused Christians to accuse Jews of murdering the Christ, the *St. Joseph Sunday Missal* is careful to explain, "We are all responsible for sin and for our Lord's suffering." The *Missal* includes an explanation that the responsibility for Jesus's death "must not be laid against all the Jewish people of Jesus's day or of our own."[11] However, the power of the dramatic reading complicates this affirmation. For while the dramatic reading lends itself to a theology in which all people are responsible for Jesus's suffering, it tends in the opposite direction as well. On the one hand, the congregation is asked to accept responsibility for Jesus's death by the fact that they are the ones reciting the lines which condemn him. On the other hand, though, the congregation is aware that it is saying those lines as part of a liturgy of worship. Even as members of the congregation call for the condemnation of Jesus, they distance themselves by the fact that they are participating in a Christian ritual.

Moreover, the drama of the reading can easily lend itself to the misunderstanding that it was Jews who crucified Jesus. Historically, of course, this is simply not the case, as the Roman government both issued the sentence and carried out the actual execution. And yet in the liturgy, the members of the congregation who were just a few moments ago identified as being the children of Jerusalem now shout for Jesus's death. It is easy to see how a misunderstanding could arise.

Furthermore, though the *Missal* affirms that blame for the death of Jesus "must not be laid against all the Jewish people of Jesus's day or of our own," in the liturgical drama there are no dissenting voices as the crowd calls for crucifixion. The people speak as a whole in condemning Jesus. Again, it is easy to see how this kind of dramatic performance of the Gospel reading could lend itself to misunderstanding and, as has happened historically, to tragic misuse.

THE PASSION OF JESUS: MUSIC, DRAMA, AND FILM

It wasn't until the late Middle Ages that the Palm Sunday liturgy developed the offshoot known as the Passion play. Passion plays incorporated speeches and characters not found in the gospels themselves, and they embellished the canonical texts in order to heighten the dramatic tension of the story. The tradition of the Passion play has continued from the Middle Ages until our own time, as drama, music, and movies have sought over and over to re-present and reinterpret the suffering and death of Jesus.

In these efforts, several questions arise. In a discussion of how Jesus is presented in film, W. Barnes Tatum highlights four questions in particular. First, says Tatum, there are artistic issues to consider. Dramatic, musical, and cinematic depictions of Jesus must have aesthetic integrity and artistic appeal if they are to move their audiences. Second, one must attend to the literary problem that arises from the diverse portraits of Jesus found within the canonical gospels, as well as in extra-canonical writings. Third, there is the historical issue to consider, or, as Tatum puts it, "the recognition that a distinction can be made between the stories about Jesus, as written in the gospels in the last third of the first century, and Jesus the historical figure who lived out his life in Roman-occupied Palestine during the first third of that century."[12] Finally, Tatum points to theological questions, or issues related to faith-claims about Jesus: Is Jesus portrayed as both fully divine and fully human? What is Jesus's message? What is Jesus's significance? Why does Jesus die, and how or in what sense does he rise again?

Post-Auschwitz, these questions take on particular urgency. As we have seen, Passion plays have at times incited hatred and violence against Jews. The fact that Jesus was a Jew has often been obscured in artistic presentations of his life. For example, in 1936, Romanian Jewish writer Mihail Sebastian attended a performance of Bach's *St. Matthew Passion* in Bucharest. He wrote afterwards, "I found in it a lot that had remained in my memory since last year, but I also discovered many new things. I felt overwhelmed. I really had the physical sense of being beneath a canopy of sounds . . . And how many sweet passages, how many graceful moments!"[13] In 1937 he attended a performance in Leipzig, noting, "I'd been afraid that spring would pass without my hearing it. Nothing could have consoled me for that. Not only is it a great musical joy; it has become a superstition that seems to bode well for me."[14] By the next year, however, Sebastian's enthusiasm for the opera had begun to wane. On April 13, 1938, after attending a performance in Bucharest, he wrote, "By now I know it too well not to notice when it is badly performed . . . It is no longer enough for me just to read the text;

it has become too familiar to deliver by itself the emotion that I used to feel."[15]

And yet four days later, Sebastian experienced something of a revelation: "There are some simple things that I have always known, but that sometimes give me the arresting sense that I am discovering them for the first time," he wrote. "I suddenly remembered that Jesus was a Jew—something of which I am never sufficiently aware, and which forces me to think again about our terrible destiny . . . I have been reading Nietzsche's *Daybreak* since yesterday evening. Somewhere it talks of the 'Jewish ballast' in Christianity. How terribly ironic is that ballast, but somehow also a kind of consolation for us."[16] Sebastian explains neither the irony nor the consolation. Presumably, what is ironic is that Christianity tossed overboard its own origins, and what consoles is that Judaism still stands as the foundational covenant between God and humans. What is even more striking about Sebastian's observations, however, is that he could have listened to so many renditions of the death of Jesus without realizing, plainly and forcefully, that Jesus was a Jew.

This problem becomes even more acute in dramatic (as opposed to musical) presentations of the Passion of Jesus, as the events that one sees enacted on stage are more easily mistaken for "what really happened." In recent years, two versions of Jesus's death have generated widespread interest on the part of both scholars and popular audiences. The first of these is the Oberammergau Passion play, which is staged in Germany. The second is the blockbuster movie entitled *The Passion of the Christ*, directed by Mel Gibson and released in 2004. What is most interesting about these two dramas is not only how they portray Jesus's death, but how their creators have responded to scholarly criticism and input.

For example, in 1978, two prominent Catholic scholars published a booklet entitled *A Commentary on the Oberammergau* Passionsspiel *in Regard to Its Image of Jews and Judaism*. In their reflections on the famous Passion play, Leonard Swidler (a specialist in Catholic thought) and Gerard Sloyan (an expert in New Testament studies) stressed the need "for us Christians not only to eliminate our distorted and false understandings of and attitudes toward Jews, and Judaism, but also to discern and propagate the Jewish-rootedness of our Christianity."[17] In subsequent performances of the Oberammergau play, numerous revisions were made so that the production would more accurately reflect the insights offered by Swidler and Sloyan (as well as the recommendations of other scholars).

In contrast, in 2003, a group of scholars was given an early draft of the screenplay for Mel Gibson's film *The Passion of the Christ*. The panel concluded that the draft was neither consistent with the gospel accounts of Jesus's death nor historically accurate, and they recommended that several changes be made. Their concerns were dismissed by the film director as "revisionist bullshit."[18]

What accounts for the difference in how the insights of scholars were received by the producers of the Oberammergau play, on the one hand, and by Gibson, on the other? At least part of the difference can be attributed to divergent reactions to the inroads that critical scholarship has made in Catholic life and thought in the past hundred years. In 1893, Pope Leo XIII attacked what was then called "higher criticism" of the Bible, calling it an "inept method" that would end up destroying faith.[19] Since then most Catholics have embraced the insights gained by historical-critical analysis; at the same time, however, a significant minority has sought a return to a pre-critical approach to the Bible. This explains, at least in part, the very different reactions that Oberammergau's producers and Gibson had when confronted by scholarly critique.

The Oberammergau production, probably the most famous Passion play in the world, is performed in Oberammergau, Germany, every ten years (as well as in significant anniversary years). It includes a variety of genres such as poetry, dialogue, and tableaux meant to connect Jesus to events and characters in the Hebrew Bible.

One cannot really speak about "the" Oberammergau Passion play, however, since the script, sets, music, and costuming have undergone a number of changes since the drama's inception in the year 1634. In that year, villagers enacted the Passion in fulfillment of a vow meant to ward off the plague.[20] Since 1860, however, productions have largely been based on the script written by a parish priest named Joseph Alois Daisenberger. The script contains long conversations among Jewish authorities who conspire to kill Jesus, as well as conversations between the Jewish High Priest and Pilate that do not appear in the New Testament. One effect of this inclusion of non-biblical elements is to heighten Jews' role in the death of Jesus. Another effect is to increase the dramatic tension in the Passion narrative by contrasting the "evil" Jews with the "good" followers of Jesus.

The contrast has at times been exacerbated through the use of lighting and costumes. As late as 1980, the production at Oberammergau set Jesus and his apostles apart by giving them costumes different from those worn by the other characters. In addition, beginning in 1900, the Temple priests wore head-dresses with appendages on them suggestive of devils' horns.[21]

Moreover, the Jewish authorities have been portrayed as eager to shed the blood of Jesus. Here is a portion of their conversations as performed in the 1934 version that Hitler attended:

CAIAPHAS: Hear then, the High Priest. Is it not better that one man die than the whole nation perish? He must die! Without his death, there is no peace in Israel, no security for the Law of Moses—no hour of peace for us!

RABBI: God has spoken through his High Priest. Only by the death of Jesus of Nazareth can and must the people of Israel be saved.

NATHANIEL: The word has been burning on my tongue—now it is spoken. He dies—the enemy of our Fathers!

ALL (excepting Joseph and Nicodemus): He must die! He must die for our safety.

ANNAS: By my grey hairs, I will not rest until the blood of this deceiver washes out the shame.[22]

Not much had changed by 1960. In the scene of Jesus's sentencing by Pilate, the (Jewish) crowd spoke with one voice in demanding the death of Jesus:

ALL: Judge! Sentence him!

PILATE: Behold! What a man!

PRIESTS and PHARISEES: To the cross—

PEOPLE: To the cross with him!

PILATE: Can not even this pitiful sight win some compassion from your hearts?

ALL: Let him die! To the cross with him!
PILATE: So take ye him and crucify him at your peril. I will have nothing to do with it, for I can find no fault in him.
CAIPHAS [sic]: Hear, O Governor, the voice of the people! They join in our accusation and demand his death.
PEOPLE: Yes, we demand his death![23]

It was this sort of dialogue that prompted Swidler and Sloyan's 1978 *Commentary on The Oberammergau* Passionsspiel. Their booklet made numerous suggestions for revising the script of the play. For example, they noted that Pontius Pilate in the script was "made to look like a very sympathetic, noble Roman who against all his best instincts was forced into allowing Jesus' death by the evil Jews." Such a portrayal, they argued, was "a gross distortion of the historical record (Josephus and Philo), from which we know that Pilate was an uncommonly cruel, bloodthirsty, self-seeking Roman ruler." They concluded that "to avoid an indirect fostering of anti-Semitism it is recommended that the dialogue of Pilate be re-written so as to portray him more accurately as the evil character he was."[24]

In addition to this change in the depiction of Pilate, Swidler and Sloyan suggested several other alterations, including translating the Greek word *Iudaioi* (identifying the group to whom Jesus says he has been handed over in John 18:36) as "Jewish authorities," rather than simply as "the Jews," and designating the group that cries for Jesus's blood as a "mob" (German: *Pöbel*), rather than as simply "the people" (German: *Volk*). They also urged that the play's one-sidedly negative portrayal of the Pharisees be addressed, noting that "this treatment of the Pharisees is unwarranted by the Gospels and other historical documents. This point has been made amply clear by modern critical scholarship, including careful Catholic scholarship."[25]

What is significant in Swidler and Sloyan's document is not simply the changes that they suggested, but also the reasons they gave for suggesting them. The two frequently cite documents written at the Catholic Church's groundbreaking Second Vatican Council, during which the Church declared that Jesus's Passion "cannot be blamed upon all the Jews then living, without distinction, nor upon the Jews of today."[26] However, as is evident from the passages cited above, Swidler and Sloyan also frequently cite the findings of historians, philologists, and biblical scholars. This is precisely the sort of evidence that, as we will see, Gibson dismisses as irrelevant.

By the year 2000, as a result of scholarly input, the play at Oberammergau had undergone significant revision. The Sanhedrin no longer condemned Jesus to death, nor was it portrayed as a body united in its thirst for blood. The crowd no longer shouted the text from Matthew 27:25, "His blood be on us, and on our children!" Moreover, to stress the Jewishness of Jesus and of the apostles, the script included a blessing recited by Jesus in Hebrew.[27]

In addition, the text of the *Passionsspiel* contained a preface acknowledging the troubling history of the drama:

> In former times the black-versus-white contrast portrayed in passion plays, the opposition of friends and foes of Jesus, led not only to accusations of collective guilt against the Jews of the era of Jesus, but also against contemporary Jews who were consequently approached with aversion, contempt and aggression . . . Even if such despicable atrocities are not part of the particular history of the Oberammergau Passion Play, we must nevertheless admit, that this Passion Play, too, contributed in various ways to preparing the soil which eventually yielded the terrible harvest of the extermination of the Jews.[28]

The 2000 version of the play was extensively rewritten so as to remove many of the more egregious elements in the script. Still, some things remained the same. In the debate over what to do with Jesus, priestly authorities spoke against Jesus sixty-five times, as opposed to his defenders, who spoke eighteen times. In Jesus's interrogation, there were nineteen statements against him and six for him. The members of the crowd who shouted "Crucify him! Crucify him!" vastly outnumbered those who tried to defend him.[29] In reaction to the script, John Pawlikowski, a Catholic priest and expert in Jewish-Christian relations, commented, "I'm still not sure that when people leave the theater, they'll have any real sense of what the church is teaching today about Christian-Jewish relations and how we better understand the dynamics of the first century. Despite the fact that the play has created more of a Jewish context for Jesus' message, it hasn't significantly changed the underlying theology."[30]

Certainly from the perspective of the scholars who have called for revisions of the Oberammergau production, there is still more work to be done. And yet, just as certainly, great strides have been made in the effort to make the play reflect more accurately the complexities of Jesus's life and times. Gerard Sloyan reports that in 1980, the town council of Oberammergau rejected all of the revisions that he and Leonard Swidler had proposed. By 1990, however, the council had accepted nearly all of them.[31] This willingness to change based on scholarly input stands in stark contrast to the reaction that Mel Gibson had when he was confronted with a scholarly critique of his *Passion of the Christ*.

The debate that erupted concerning the movie began long before the film was ever released. Controversy about the production began when a group of scholars, all of whom were involved in Catholic-Jewish dialogue, was given an early draft of the movie's screenplay. The group composed and sent to Gibson, himself a Roman Catholic, a summary statement in which it concluded that the script was neither consistent with the gospel accounts of Jesus's death nor historically accurate.

What happened next played itself out in the language of court orders and legal threats rather than academic debate. Members of the group were told to return their copies of the movie script, and they were accused of attempting to force Gibson to change the movie to suit their own religious views.[32] Soon after, the popular media got hold of the story, and Gibson gave several interviews both on television and in print. These interviews, I will argue, indicate that he and the scholars who had examined his script were operating not only out of different understandings of the nature of the Bible, but, even more fundamentally, different understandings of the role of reason in religious faith.

For their part, the scholars offered several criticisms of the script that they had read. For one thing, they noted that when faced with discrepancies in the gospel accounts, the movie made choices "haphazardly in ways that increase and sensationalize 'Jewish' culpability."[33] Any movie that hopes to portray the last few hours of Jesus's life as they have been presented in the gospels is immediately faced with the fact that the accounts cannot easily (if at all) be reconciled with one another. Given such diverse accounts, no single presentation of the Passion could tell the story in a way consistent with all four gospels. What the committee objected to was not simply that Gibson's script chose one narrative line over another. Such choices would be inevitable unless one opted simply to stick to one gospel's version of events. What troubled them more was the *kinds* of choices that Gibson had made. For example, the committee noted that the script incorporated the Gospel of John's interpretation of Jesus's scourging: that Pilate, reluctant to execute the man who stood before him, called for the scourging as a device to satisfy the crowd while at the same time sparing Jesus's life. This interpretation minimizes Pilate's role in the death of Jesus and, at the same time, increases the role of the Jews. The scholars' report remarks, "Mark and Matthew, probably with greater historical accuracy, present the scourging as a normal preliminary to a Roman crucifixion, while Luke omits it entirely." The report also accused the movie script of taking a naive approach to the gospel writings, by presenting them as historical tracts, rather than as theological interpretations written decades after the events that they portray took place.[34]

On the subject of historical accuracy, other problems arose. For example, the committee took issue with the movie's depiction of Pontius Pilate (much as Swidler and Sloyan had done in their response to the Oberammergau play), particularly the film's placing him in an apparently subordinate relationship to the High Priest Caiaphas. It also pointed out that the movie's version of the Jewish Temple did not correspond to archeological findings, and that the details of the crucifixion were inaccurate.[35] In addition, committee member Paula Fredriksen objected to Gibson's plan to have the Jewish high priest and the Roman prefect speak to each other in Latin. She argued that they would instead have conversed in Greek, or what she called "the English of antiquity."[36]

In response, Gibson defended his version of Jesus's Passion with a mixture of biblical literalism and devout anti-intellectualism. Regarding the origins of the gospels, he asserted, "John was an eyewitness. Matthew was there. And these other guys? Mark was Peter's guy, Peter's scribe. And Luke was Paul's guy. I mean, these are reliable sources. These are guys who were around."[37] Regarding the varying accounts of the Passion offered by the four gospels, he stated, "The Gospels don't contradict one another. They mesh. There's a couple of places where, yeah, that's not quite the same scene. But they just complete parts of the story that the other guy didn't complete . . . If you read all four of those, they mesh. Because if they didn't, you wouldn't have so many people hooked into this."[38] With reference to the claim by scholars that Pilate was a brutal dictator who would not have been intimidated by the Jewish High Priest, Gibson asserted, "Basically, what it comes down to is he actually said, you know, I find no cause in this man, he's innocent, all this kind of stuff. He actually condemned a man to death who he had proclaimed he thought was innocent."[39]

He does not explain on what basis he knows these assertions to be true. It is safe to say, however, that his conclusions do not result from the kind of historical-critical analysis that guided the committee of scholars. Referring to the academics who had criticized the movie script, he exclaimed, "It was like they were more or less saying I have no right to interpret the Gospels myself, because I don't have a bunch of letters after my name. But they are for children, these Gospels. They're for children, they're for old people . . . Just get an academic on board if you want to pervert something!"[40]

It should be noted that in the time between when the controversy began and when the film was released, Gibson did delete a scene which at least one member of the scholarly group had deemed historically inaccurate. Amy-Jill Levine, a professor of New Testament and part of the group of scholars who responded to Gibson's script, observed that in the version of the screenplay seen by the committee, Jesus's cross was manufactured in the Jewish Temple.[41] This detail not only contradicted historical practice, but, Levine felt, also unfairly increased Jewish culpability for the death of Jesus. In the final cut of the movie, the scene was removed.[42]

On the other hand, another controversial element, one that was not in the version of the script reviewed by the panel of scholars, was added by Gibson to the final cut of the film, though in a subtle form. The scene in question depicts the moment in the Gospel of Matthew when Pilate refuses responsibility for the death of Jesus. Having found Jesus innocent of any crime, Pilate stands before the assembled (Jewish) crowd and washes his hands, declaring, "I am innocent of this man's blood; see to it yourselves." To this, the crowd (that is, "the people as a whole," according to Matthew) replies, "His blood be on us and on our children!" (27:24–25). The episode has only dubious historical value, as many scholars attest.[43] However, it has been invoked innumerable times to justify violence by Christians against Jews.

When discussing this section of Matthew's gospel, Gibson told an interviewer that he had initially planned to include it, with the High Priest Caiaphas uttering the infamous lines. Gibson explained, "I wanted it in. My brother said I was wimping out if I didn't include it. It happened; it was said. But, man, if I included that in there, they'd be coming after me at my house, they'd come kill me."[44] (According to the interviewer, "they" referred to critics such as the Anti-Defamation League and the Simon Wiesenthal Center, as well as various academics.) When the film was released, the words from Matthew are included after all. They are in Aramaic, however, and do not appear in the English subtitles.[45]

THE PASSION OF JESUS: HISTORY

I asserted above that Gibson's comments about the nature of the gospels seem to stem from a combination of biblical literalism and anti-intellectualism. It is this mixture that I would like to explore next, showing both how and why it differs so dramatically from the approach to reason and revelation that has dominated Catholic thinking for the past several decades.

As early as 1893, Vatican authorities were reacting to the kinds of historical-critical scholarship that were then calling into question traditional assumptions about how, when, and by whom the Bible was written. In his encyclical entitled *Providentissimus Deus*, Pope Leo XIII warned that such criticism would not throw light on the scriptures but would, instead, "resolve itself into the reflection of the bias and the prejudice of the critics."[46] *Providentissimus Deus* meant to steer faithful Catholic interpreters away from such suspect tools.

At the same time, however, the encyclical encouraged serious study of the biblical texts in their original languages. It also professed, in response to scientific developments, that no real conflict could exist between reason and revelation, as "truth cannot contradict truth."[47] *Providentissimus Deus* acknowledged that science might raise legitimate questions about the literal accuracy of various biblical statements, since the Bible's writers "did not seek to penetrate the secrets of nature, but rather described and dealt with things in more or less figurative language, or in terms which were commonly used at the time . . ."[48] The papal document is thus seen as opening the door to modern biblical scholarship.

A less sanguine assessment of the value of independent investigation into scriptural matters came in the form of another encyclical, this one issued in 1907 by Pope Pius X. *Pascendi Dominici Gregis* was an extended critique of the beliefs and techniques of those scholars it called "Modernists," many of whom were Catholics. Modernists, asserted the encyclical, do not hesitate to affirm that the books of the Bible "have been gradually formed by additions to a primitive brief narration—by interpolations of theological or allegorical interpretation, by transitions, by joining different passages together."[49] (This has since, of course, become a commonly accepted position in biblical studies.) As the encyclical saw the matter, this was the same as asserting that truth *evolves*—that faith has undergone changes rather than having been true for all time. Such a claim the encyclical could not abide, and it declared that anyone who embraced this claim "makes profession thereby of the errors contained in it, and places himself in opposition to Catholic faith."[50]

Matters changed significantly in the years that followed, however. In 1943 Pope Pius XII issued *Divino Afflante Spiritu*, an encyclical written in honor of the fiftieth anniversary of *Providentissimus Deus*. In his letter the pontiff urged that interpreters "with all care and without neglecting any light derived from recent research, endeavor to determine the peculiar character and circumstances of the sacred writer, the age in which he lived, the sources written or oral to which he had recourse and the forms of expression he employed."[51] In other words, Catholic theologians and exegetes were free to pursue the kinds of work that now constitute contemporary biblical studies: textual criticism, which tries to uncover the original wording of a document; literary criticism, which examines varying literary genres; source criticism, which attempts to discern the origins of material in a biblical work; redaction criticism, which looks at the "editorial positions" that shaped the construction of texts; and so on.[52]

The steps taken in *Divino Afflante Spiritu* were ratified by the Second Vatican Council's "Dogmatic Constitution on Divine Revelation," also known as *Dei Verbum*. Here the Council affirmed that God speaks in the scriptures through human beings, and thus that investigation of the Bible must take into account literary forms, as well as the historical situations of the biblical writers: "For the words of God, expressed in human language, have been made like human discourse, just as the word of the eternal Father, when He took to Himself the flesh of human weakness, was in every way made like men."[53] Since Vatican II, Catholic scholars have been free to use whatever tools are available to them as they pursue the meanings of biblical texts.

In fact, it was just such tools that guided the scholars' committee that responded to the script of Gibson's *Passion*. In its statement, the committee recommended that Gibson change the film and justified its recommendation by appealing to precisely the kinds of scholarship that Vatican II endorsed. It also, however, invoked the United States Catholic Bishops' "Criteria for the Evaluation of Dramatizations of the Passion." This document, published in 1988, stressed the importance of recent developments in biblical scholarship in dealing with the death of Jesus. It cautioned that producers cannot use biblical texts uncritically and that, on the contrary, they must be sensitive to the variant accounts of the Passion offered by the gospels, and must justify any decision about what to include in a dramatic presentation and what to leave out. The document stated that "it is not sufficient for the producers of passion dramatizations to respond to responsible criticism simply by appealing to the notion that 'it's in the Bible.' One must account for one's selections."[54]

The guidelines also pointed to recent historical discoveries that "place in doubt a more literalist reading of the biblical text."[55] The gospels were not written as history, the statement affirmed. They were written rather with theological and spiritual claims in mind, and any interpretation that ignores that fact will be a misinterpretation of the scriptures. The document concluded by quoting a statement issued by the Vatican in 1985 entitled "Notes on the Correct Way to Present the Jews and Judaism in Preaching and Catechesis of the Roman Catholic Church." It directed that "because the Church and the Jewish people are 'linked together at the very level of their identity,' an accurate, sensitive, and positive appreciation of Jews and Judaism 'should not occupy an occasional or marginal place in Christian teaching,' but be considered 'essential' to Christian proclamation."[56] The panel of scholars that examined the draft of Gibson's work was able to appeal both to the authority of the Catholic Church and to historical-critical scholarship without encountering any contradictions. It was able to draw on both sources in its effort to convince Gibson that the gospels should not be read as historical transcripts, and that any depiction of the crucifixion of Jesus has to be done with great care and sensitivity to the history of Christians' persecution of Jews.

Indeed, Swidler and Sloyan had made much the same point in their second response to the performance at Oberammergau, written with reference to the 1984 production. In that document, they explained, "The gospels are closer to the dramatic medium than to the historical. It would be a betrayal of both the gospels and the medium of drama to convert them into jejune historical tracts . . . The gospels must be presented for what they are, dramatic writing that hopes to foster faith."[57] The irony, in other words, is that those who defend a dramatic production as based on the New Testament and *therefore* as historically accurate have misunderstood both the gospels and the play itself.

This raises, however, a serious question. If the gospels should not be read as historical transcripts—if they are instead a mixture of history, theology, poetry, and drama—then why should scholars complain if Gibson's movie is not historically accurate? After all, one might fairly claim that because it is a dramatic presentation of the death of Jesus, *The Passion of the Christ* need not concern itself too much with the details of history. Few people take *Gone with the Wind* to task for not accurately representing antebellum Atlanta. No one cares if the events in *The Wizard of Oz* "really" took place. Why then should historical considerations enter into Gibson's film?

The answer is twofold. First, Gibson himself has asserted several times that his movie is simply a cinematic version of history. When asked how *The Passion* differed from the many previous versions of the life of Jesus, Gibson stated, "This film will show the passion of Jesus Christ just the way it happened. It's like traveling back in time and watching the events unfold exactly as they occurred." When asked how he could be so sure that his version was accurate, Gibson replied, "We've done the research. I'm telling the story as the Bible tells it. I think the story, as it really happened, speaks for itself. The Gospel is a complete script, and that's what we're filming."[58] Thus, Gibson asserts that his movie is not only an accurate version of the Bible, but also of history as it really happened. More: it is history as it really happened precisely *because* it is an accurate version of the Bible.

Admittedly, this claim is mitigated in other interviews. For example, when he was asked specifically about the balance between staying true to scripture and his own creative vision, Gibson answered, "Wow, the Scriptures are the Scriptures— I mean they're unchangeable, although many people try to change them. And I think that my first duty is to be as faithful as possible in telling the story so that it doesn't contradict the Scriptures. Now, so long as it didn't do that, I felt that I had a pretty wide berth for artistic interpretation, and to fill in some of the spaces with logic, with imagination, with various other readings."[59] This would seem to contradict his other statement that "the Gospel is a complete script," which, presumably, would require no such supplementary material. In any case, the fact that Gibson in at least some interviews asserts that the movie is nothing other than accurate history means that historians have a responsibility to weigh in with their own assessments.

There is a second reason why historians must offer critical evaluations of Passion dramas, and this has to do with the impact that such artistic representations have had on Jewish-Christian relations. Perhaps in theory historical considerations should not play a role in assessments of art; but in fact, they must. As biblical scholar John Dominic Crossan has put the matter, there is, post-Auschwitz, a "moral necessity of making a judgment on what actually happened."[60] The charge that Jews killed Jesus has led to horror and bloodshed. When treading on such dangerous ground, one has a moral obligation to step with care.

In numerous media reports, Gibson has been described as a "traditionalist" Catholic. This means, for example, that he rejects contemporary celebrations of the Mass in the vernacular, opting instead for the Latin Mass as celebrated before Vatican II. It means that he rejects contemporary theologies of salvation in which non-Catholics can be admitted to heaven.[61] And, as we have seen, he rejects the kind of biblical scholarship that has become not only commonplace but officially sanctioned by the Vatican.

What must be pointed out, however, is that such traditionalist Catholicism is not simply the same as Catholicism as practiced in previous generations. It is, on the contrary, a new movement that arose precisely in reaction to the changes that took place within Catholic life and thought in the nineteenth and twentieth centuries. It is, in other words, not "old-time" religion, but rather a very contemporary movement. It seeks to adopt certain elements of Catholic history as a reaction to and protest against the path that Catholic tradition has taken.

Behind this movement seems to be the same kind of fear that characterized Pius X's condemnations of Modernism. Over and over again in his encyclical *Pascendi Dominici Gregis*, the pope raised the spectre of doctrinal evolution as the enemy against which the Church must defend itself most vigorously. Change, and its twin danger, relativity, were to be feared above all else, as they implied that "there is to be nothing stable, nothing immutable in the Church."[62]

Underlying this fear lies an understanding of divine revelation as a body of knowledge that is fixed and immutable. *Pascendi Dominici Gregis* began by reminding the Catholic faithful that God had entrusted the office of the pope with a special duty: "namely, to guard with the greatest vigilance the deposit of the faith delivered to the saints, rejecting the profane novelties of words and oppositions of knowledge falsely so called."[63] In such a model of revelation, truth is firm and unalterable, and it has been deposited with the one true Church to be guarded at all cost. Change is by definition the enemy of this truth, and "progress" is simply another word for deviation.

This seems to be the model that Gibson has adopted, at least insofar as one can discern his theological positions from the interviews he has given. Again, however, it must be stressed that opting for this model at the beginning of the twenty-first century is a deliberate choice against the flow of Catholic tradition.

For, in fact, Catholic thinking has for the past sixty or seventy years moved in a quite different direction. While generalizations are always hazardous, one can say with confidence that numerous contemporary theologians, as well as at least some of the pronouncements of Vatican II, understand revelation as an ongoing process in which God reveals God's self and God's will for the world in very human terms: terms which adapt themselves to the often very messy details of history. Revelation is less a body of pronouncements than it is contemporary experience, understood as ever-fuller participation in the life of God, and illuminated by scripture and tradition.[64]

If one accepts this model of revelation, then the ongoing discoveries of science and history can only deepen one's experience of revelation. Faith has nothing to fear from scholarly debate. Breakthrough discoveries made by archeologists, philologists, theologians, philosophers, and students of antiquity are all sources for deepening faith, rather than intruders threatening to destroy it.

Unfortunately, it is the nature of scholarship that such breakthroughs usually provide only tantalizing hints, rather than definitive conclusions. Not surprisingly, then, when it comes to the question of "what really happened" during Jesus's last hours, one finds widely divergent accounts.

Two of the more sharply differentiated views on this question can be found in Raymond E. Brown's two-volume work, *The Death of the Messiah: From Gethsemane to the Grave* (1994), on the one hand, and in two of John Dominic Crossan's books, *The Cross That Spoke: The Origins of the Passion Narrative* (1988) and *Who Killed Jesus?: Exposing the Roots of Anti-Semitism in the Gospel Story of the Death of Jesus* (1995), on the other. The latter of the two books by Crossan was written explicitly in reaction to Brown's work. Crossan himself has characterized his differences with Brown by explaining, "Basically the issue is whether the passion accounts are prophecy historicized or history remembered. Ray Brown is 80 percent in the direction of history remembered. I'm 80 percent in the opposite direction."[65] At issue is whether the accounts of the arrest, trial(s), and execution of Jesus are based on memories of what really happened, or if they are rather fictional stories written to make a theological point.

Putting the matter that starkly does not really give an accurate description of the differences between Brown's and Crossan's agendas, however. Brown, though he acknowledges that questions of historicity are important, gives only scant attention to them. His interest is rather "to explain in detail what the evangelists intended and conveyed to their audiences by their narratives of the passion and death of Jesus."[66] Thus he devotes most of his two volumes to commentary rather than to historical analysis. As he sees the matter, "[T]he primary concern of a commentary is making sense of what the biblical writers have given us, not in reconstructing pre-Gospel traditions or in detecting history."[67] For his part, Crossan focuses far less on the theological nuances of particular gospels and far more on a search for the historical Jesus.

Thus, there is a marked divergence in the aims and motives of the two authors, and a corresponding difference in the material that each includes in his work. It would be unfair to give the impression that the two pore over the same texts with the same questions. Despite this, however, we can nonetheless discern some points of direct confrontation.

The first of these has to do with the authors' views regarding the relations among the four canonical gospels (Matthew, Mark, Luke, John). Both Brown and Crossan agree with the nearly universally accepted position that the Gospel of Mark was written before the other three, that Matthew and Luke incorporated Mark into their own gospels, and that Matthew and Luke also drew on material from another text, designated by scholars as the "Q" Gospel. No independent copy of Q has ever been found, but its existence has been inferred from the fact that Matthew and Luke share some material in common that is not found in Mark. Thus most biblical experts believe that Matthew and Luke both had access to a source ("Q" is a shortened form of *Quelle*, the German word for "source") in addition to Mark.

However, Brown and Crossan part ways when it comes to the origins of the Gospel of John. Brown believes that John was written independently of the other three gospels, which are usually called "synoptic" because they share a common vision.[68] Crossan, on the other hand, believes that John incorporates several different sources, including some that provided the miracle stories and sayings of Jesus, and one from which the story of Jesus's death and resurrection was drawn.[69] That last source, he believes, also shaped the synoptic gospels as well as the extra-canonical Gospel of Peter. Crossan calls this hypothetical earlier source the "Cross Gospel." Moreover, Crossan posits a direct literary dependence of John on Mark.[70]

The difference between Brown and Crossan regarding sources is not trivial; rather, it affects how each writer imagines what actually happened to Jesus. For, when Brown explains what criteria he uses to determine the historicity of events narrated in the gospels, he points first to the principle of multiple attestation.[71] This criterion, widely used by contemporary biblical scholars, holds that an event is more likely to have happened if it is attested to in more than one source. Thus, for example, if the canonical Gospel of Mark and the extra-canonical Gospel of Thomas both contain the same version of a parable of Jesus, then that version is thought more likely to be authentic. Recall that Brown believes that the Gospel of John was written independently of the synoptic tradition. Thus, if he finds the same story told in both the synoptic gospels and in John, he deems that story to be more authentic.

And indeed he does find the same story told in all four gospels, at least in broad outline. He explains:

> All the Gospels agree that the Jewish authorities, particularly the priests, disliked Jesus and that there were earlier attempts to stop his teaching. All agree on a judicial action by the Sanhedrin, and (if we join Acts [of the Apostles] to Luke) all agree that one of the issues against Jesus was the threatened destruction of the Temple sanctuary. All agree that the Jewish authorities gave Jesus over to Pilate, who sentenced him to death.[72]

It is no wonder, given this evidence, that Brown contends, "When the Jewish, Christian, and pagan evidence is assembled, the involvement of Jews in the death of Jesus approaches certainty."[73] This involvement, Brown says, should be thought of in terms of "responsibility" rather than "guilt," however. He explains, "At any time and in any place those who contribute to the execution of an accused are responsible for that death; they are guilty only if they know that the accused is undeserving of such punishment or have been negligent in discerning innocence."[74] He assumes that most of the members of the Sanhedrin acted in good faith in condemning Jesus, believing that they were doing the will of God. Thus they were responsible for his death, but not guilty of it.

If we turn to Crossan's understanding of the Passion narratives, we find an entirely different perspective on their historicity. Crossan argues that there was one source, the as-yet-undis-
covered Cross Gospel, that found its way into all four canonical
gospels and also into the Gospel of Peter. (Brown, in contrast to
Crossan, considers Peter to be a later, popularized digest of three
of the canonical gospels.)[75] Moreover, Crossan believes that John
incorporated parts of Mark's Passion narrative just as Matthew
and Luke did. Thus if we find stories in John that are similar to
those in the synoptics, we should not read this as independent
corroboration of facts but rather as the perfectly natural result
of the gospels' sharing the same source and of their having borrowed from each other. For Crossan, the fact that all the gospels
agree that religious authorities disliked Jesus, that there was a
judicial action by the Sanhedrin, and that Jewish authorities
handed Jesus over to Pilate to be sentenced does not mean that
those things actually happened. What it means is that one source
said that they happened, and that this one account was repeated
several different times by several different authors.

Moreover, Crossan contends that the Cross Gospel was not
based on memories of what had happened during the last few
days of Jesus's life. It was rather a theological attempt to make
sense of the fact that Jesus had died but that faith in him had
not. As Crossan sees it, the Passion narrative underwent several
stages. First came what he calls the *historical Passion*, or events
as they actually unfolded. Of those events, he imagines that those
closest to Jesus knew very little. Next came the *prophetic Passion*,
or a vision in which the Passion of Jesus was understood as the
fulfillment of biblical prophecy. Out of this developed what
Crossan calls the *narrative Passion*, or a story that wove the
prophetic Passion into a cohesive, dramatic whole. Such a narrative Passion, he contends, could be found in the Cross Gospel.[76]
The Cross Gospel was incorporated—though to what extent isn't
clear—into the Gospels of Peter and Mark, and then into
Matthew, Luke, and John.[77]

In sum, then, the canonical gospels appear to Brown as two
independent versions (Mark and John) and two dependent versions (Matthew and Luke) of a more-or-less accurate memory of
the death of Jesus. To Crossan, they appear as four different vari-
ations of the same narrative account, which was not written with

any intention of explaining what had "really" happened. As Crossan sees the matter, the trial of Jesus before the Sanhedrin and Jesus's interrogations before Herod and Pilate are dramatic stories created to meet theological rather than historical needs. These events are not history remembered, but prophecy historicized.

Brown, it should be noted, has no stomach for Crossan's thesis that the apostles knew very little about what had happened to Jesus, which brings us to a second key difference between the two. Brown writes,

> It is inconceivable that they showed no concern about what happened to Jesus after the arrest. True, there is no Christian claim that they were present during the legal proceedings against him, Jewish or Roman; but it is absurd to think that some information was not available to them about why Jesus was hanged on a cross. The whole purpose of crucifixion, after all, was to publicize that certain crimes would be severely punished.[78]

And yet, despite what Brown says, it does not seem inconceivable at all that the apostles would have known very little about Jesus's fate. Surely in our own day untold thousands have been executed by oppressive regimes in El Salvador, China, South Africa, Cambodia, the Soviet Union—the list could go on and on. Often those who care the most about what happened to the "disappeared ones" have the least access to information. Even knowing what happened to the loved one's body is a privilege often denied to friends and family. Given the brutality of the Roman empire in Jesus's day, and given the frequency with which executions were carried out without the nicety of a trial (see Josephus's *Jewish Antiquities*[79]), it does not seem at all implausible that Jesus's followers would have had no details about his last hours. Surely they knew that he had been crucified as a troublemaker, as had been thousands of Jews before him. Beyond that, perhaps they knew nothing at all.

Crossan's point is not to discount any possibility that someone might have witnessed the events that took place between Jesus's arrest and his execution. His point is rather that the Passion stories told in the gospels can, for the most part, be attributed to prophecy turned into narrative. What cannot be accounted for in this way can, he believes, be traced instead to Christian attempts to minimize Roman responsibility for Jesus's death and to maximize Jewish responsibility. After all, the canonical gospels were written shortly after the Romans had successfully and brutally defeated a Jewish insurgency, destroying the Temple in the process. It would have been prudent at such a time to show deference towards Roman authorities while at the same time putting some distance between the followers of Jesus and other Jewish groups.

Consider, for example, the scene in all four canonical gospels in which an assembly demands that Jesus be crucified. The composition of the assembly varies somewhat. In Mark 15:8–11, it is a crowd that has been stirred up by the chief priests. In Matthew 27:20, the crowd has been stirred up by the chief priests and the elders. In Luke 23:13 the crowd is itself the chief priests, the leaders, and the people. In John 19:14–15, it is simply "the Jews." In each gospel, to a varying degree, there is an effort to show that Pilate was reluctant to kill Jesus, but that in the end he acquiesced to the blood-thirsty demands of those gathered before him.

Such a portrait is decidedly not in keeping with what historians know about Pilate from other sources, which indicate that he was a brutal administrator who did not waste time dithering over the guilt or innocence of an accused rabble-rouser. Crossan explains his assessment of the historicity of that event:

> Knowing, on the one hand, what I do about Pilate as an ordinary second-class governor, of his ten-year tenure and his eventual removal, of his attitude toward Jewish religious sensitivities and his tactics toward unarmed but demanding crowds, and, on the other hand, of Christian reasons for increasing the responsibility of Jewish and decreasing that of Roman participants in the crucifixion, there can be only one *relatively plausible* conclusion. That reiterated juxtaposition of Jewish demands for Jesus' crucifixion and Roman declarations of Jesus' innocence is not prophecy, and neither is it history. It is Christian propaganda.[80]

Moreover, it is propaganda that has become lethal. According to Crossan, "What was at stake in those passion stories, in the long haul of history, was the Jewish Holocaust."[81]

I have focused on the debate between Brown and Crossan not in order to come to a conclusion regarding the existence of the hypothetical Cross Gospel or on whether the Gospel of Peter was written before or after the synoptics. Many scholars find Crossan's arguments about these matters less than persuasive.[82] On the other hand, Crossan's basic assertion that in the synoptic tradition we are dealing with only one source for the Passion narrative, found in Mark and borrowed by Matthew, Luke, and John, finds wider, if still hotly contested, affirmation.[83] Moreover, Crossan's contention that the events in the Passion narrative are "prophecy historicized" rather than history remembered is supported by Helmut Koester, who writes, "One can assume that the only historical information about Jesus' suffering, crucifixion, and death was that he was condemned to death by Pilate and crucified. The details and individual scenes of the narrative do not rest on historical memory, but were developed on the basis of allegorical interpretation of Scripture."[84]

I have examined the different approaches of Crossan and Brown not to side definitively with the various conclusions of one or the other, but rather to show how radically different a perspective one gains if one begins with a basic suspicion in reading Christian sources. This is a central criticism that Crossan levies against Brown's work. He writes, "I do not find any unfair, illegitimate, or invalid criticism of Judaism's religious tenets anywhere in Brown's book, and I emphasize that most strongly to offset any misunderstanding. *What is lacking, however, is a fair, legitimate, and valid criticism of Christianity's passion stories.*"[85] In other words, Crossan does not allege that Brown's writings are antisemitic or that he portrays Judaism in an unfairly negative light. The problem is not that Brown is critical of Judaism, but rather that he is not critical enough of Christianity.

By way of my own conclusion, I can do no better than to echo what the bishops have written. There is great power in liturgical and dramatic presentations of the death of Jesus. That power has been used for terrible ends. After Auschwitz, we cannot afford a naiveté about the Passion narratives. The only hope lies in careful, thoughtful examinations of the texts and of Christians' use of them.

CHAPTER 4

Holy Thursday, the Chrism Mass

On October 12, 1940 (Yom Kippur), the Nazis announced that a special area of Warsaw would be sectioned off to house the city's Jews. The head of the Jewish orphanage, Janusz Korczak, petitioned to be able to continue to operate outside of the soon-to-be-created Ghetto. Korczak was both a medical doctor and the author of several books for and about children, and he hoped that his reputation might gain him some leniency. His request, however, was denied.

Shortly before Korczak was forced to relocate the orphanage to within the Ghetto, a non-Jewish friend approached him and offered to procure false identity papers for him so that he could escape the Nazis' mounting campaign against Jews. Korczak asked, "And the children?" Told that it would be impossible for the friend to find hiding places for all of the 170 Jewish orphans, Korczak declined the offer.[1]

In July of the following year, Korczak's friend again visited and begged him to escape: "I explained that this was the very last chance to save even a few from perishing," the friend later recalled. "There could be no postponement. If the doctor would close the orphanage, some of the children and teachers would perhaps have a chance to escape to the other side. He had only to give the order and come away with me at once." In response, the friend remembers, Korczak "looked at me as though I had proposed a betrayal or an embezzlement." Part of Korczak's concern seems to have been the peril he would have been imposing on anyone who had agreed to hide even one child.[2] Whatever his reasons, the doctor declined the offer.[3]

While he was in the Warsaw Ghetto, Korczak did what he could for the children under his care, but conditions grew desperate. On August 4, 1942, he wrote in his diary, "Our Father who are in heaven . . . This prayer was carved out of hunger and misery. Our daily bread. Bread."[4] It was one of his final entries. On August 6, Korczak and his children were taken to the Umschlagplatz and loaded into cattle cars. According to some accounts, at the last moment, a German officer handed Korczak a piece of paper giving him permission to return home—without the children—but Korczak waved him away.[5] The train headed towards Treblinka, and Korczak and his orphans were never heard from again.

Who can possibly understand fully what motivated the doctor to accompany those children to their deaths? At that point, of course, he had been exhausted by his daily struggle with starvation and illness. When an old tailor of Korczak's acquaintance had succumbed to the conditions in the Ghetto, the doctor had written, "Oh, how hard it is to live, how easy to die!"[6] And yet this does not explain why he did not flee when given the chance even before the Ghetto had been created.

Dare we believe, as we consider Korczak's story from our own comfort and safety, that as he headed towards the cattle cars, "head held high, holding a child by each hand, his eyes staring straight ahead with his characteristic gaze, as if seeing something far away,"[7] he did so simply because he was the leader of the community of orphans and that he could not (would not) abandon them? Is it possible to believe that he would prefer to die than to desert the children in his care? Surely at that point he knew that there was no question of his being able to save the children. Surely he knew that there was nothing he could do even to influence the Nazi guards to be less brutal in their treatment. And yet he stayed.

Korczak's story is particularly relevant as we consider the Holy Week liturgy known as the Chrism Mass, during which priests renew their commitment to service. One of the questions the priests are asked by their bishop during the liturgy is, "Are you resolved to unite yourselves more closely to Christ and to try to become more like him by joyfully sacrificing your own pleasure and ambition to bring his peace and love to your brothers and sisters?" They are to answer, "I am."[8]

What is particularly significant in this promise is the connection made between self-sacrifice and the building up of the community. The priest's role is to foster relationships among the people in his care, and to create an environment in which peace and love can flourish. The priest's sacrifice is not simply an offering made to God, but it is a gift given to and in the interest of the people whom he serves. This model of ministry is based in the solidarity between leader and congregation; furthermore, I will argue, this model offers a compelling alternative to conceptions of the priesthood that are primarily ritual or cultic in nature. When the role of the priest is described using language taken over from the Jewish Temple, a kind of supersessionist view often develops. The Catholic priesthood is then seen as the continuation of—but at the same time a replacement for—the Jewish priesthood, which is thereby rendered null and void. The Chrism Mass of Holy Thursday, however, includes resources for thinking of ministry as what liberation theologians have called "solidarity with the oppressed." This is a model of leadership that Janusz Korczak knew something about.

THE CHRISM MASS

Holy Thursday marks a high point in the Church's liturgical cycle. On this day two separate liturgies take place, the first of which is known as the Chrism Mass. During this ceremony, each community's bishop consecrates the chrism—an ointment usually made from a mixture of olive oil and balsam—that will be used throughout the year in the sacraments of Baptism, Confirmation, and Holy Orders. The oils used to anoint catechumens (those undergoing instruction in the faith) and to anoint the sick are also blessed during this ritual.

The readings for the Chrism Mass do not vary from year to year. The first reading is taken from the Book of Isaiah (61:1–3ab, 6a, 8b–9) and begins,

> The spirit of the Lord GOD is upon me,
>   because the LORD has anointed me;
> he has sent me to bring glad tidings to the poor,
>   to heal the brokenhearted,
> to proclaim liberty to the captives
>   and release to the prisoners,
> to announce a year of favor from the LORD
>   and a day of vindication by our God,
>   to comfort all who mourn . . ."[9]

This theme is picked up by the Gospel text (Luke 4:16–21), in which Jesus reads the same passage from Isaiah in the synagogue of his hometown of Nazareth. Jesus does not stop with reading the Torah scroll, however. According to Luke, he then sits down and says to those assembled in the synagogue, "Today this Scripture passage is fulfilled in your hearing."

What precisely had been fulfilled is a matter worth pondering. It was not the case that at that point the poor had all heard good tidings and the brokenhearted had been healed. Captives had not all been set free, and prisoners had not all been released. What Jesus seems to be saying is not that the world had changed, but rather that as of that day, he himself had changed. He understood himself to be one charged with proclaiming God's will for the world. He, like the prophet Isaiah, had been given the sacred responsibility of letting people know that their deepest longings were shared by God. Not only did he feel this inwardly, Luke's gospel seems to say, but as of that day he was committed to proclaiming his vocation publicly.

The conjunction of the first reading from Isaiah and the Gospel reading from Luke indicates that to be a follower of Jesus is to serve those who are most in need of aid, and to uplift those who are most in need of good news. To be a disciple is to understand oneself as having a calling to empower and to heal. These texts tell us that the world is not the way that either we or God would wish it to be, and that the task of those who serve God is to help change it.

The second reading, however, coming between the portion from Isaiah and the portion from Luke, and taken from the Book of Revelation (1:5–8), offers something of a different message. Here Jesus is portrayed as one who has already overcome the tomb; he is "firstborn of the dead." Verses 5–6 proclaim,

> To him who loves us and has freed us from our sins
>   by his blood,
>   who has made us into a kingdom, priests for his
>   God and Father,
>   to him be glory and power forever and ever.
>   Amen.

The text is distinct in that it offers an apocalyptic vision in which Jesus has already accomplished his work. We have already been freed from sin, and the kingdom of God has already been accomplished.

Elisabeth Schüssler Fiorenza argues convincingly, however, that the author of Revelation later amends this view to discourage the idea that final redemption and salvation have already taken place. She points out that in Revelation 5:9–10, one finds a hymn similar to that found in 1:5–6. This later text, however, which is another song of praise to Jesus, includes a promise for the future: "[Y]ou were slaughtered and by your blood you ransomed for God saints from every tribe and language and people and nation; you have made them to be a kingdom and priests serving our God, and they will reign on earth." Schüssler Fiorenza contends that by including the future tense ("they will reign"), the author recognizes that at this point the victory has not yet been achieved. She concludes, "To pretend that redemption and salvation are already accomplished in baptism would therefore be an illusion. According to [the Book of Revelation] fully realized redemption and salvation presupposes not only the liberating and dignifying of individual persons, but also the creating of a new world."[10] Thus what looks like a claim of victory is better read as a longing for the kind of future spoken of in both Isaiah and Luke.

The passage from Revelation is unusual in that it is one of the few places in the New Testament where the followers of Jesus are referred to as "priests." Obviously the term alludes to the Jewish Temple priesthood. And yet the Temple does not seem to be the most immediate context for the reference. Schüssler Fiorenza points instead to Exodus 19:5–6, in which God says, "Now then, if you will obey Me faithfully and keep My covenant, you shall be My treasured possession among all the peoples. Indeed, all the earth is Mine, but you shall be to Me a kingdom of priests and a holy nation." God speaks these words to Moses, but Moses is to pass them on to the children of Israel (19:3). In other words, they are addressed not just to the cultic priesthood but to the people as a whole.

This focus on the priestly vocation of all of God's people is blurred, however, in the rest of the Chrism Mass. After the three scriptural portions have been read and the homily expounding upon them has been completed, the Renewal of Commitment to Priestly Service takes place. During this part of the liturgy, those who have been ordained reaffirm their vocation as leaders in the

Catholic community. The presiding bishop begins by addressing them: "My brothers, today we celebrate the memory of the first eucharist, at which our Lord Jesus Christ shared with his apostles and with us his call to the priestly service of his Church."[11] Here priesthood is explicitly understood as the power to offer the sacrifice of the Mass, just as Jesus offered himself at the Last Supper. This connection is furthered later on when the presider addresses himself to God, the Father of Jesus:

> By your Holy Spirit
> you anointed your only Son
> *High Priest of the new and eternal covenant.*
> With wisdom and love you have planned
> that this one priesthood should continue in the
>   Church.
>
> Christ gives the dignity of a royal priesthood
> to the people he has made his own.
> From these, with a brother's love,
> *he chooses men to share his sacred ministry . . .*
>
> *He appoints them to renew in his name*
> *the sacrifice of our redemption*
> *as they set before your family his paschal meal.*[12]

Here Jesus is the new High Priest in that he offers himself as a sacrifice to ratify "the new and eternal covenant." Jesus extends the dignity of the priesthood to the people as a whole, but some of these people are specially chosen to be priests in the same sense that (according to the prayer) Jesus was, as they re-present the sacrifice of Jesus at his last Passover meal.

This understanding of priesthood lends itself to a supersessionist view in which Jewish tradition is both invoked and diminished. The old covenant has been replaced by the new covenant. The old Temple priesthood has been replaced by the High Priesthood of Jesus and his disciples. The old Passover has been replaced by the new paschal meal at which Jesus is both priest and lamb, both the one who sacrifices and the one who is sacrificed, and this paschal meal is continually renewed by the men (Roman Catholics do not ordain women) chosen to celebrate the eucharist. Indeed, celebrating the eucharist is portrayed as the primary task of the priesthood, as the purpose of the Chrism Mass is to recall Jesus's Last Supper at which Jesus initiated his call to priestly service.

This conception of priestly service surely has the weight of tradition behind it, but just as surely this interpretation is not the only one available within Catholic tradition. As Edward Schillebeeckx has shown, Catholic notions of the priesthood were not handed down in the scriptures but evolved over centuries. Whereas today priesthood is thought of primarily in its relation to the sacrifice of the Mass, this was not always the case. In the first Christian communities, Schillebeeckx contends, leaders presided at the eucharist by virtue of their being leaders, rather than by virtue of "ordination" in the sense that we think of it now. Schillebeeckx explains, "If we remember that the early eucharist was structured after the pattern of Jewish grace at meals—the *birkat hamazon* [Hebrew: blessing of the food]—at which just anyone could preside, it is evident that the leaders of house communities *ipso facto* also presided at the eucharist, and this is also evident from the texts written at the same time as the last part of the New Testament [e.g. the first-century document called the *Didache*]."[13] In other words, hosts in the Christian house communities, by virtue of their being hosts, would naturally be the ones to offer eucharistic prayers on behalf of the gathered faithful. The primary connection was not between leader and eucharist, but rather "between the community and its leader, and therefore between the community leader and the community celebrating the eucharist." Schillebeeckx concludes, "This nuance is important."[14]

The nuance was lost, however, in the fourth century when Christianity became the law of the empire. Gradually, following Jesus became a *religio* along the lines of the pagan religions, and Christian ministers came to be seen as analogous to the pagan priests who presided over the temple cultic rituals. As a result, argues Schillebeeckx, "the [Christian] priesthood itself was connected one-sidedly with the eucharist as the high point of the cult."[15] Formerly, ministers were charged with building up the life of the community, and as leaders they also hosted the eucharist. In the fourth century, by contrast, the primary role of the minister came to be offering the sacrifice of the Mass.

I use the term "sacrifice" deliberately, because by the fourth century the eucharist was described using terminology borrowed from Jewish Temple worship. Schillebeeckx points out that in the New Testament one finds references to the priestly character of Jesus as well as to the priesthood of the people of God, but there is no mention of priests as ministers within the community.[16] He notes that Cyprian (d. 258) was one of the first to compare the eucharist to the sacrifices formerly offered in the Jewish Temple and to say that the priest (*sacerdos*) presides in Jesus's place.[17]

Because such language connecting ministry with sacrifice does not appear in the earliest Christian sources, at the very least one can conclude that it is not *essential* to a Christian understanding of ministry. One might, in other words, conceive of Catholic ministers without comparing them to the Jewish priests who offered sacrifices in the Jerusalem Temple, and thus avoid the supersessionism that such comparisons invite. If Schillebeeckx is correct that in early Christian churches the primary concept of ministry had to do with leadership and service to the community, then there is no reason why a contemporary theology of the priesthood cannot be based in these values as well. Indeed, both the reading from Isaiah and the Gospel text proclaimed at the Chrism Mass point in precisely this direction. They issue calls to build up the community by healing the sick, curing the blind, and preaching good news to prisoners and the poor. Even the text from Revelation, which might be interpreted as offering a "spiritual" view of redemption, is best understood as speaking of salvation, as Schüssler Fiorenza says, "in political terms and in socio-economic categories."[18]

This brings us back to the model of leadership exhibited by Janusz Korczak. Korczak's death, his "sacrifice," was of a piece with his life. His primary allegiance was to the children whom he served, and when faced with the choice of leaving them or accompanying them, he chose to board the train. This example of solidarity with those who are most vulnerable, even unto death, is a challenge to any theology of ecclesial leadership.

In summary, the Chrism Mass attempts to combine two themes. The first is the urgent need for the people of God to serve the neediest of the world. The second is that Jesus instituted the ritual of the eucharist and intended for an ordained priesthood to continue it. This second theme, however, is heavily loaded with supersessionist assumptions, as it both borrows language from Jewish Temple rites and claims to have replaced those rites with the "new and eternal" sacrifice of Jesus. What I have tried to show is that these supersessionist assumptions are not necessary to Catholic notions of ministry or of the eucharist. This is not to say, of course, that they do not have the weight of history and tradition behind them. It is merely to say that it is possible to rethink theologies of the priesthood in ways that do not co-opt language and images from the priesthood of the Jewish Temple.

In the next chapter, I will examine how Catholic tradition has used symbolism borrowed from the Jewish Passover in illustrating the significance of Jesus. For the most part, this borrowing takes place without a recognition of how the meanings of Passover have changed in the post-Holocaust world. In the Catholic liturgy, Passover functions as the answer to the question of who Jesus was. After Auschwitz, however, Passover is not so much an answer as it is a question.

CHAPTER 5

Holy Thursday, the Mass of the Last Supper

By the spring of 1943, the Jewish Ghetto in Warsaw had been ravaged. The summer before had seen three hundred thousand Jews deported for "the East," a code name for the death chambers at Treblinka.[1] Many of those left behind were determined to fight, and they began to plot what would become known as the Warsaw Ghetto Uprising. One uprising had taken place in January of 1943, and another opportunity for revolt came towards the end of April. The Nazis had chosen the week of Passover for the final destruction of the Ghetto, and as the German soldiers moved in with their machine guns and howitzers, the resistance fighters put their plans into action. On the evening of April 19, one of them, Tuvia Borzykowski, went in search of flashlights:

> Wandering about there, I unexpectedly came upon Rabbi Maisel. When I entered the room, I suddenly realized that this was the night of the first Seder.
> The room looked as if it had been hit by a hurricane. Bedding was everywhere, chairs lay overturned, the floor was strewn with household objects, the window panes were all gone. It had all happened during the day, before the inhabitants of the room returned from the bunker.
> Amidst this destruction, the table in the centre of the room looked incongruous with glasses filled with wine, with the family seated around, the rabbi reading the Haggadah. His reading was punctuated by explosions and the rattling of machine guns; the faces of the family around

the table were lit by the red light from the burning buildings, nearby.

Borzykowski concluded his story by saying, "As I was leaving, the Rabbi cordially bade me farewell and wished me suc-
cess. He was old and broken, he told me, but we, the young people, must not give up, and God would help us."[2]
The sight of the rabbi calmly celebrating Passover in the midst
of the devastation of the Ghetto must have seemed extremely
odd. And yet, according to the Book of Exodus, Passover itself
was born amid danger and destruction. On the night that gave
the festival its name, says the Bible, God visited a terrible plague
upon Egypt in an attempt to persuade the pharaoh to free the
Hebrew slaves led by Moses. The display of divine power was
effective, and the slaves were liberated. However, the Lord then
hardened the heart of the pharaoh, and the Egyptians gave chase
in chariots. Only the miraculous intervention of the Lord at the
last moment was able to save the Israelites.
The story of that miraculous deed, the parting of the Red Sea,
had nourished Jewish communities for thousands of years by the
time Rabbi Maisel offered his words of hope to the Warsaw resistance fighter in April of 1943. The Ghetto Uprising was, of course,
doomed to failure. By the time it ended, several thousand Jews
had been killed in the fighting, and several thousand more were
captured and then shot. More than twenty thousand others were
rounded up and sent off to Treblinka or Majdanek, and many
thousands of others were sent to work camps.[3] The Ghetto itself
was razed. Importantly, though, the resistance of the Jews forced
the Nazis to fight for nearly a month to take the ground that they
had hoped to seize in just one day.
Years later, when the Israeli government was faced with the
task of assigning a date on which the Holocaust would be officially remembered, one option under consideration was the first
day of Passover (15 Nissan), in honor of the Warsaw Ghetto
Uprising. Many Israelis, however, objected. They did not want
the joy of Passover to be replaced with remembrance of the
Holocaust. In the end, Yom Hashoah Ve Hagevurah (Destruction
and Heroism Memorial Day) was assigned to 27 Nissan, coming on the heels of Passover but not negating it. Irving Greenberg
writes that the choice of that date was wise: "In effect, Passover

is wounded but not destroyed, which is the truth witnessed by Jewish life after the catastrophe."[4]

The image of a Jewish leader and his small community gathered around a table set for Passover, sharing cups of wine and praying to the God of Moses even as tragedy looms before them, is very familiar to Catholics. It is so familiar, in fact, that many of them hang paintings of it on the walls of their homes. The Last Supper of Jesus has been depicted in countless works of art and is specially commemorated in the Catholic liturgical cycle with the celebration of Holy Thursday.

For, according to the Gospel of Mark, "On the first day of Unleavened Bread, when the Passover lamb is sacrificed, [Jesus's] disciples said to him, 'Where do you want us to go and make the preparations for you to eat the Passover?'" Jesus gave the disciples instructions regarding a room in the city, and the disciples set out "and found everything as he had told them; and they prepared the Passover meal" (Mark 14:12–16). According to Mark, it was the last time that Jesus would ever share a meal with his friends and followers. The next day he would be crucified.

The Gospels of Matthew and Luke also portray the Last Supper as a Passover meal. Only John situates Jesus's Last Supper differently, placing it on the evening before the first Passover celebration. Scholars have debated which account is more likely to be historically accurate, and opinion at this point leans towards John's chronology: that Jesus's final gathering with his friends was not a Passover meal.[5] Even if John does not equate the Last Supper with the celebration of Passover, however, he nonetheless connects the two events by noting that Jesus's final meal with his friends took place "before the festival of the Passover" (13:1).

Above, I said that the image of a Jewish leader celebrating a final Passover meal is very familiar to Catholics. And yet immediately I must clarify. There is a profound difference between the Passover celebrated by Rabbi Maisel and that celebrated (at least according to the synoptic gospels) by Jesus. In Jewish memory, the destruction of the Warsaw Ghetto is part of the larger destruction of the Jews of Europe. It is a disaster of monumental proportions. The Uprising's heroes are honored, to be sure, yet their stories can be told only as part of the larger sorrow of the *Shoah*. The Passover celebrated by Rabbi Maisel, while perhaps remembered with admiration, is overshadowed by the fate that awaited all those who sat at his table. His Passover ended in flames and poison gas.

In the memory of Catholics, by contrast, the Last Supper was a moment of triumph: Jesus instituting a ritual through which, Christians believe, he would be present to them for all time to come. It was tragic in that it signaled that the end of Jesus's earthly life was drawing near, and yet the tragedy appears as only one moment in a story of glorious resurrection and redemption. What might be recalled in Catholic minds as an evening of treachery culminating in blood and death is remembered rather as a victorious episode in an ultimately happy story. Even the betrayal of Jesus by Judas and the subsequent crucifixion are often viewed as foreordained events for which Christians should be grateful.

This assurance of victory can lead at times to a morbid fascination with the suffering of the Christ. Because a happy ending has already been accomplished, there is leisure to linger over the details of the Passion. The thorns, the whips, the bloody cloak, and broken limbs—these would be unbearable if Jesus's story ended with his naked and rotting body being dumped unceremoniously into a mass grave. Tradition can afford to present and re-present the details only because it deems them, in the end, insignificant in light of the resurrection.

Later in this book I will argue that this basic tendency within Catholic thought to skip quickly from tragedy to victory, from death to resurrection, has serious consequences, many of them negative. It can lead to a kind of triumphalism in which the suffering of the world is swept aside as inconsequential. More specifically, Jewish suffering can appear either as insignificant or, worse, as part of a divine plan. As I will argue, such triumphalism actually undercuts the meaning of Christian faith. For the moment, however, it is enough to keep in mind the danger inherent in presuming to know at the outset the significance of anyone's suffering, whether it be the suffering of Rabbi Maisel or the suffering of Jesus.

That said, the final meal that Jesus ate with his followers has attained enormous ritual and theological importance in Catholic life. It is commemorated as one of the central events in all of human history, and it is re-presented every time the Mass is celebrated. During the most sacred moment of that central Catholic liturgy, the priest, acting *in persona Christi*, consecrates the bread and wine on the altar by recalling Jesus's words at the Last Supper, saying, "Take this, all of you, and eat it: this is my body which will be given up for you . . . Take this, all of you, and drink from it: this is the cup of my blood, the blood of the new and everlasting covenant. It will be shed for you and for all so that sins may be forgiven. Do this in memory of me."[6] Day in and day out, in every corner of the earth, the Last Supper is remembered by Catholics as the meal during which their holiest ritual was instituted. The meal is also commemorated each year on the Thursday before Easter, on the day known as Holy Thursday.

What I will try to show in this chapter is that the Holy Thursday liturgy has appropriated the language, images, and festivals of Judaism in ways that are problematic. They are problematic first because by adopting elements of Jewish tradition, Catholicism has also frequently understood itself as having superseded Judaism. And, as Franklin Littell has pointed out, it is a short step from deeming a religion superfluous to deeming those who practice it to be superfluous as well.[7]

These appropriations of Jewish tradition are also problematic because Judaism itself has undergone significant transformations since the time of Jesus. It has grown and changed just as Christianity has, and the meanings of its rituals and practices have changed as well. Not to take account of this fact is to freeze Judaism in the past. Not recognizing Judaism's ongoing vitality can also lead to a view of the religion as merely a "fossil" that by all rights should have died out with the advent of Christianity.

Finally, Christian liturgy's use of Passover imagery is problematic because some of the changes that Judaism has undergone have been the direct result of Christian antisemitism. When Catholics invoke Passover symbols and images, they should be aware that medieval Jews told the Passover story by comparing the evil pharaoh to the marauding Catholic crusaders who slaughtered entire Jewish villages. Catholics should know that it was shortly after the first Crusades that the section of the Haggadah in which Jews beg God, "Pour Your anger and Your wrath on the heathen nations that do not know You and the sinful kingdoms that do not call Your name"[8] was first included.[9] And, of course, Catholics need to confront the fact that, post-Holocaust, the phrase "Angel of Death" no longer evokes only the spirit who, according to tradition, slew the first-born of the Egyptians at God's behest. It now also revives the memory of the devout Catholic doctor Josef Mengele[10] who stood on the platform at Auschwitz and decided which Jews would be gassed immediately and which would instead be worked to death as slaves.

In sum, the Holy Thursday liturgy relies on a rich history of symbols and images. The point of this chapter is to show that that history is more complex and far more troubling than might be apparent.

EVENING MASS OF THE LORD'S SUPPER

On Holy Thursday, the season in the Catholic calendar known as the Easter Triduum is inaugurated with the Evening Mass of the Lord's Supper. This ritual formally commemorates Jesus's last meal with his disciples, and it is from this service that Holy Thursday gets the name Maundy Thursday. The term "Maundy" is derived from the Latin *mandatum* or "command"; according to the Gospel of John, after sharing his final meal with his disciples and washing their feet, Jesus said to them, "I give you a new commandment, that you love one another" (13:34). That commandment is included as one of the antiphons that can be sung in the liturgy during the washing of the feet.

The readings for the Mass of the Lord's Supper are the same each year. The first connects the sacrifice of Jesus with the sacrifice of the lamb at Passover. The Responsorial Psalm that follows thanks God for many gifts bestowed and explains how to interpret the deaths of God's faithful ones. Next, the second reading extends the connection made between the Passover and the eucharist (the ritual which Catholics believe makes present once again the offering Jesus made). Finally, the Gospel reading tells the story of how Jesus washed the disciples' feet. Let us look at each of these readings in turn.

I. Jesus and the Passover: Exodus 12:1–8, 11–14

The Liturgy of the Word on Holy Thursday commences with a reading from the Book of Exodus. That reading recalls the night of the first Passover, when God freed the Israelites from slavery in Egypt. The text's purpose in the liturgy is to associate the sacrifice of Jesus with the sacrifice of the Passover lambs. Just as the lambs' blood was shed to save the Israelites from death, so the analogy goes, Jesus's blood was shed to save the world from death. As we will see in this section, however, some of the details of the Passover festival have changed from century to century. Passover in Jewish tradition has been linked with the biblical story of the *Akedah* (the binding of Isaac) as well as with the martyrdom of Jews at the hands of Christians. More recently, the celebration of Passover has been forced to confront the events of the Holocaust. When Catholics invoke the Passover in their understanding of Jesus, therefore, they need to take account of the entire complex of images, events, and questions that accompany it.

The story of the first Passover is well known. The portion of scripture read at the Mass of the Last Supper includes God's instructions to Moses and Aaron:

> Tell the whole community of Israel:
>> On the tenth of this month every one of your families
>> must procure for itself a lamb, one apiece for each
>> household . . .
> They shall take some of its blood
>> and apply it to the two doorposts and the lintel
>> of every house in which they partake of the lamb . . .
> It is the Passover of the LORD.
> For on this same night I will go through Egypt,
>> striking down every firstborn of the land, both man
>> and beast,
>> and executing judgment on all the gods of Egypt—
>> I, the LORD! . . .
> Seeing the blood, I will pass over you;
>> thus, when I strike the land of Egypt,
>> no destructive blow will come upon you.[11]

The blood of the lambs brings protection to the houses of the Jews. Ultimately it brings the Israelites freedom from their Egyptian masters, as the Angel of Death that passes over the land that night (according to tradition, though not scripture) causes such widespread affliction that the pharaoh tells Moses to take his people and to go. This Moses does, but when the pharaoh changes his mind and pursues the fleeing slaves, God must intervene again to ensure that the escape is successful.

In Jewish life and thought, the memory of God's victory over Egypt is continually reshaped as the context in which the Passover is celebrated changes. Thus, for example, in the Middle Ages, the Passover story was invoked as a plea for God to end the suffering of Jews at the hands of Christians. Ephraim of Bonn, after recounting the massacres of Jews in the twelfth century, prayed, "May the jealous and vengeful God reveal to us His vengeance . . . as He did against Pharaoh and all of Egypt . . ."[12] Praying in the fifteenth century, Akiva ben Eliezer recalled Jews who had been executed at Trent, and he asked of God, "Execute revenge upon our enemies in the near future, as when I left Egypt!"[13] In the minds of medieval Jews, Christians were the new pharaoh who sought to destroy them. Passover was both a remembrance of God's destruction of Egypt and a prayer that God rescue God's people once again from oppression.

Likewise, and more directly relevant to our purposes, in contemporary Jewish life the celebration of Passover has been affected profoundly by the events of the twentieth century. Numerous works of art as well as modern versions of the Haggadah make the connection between Passover and the *Shoah*. Examining a few of these will provide some context for understanding the multiple connotations that Passover has today, and why it is important for Christians to be aware of these.

For example, a version of the Passover service written shortly after the end of World War II asks why God did not intervene in Auschwitz. *A Survivors' Haggadah*, composed by a Lithuanian Jew who had endured four years in concentration camps, offers a bitter rendition of the traditional *dayenu* ("it would have sufficed"), the prayer that offers thanks for God's redemption of the Israelites from slavery. The traditional version proclaims that it would have been enough if God had merely rescued the Jews without also punishing their captors; it would have been enough if God had merely led the Israelites through the desert without also providing manna; it would have been enough if God had fed them manna without also giving them the Sabbath; and so on. However, the Haggadah used in 1946 by the remnant that Hitler did not have time to murder prays instead, "Had He scattered us among the nations but had not given us the First Crusade, we would have been content . . . Had He given us the Inquisition but not the pogroms of 1648–49, we would have

been content . . . Had He given us gas chambers and crematoria, but our wives and children had not been tortured, we would
have been content . . ."[14] The Haggadah does not wait for an
answer from God about why such atrocities were allowed to
occur. It finishes the *dayenu* simply by vowing, "All the more so,
since all these have befallen us, we must make *Aliyah* [emigra-
tion to Israel], even if illegally, wipe out the *Galut* [exile], build
the chosen land, and make a home for ourselves and our children for eternity."[15] The question of why these events occurred
is asked of God but never answered.

Similarly, the 1999 film *The Devil's Arithmetic*, based on the
children's novel of the same name, incorporates memories of the
Holocaust quite literally into its presentation of a contemporary
Passover celebration. The main character in the made-for-tele-
vision movie is Hannah (played by Kirsten Dunst), a typical
American teenager who resists her parents' insistence that she
accompany them to her relatives' home for the Seder meal. As
she arrives at the house and is greeted by her elderly aunts and
uncles, she appears ill at ease, and she brushes off the old people's attempts to tell her about their experiences in the Nazi concentration camps.

All that changes, however, when Hannah is asked by her Aunt
Eva to open the door for Elijah as part of the ritual meal. As she
grudgingly obeys the request, she suddenly finds herself trans-
ported back to 1941, to the Polish village where her aged relatives had lived in their youth. She does not have much opportunity to explore the town, however, as immediately she and the
rest of the Jews are rounded up by Nazi soldiers and taken to a
concentration camp. There she experiences the horrors of the
Holocaust: slow starvation, exhausting labor, and the constant
threat of death either at the whim of a passing soldier or as part
of the bureaucratic calculations of the camp commandant (i.e.,
"the devil's arithmetic"). Her only source of comfort is her cousin
Rivkah (played by Brittany Murphy), who vows that if she sur-
vives the war she will change her name to Eva. That name, of
course, means "mother of all the living" (see Gen. 3:20).

Hannah's days in the camp come to an end when she takes
Rivkah's place during a selection and is marched to the gas chamber along with several other women and children. We watch as
she and the others are locked into the chamber and as the gas

pellets begin to emit their poison. Finally, we see Hannah's body tangled among the other corpses lying on the floor, one more victim of the Nazi machine.

In an Oz-like return to home, however, Hannah then awakens and finds herself once again in the house of her relatives. The uncles and aunts are gathered anxiously around her, and they explain that she fainted from drinking too much wine at the Seder. Only Aunt Eva (who as a girl was named Rivkah) seems to understand the journey she has taken, and she and Hannah share a quiet moment of wonder at and gratitude for the miracle that has occurred. Hannah then vows always to remember the suffering of the Holocaust, and she eagerly rejoins her relatives in their celebration of the Passover Seder. *The Devil's Arithmetic* explicitly connects the telling of the Passover story with the story of the Holocaust. Both narratives, the film suggests, are crucial to the identity of contemporary Jews.

In her analysis of *The Devil's Arithmetic*, Liora Gubkin questions the film's use of the Holocaust as a means to teach a lesson to young Hannah. She notes that "people confronted with the Holocaust often try to rescue 'hope' or at least 'meaning' from the ashes of Auschwitz, and thus redeem the Holocaust." This is understandable, she says, as it is "a desperate attempt to hold on to an optimistic view of humanity."[16] And yet the strategy also prevents one from confronting the singular and irreducible horror of the *Shoah*.

It is true that *The Devil's Arithmetic* uses the Holocaust as a way of resolving Hannah's conflict about her identity as a Jew. On the other hand, the movie leaves open and unresolved one of the most important questions raised by its characters. While in the concentration camp, Hannah asks why she and her fellow Jews are being subjected so such suffering. She is convinced that she is being punished by God for having been "a foolish girl" in her earlier life. Her cousin Rivkah, however, rebukes her, pointing out that surely the children in the camps had done nothing to deserve their fate. Hannah persists, asking, "Then why? Why?" Rivkah answers, "Ask them. Why? Ask the Nazis, not me."

Later in the film, however, after her ordeal is over and she is speaking with her Aunt Eva, Hannah asks the same question. How could so many people have been punished as they were? Aunt Eva (née Rivkah) answers, "Once I would have said you have to ask the Nazis. But now I know better. And I say you have to ask God. There is no one else." The film resists closure to the theological question of evil even as it resolves Hannah's Jewish identity. One might conclude that asking God difficult questions is precisely the core of what it means to be a Jew.

A contemporary version of the Seder ritual also refuses to bring closure to the question of God's involvement in history. In *A Passover Haggadah*, Auschwitz survivor Elie Wiesel considers why the traditional Seder urges, "In every generation, every individual must feel as if he personally had come out of Egypt." The fact that the text does not say "every Jew" but rather "every individual" shows, says Wiesel, that the experience of the Jews is universal. He explains, "This lesson is especially relevant for those of our contemporaries who declare that all of us 'are survivors of the Holocaust.' No, all of us are not . . . Only those who knew death in Auschwitz survived Auschwitz. But all of us should think and act 'as if' we had all been there."[17]

To think and act as if we had been in the Holocaust is to respond always with compassion, Wiesel says, and that includes compassion for one's enemies. Significantly, in the celebration of Passover one is prohibited from expressing glee at the defeat of the Egyptians. Neither the slaying of the first-born nor the drowning of Pharaoh's soldiers in the Red Sea is recalled as a cause for joy. Numerous midrashim stress that God had given the Egyptians many opportunities to repent before visiting the last, most terrible plague upon them. For example, one reminds, "Despite all the lashings of punishment which the Holy One, blessed be He, inflicted upon the Egyptians in order to cleanse them of evil, so that the Egyptians would let Israel go from their midst . . . the Egyptians did not consent to let them go. When did they let them go? After . . . the smiting of the first-born."[18] Another midrash explains that when the Red Sea swallowed up Pharaoh's men, "The ministering angels wanted to chant their hymns, but the Holy One, blessed be He, said, 'The work of my hands is being drowned in the sea, and shall you chant hymns?'"(Megillah 10b). According to Jewish tradition, at the recitation of each plague during the Seder meal, a few drops of wine are spilled to remind the celebrants that their joy came at the cost of others' suffering. Likewise, while on the first two nights of Passover six psalms are sung in praise of all that God has done, for the rest of the festival this *Hallel* is shortened as a mark of mourning for the Egyptians.[19]

Passover thus seems to be a festival of contradictions: joy at liberation, and sorrow at the suffering that led to it; proclamations that God saves God's people, and memories of when God did not. Wiesel sees these contradictions as at the heart of Jewish faith. Reflecting on how the meaning of the holiday has changed for him as a result of his experiences in the camps, he writes, "Do I love it less than before? No. Let's just say I love it differently. Now I love it for the questions it raises, which are, after all, its *raison d'être*."[20] Passover is now, if it was not always, more of a question than an answer.

This becomes even clearer when one considers that the story of the Passover has in Jewish literature and lore been linked with Abraham's near-slaying of Isaac in Genesis 22. (It should be pointed out that the Passover Haggadah itself does not make this connection.) According to Genesis 22, God told Abraham to slaughter his son as a sacrificial offering. Abraham complied and prepared to kill Isaac, but at the last moment God intervened and directed him to a ram instead. In his classic commentary on this text, entitled *The Last Trial*, Shalom Spiegel notes an ancient tradition in which the *Akedah* (the binding of Isaac by Abraham to ready him for sacrifice) took place in the same month as did the redemption of Israel from Egypt generations later. Spiegel argues that the Book of Jubilees, a Jewish text probably written in the second century BCE, makes the same connection.[21] Other scholars doubt Spiegel's conclusion and believe that Judaism associated the Passover with the *Akedah* somewhat later, in the late second century CE.[22] Nonetheless, from at least that point on the association became common.

For example, when commenting on a passage from Exodus 12:3 in which God orders the Hebrews to "take a lamb to a family, a lamb to a household," to slaughter it and to place its blood on their doors, Rabbi Ephraim explains that God "will remember the merit of their Fathers in their favor: the merit of Abraham, [who said to Isaac,] 'God will see to the *lamb*' (Genesis 22:8); the merit of Isaac, who was bound like a *lamb* . . ."[23] Similarly, when interpreting Exodus 12:13, in which God promises, "[W]hen I see the blood I will pass over you, so that no plague will destroy you when I strike the land of Egypt," the Mechilta explains, "What did He see? He saw the blood of the binding of Isaac, as it is said, 'God will see to a lamb for himself' (Gen. 22:8)."[24]

Like the Passover, the *Akedah* is also not remembered as an occasion for unmitigated joy. Tradition says that after his ordeal was over, Abraham was angry with God for ordering him to kill his own son. He wanted to know why God, who surely knew beforehand how events would unfold, would test him in such a manner. God responded that of course the outcome was already known to the divine mind, but that human beings also had to be shown Abraham's worthiness. This answer did not satisfy Abraham, however, and he demanded that God hear him out. "I might have reproached Thee," he tells God, "[b]ut I refrained myself, and I said nothing." In return for his forbearance, Abraham requires that God be equally patient with the trespasses of future generations. God agrees to this and promises that in years to come, if Abraham's children blow a ram's horn on New Year's Day and ask for pardon, then God, remembering the ram that was substituted for Isaac as a sacrifice, will forgive them.[25] In this tradition, even God seems to recognize that asking some-one to commit human sacrifice is beyond the pale.

As we saw earlier, the meaning of the Passover story acquired different shadings depending on the context in which it was read; so too the meaning of the *Akedah*. For example, in the Middle Ages, Jews drew on Genesis 22 to describe their suffer-ing at the hands of Christians. Rabbi Ephraim of Bonn was thir-teen years old at the time of the Second Crusade, and by his own account he was an eyewitness to some of its atrocities. One of his poems recalls the binding of Isaac by Abraham and then con-nects that event to the ongoing martyrdom of Jews. The poem portrays Isaac assuring Abraham regarding his impending immo-lation, "Oh, my father, fill your mouth with praise, For He [God] doth bless the sacrifice." In this version of the *Akedah*, as in many others, Abraham actually goes through with the killing of Isaac. Recounts the poem, "With steady hands he slaughtered him according to the rite, Full right was the slaughter." When Isaac is revived by the resurrecting power of dew that falls upon him, Abraham seizes him again "to slaughter him once more." At that point, the ministering angels cry out in horror, "Even animal victims, were they ever slaughtered twice? . . . We beg of Thee, have pity upon him!" The poem ends with the author remembering the many murders that have taken place since Abraham killed Isaac and imploring that God allow no more martyrdoms at all: "Recall to our credit the many Akedahs, the saints, men and women, slain for Thy sake . . . Break the yoke and snap the bands of the bound flock that yearns toward Thee."[26]

Other Jewish medieval accounts of the slaughter of Jews by Christians likewise invoke the sacrifice of Isaac. For example, when the Jews of Mainz were attacked by Christian crusaders, some of them chose to be killed by their own friends or family rather than submit to death (or baptism) at the hands of the marauders. Later, Solomon bar Simson described the carnage at Mainz:

> Let the ears hearing this and its like be seared, for who has heard or seen the likes of it? Inquire and seek: was there ever such a mass sacrificial offering since the time of Adam? Did it ever occur that there were one thousand and one hundred offerings on one single day—all of them comparable to the sacrifice of Isaac, the son of Abraham?[27]

To die for the unity of God's name (i.e., the *Shema:* "Hear, Israel, the Lord is our God, the Lord is One") was to offer oneself for God in the same way that Isaac was offered. And yet such offerings were tragedies that called not for rejoicing but rather for cries to heaven. Solomon bar Simson reproached God for not doing more to prevent the murders of Jews by Christians: "Wilt Thou restrain Thyself for these things, O Lord? It was for You that innumerable souls were killed! May You avenge the spilt blood of your servants, in our days and before our very eyes—Amen—and speedily!"[28]

Just as the memory of the Holocaust has been incorporated into contemporary interpretations of the Passover Seder, so has it affected contemporary portrayals of the *Akedah* as well. In many post-Holocaust works, the *Akedah* is both honored as a trial of faith and mourned as an omen of the many slaughters to come. For example, Jacob Glatstein, who was born in Lublin, Poland and whose parents were murdered in the Holocaust, composed a poem called "My Father Isaac," in which he imagined an elderly Isaac being led to sacrifice. Unlike in the Genesis story, however, this time "No good angel came flying; / the flames burned more brightly and higher." Nonetheless, as the old man dies, he calls out "in a tired voice: / 'Here I am—prepared to be your ram.'"[29] There is no joy in the poem, but rather what might be termed steadfast resignation: obedience even unto death.

Like Jews, Christians have also linked Passover with the sacrifice of Isaac. However, they have gone a step further and linked both events with the death of Jesus. Carol Delaney points out that some early Christians used the Passover/*Akedah* association to confirm that Jesus, who was killed at Passover, was truly the messiah.[30] Indeed, the interpretation of Isaac as a "type" or forerunner of Christ goes back nearly to the inception of Christianity. Clement of Alexandria, writing at the end of the second century, wrote regarding Jesus,

> He [Isaac] was a son, just as is the Son (he is the son of Abraham; Christ, of God); he was a victim, as was the Lord . . . All he did was to carry the wood of his sacrifice, just as the Lord bore the wood of the Cross . . . Isaac did not actually suffer, not only to concede the primacy of suffering to the Word, but also to suggest, by not being slain, the divinity of the Lord; Jesus rose again after His burial, as if He had not suffered, like Isaac delivered from the altar of sacrifice.[31]

Jesus, according to Clement, was the new Isaac who, like his predecessor, was sentenced to death by his own father. And like Isaac, Jesus emerged from the trial alive. In this view Jesus is not executed but rather is sacrificed, and the sacrifice ends not in the grave but in the salvation of the world.

The connection made in Christian thought between sacrifice and salvation troubles Elie Wiesel. In a commentary written on the *Akedah* entitled "The Sacrifice of Isaac: A Survivor's Story," Wiesel writes,

> In Jewish tradition man cannot use death as a means of glorifying God. Every man is an end unto himself, a living eternity; no man has the right to sacrifice another, not even to God. Had he killed his son, Abraham would have become the forefather of a people—but not the Jewish

people. For the Jew, all truth must spring from life, never from death. To us, crucifixion represents not a step forward but a step backward.

He continues, "To invoke the *Akeda* is tantamount to calling for mercy—whereas from the beginning Golgotha [where Jesus was crucified] has served as pretext for countless massacres of sons and fathers cut down together by sword and fire in the name of a word that considered itself synonymous with love."[32]

Wiesel is overstating the case when he says that in Jewish tradition one cannot use death as a way of glorifying God. Judaism in fact has a long tradition of *Kiddush haShem*, or the sanctification of the divine name through martyrdom. In the first few centuries of the common era, as Christians and Jews struggled to define themselves both in relation to each other and in the wake of the destruction of the Temple, Jewish portrayals of Isaac as a martyr began to proliferate, as did Christian interpretations of Jesus as the new Isaac. Some scholars suggest that the Passion narratives of Christians directly influenced the development of *Akedah* narratives in which Isaac is offered as an atoning sacrifice.[33] Others, such as Daniel Boyarin, suggest that since what came to be known as "Christianity" took hundreds of years to emerge as a religion distinct from Judaism, it is better to speak of "recirculating motifs, themes and religious ideas," rather than a clear line of origin and influence.[34] Nonetheless, Boyarin agrees that by the end of the third century, a new model of martyrdom had evolved in rabbinic literature. In previous narratives, he says, "the martyr refused to violate his or her religious integrity and was executed for this refusal." In the third century, however, "we find martyrdom being actively sought as a spiritual requirement and as the only possible fulfillment of a spiritual need."[35]

Significantly, Boyarin also points out that martyrdom is not presented as an unmitigated good in these early rabbinic texts. He cites as an example the story of the execution of Rabbi Akiva in the second century of the common era, as it is told in the Babylonian Talmud. When Rabbi Akiva is arrested by the Romans and is sentenced to death, his students question his resolve to die, asking, "Our teacher, so far[?]" Even the angels in heaven protest to God: "This is Torah, and this is its reward!?"[36] These voices do not prevent Akiva's martyrdom, but they do at least raise some doubts about its wisdom. Boyarin also considers two talmudic accounts of other rabbis arrested by the Romans, Rabbi El'azar, the son of Perata, and Rabbi Chanina, the son of Teradyon. The former escapes death by tricksterism, and the latter is burned alive. But the Talmud, says Boyarin, "never quite rules for tricksters or for martyrs."[37] Neither rabbi is presented as having the "correct" approach.

Even in later, medieval accounts of martyrdoms, in which Jews are praised for choosing to die by their own hands rather than submit to baptism, those who took a different path merit approval. Solomon bar Simson writes, "It is now fitting to recount the praises of those who were forcibly converted. They risked their lives even in matters pertaining to food and drink . . . He who speaks evil of them, it is as though he spoke thus of the Divine Countenance."[38]

Likewise, in the mid-twelfth century, Maimonides wrote his "Epistle on Martyrdom" regarding Jews who lived in areas where rulers demanded that they convert to Islam. In his letter, he praised those who chose death over conversion, assuring them that God held great rewards in store for them. At the same time, however, he wrote, "But if anyone comes to ask me whether to surrender his life or acknowledge [the apostleship of Muhammad], I tell him to confess and not choose death. However, he should not continue to live in the domain of that ruler."[39]

In the twentieth century, Rabbi Ephraim Oshry, who was living in Kovno, Lithuania, when the Nazis invaded, considered several questions regarding conversion and martyrdom. One case involved a Jewish man who wished to write "R.C." on his passport in order to pass as a Roman Catholic. Rabbi Oshry ruled that this was permissible because "even though the non-Jews would think they mean that he is a Roman Catholic, he was free to have in mind the Hebrew meaning of the two letters. It was irrelevant how the non-Jews would construe those letters."[40]

The rabbi also considered cases of parents who wished to entrust their children to non-Jews in order to save them. If the non-Jew was a priest, and if handing the children over meant that they would not be raised as Jews, then he ruled in the negative. However, if the non-Jews were gentile friends of the parents, and if the children were hidden with the intention of their being returned to their parents after the war, then the practice was permissible: "With life at stake, one must follow the lenient alternative."[41] Even in the case of an adult Jewish man who was a *kohein* (a descendant of Aaron, brother of Moses) but who had undergone baptism, Rabbi Oshry ruled on the side of leniency. He reasoned that the man "had acted only under the greatest of duress, fearing for his life. That had been a clear act of compulsion of which the man repented completely without any attempt at deception."[42]

By contrast, Christian tradition is nearly univocal. In Christian martyr tales, the martyr dies *in imitatio Christi* and is the ideal follower of Jesus. In martyr tales in which the protagonist manages to avoid being seized by his or her persecutors, that escape is always followed by a return and a voluntary, deliberate, and even joyful acceptance of death. In making this point, Daniel Boyarin points to the story of the martyrdom of Polycarp, who was executed in the second century. Polycarp, eighty-six years old by his own reckoning, was bishop of Smyrna when persecutions of Christians flared up. At first, at the urging of his friends, Polycarp fled the city for a farm in the country. His pursuers followed him there, however, and they closed in on him during the night. At that point Polycarp could have made another escape, but he refused, saying, "God's will be done." After the arrest, the governor tried to persuade the prisoner to deny his Christian faith, but the old man held fast. Polycarp was then burnt alive, praying amidst the flames, "O Lord God Almighty . . . I bless thee for granting me this day and hour, that I may be numbered amongst the martyrs, to share the cup of thine Anointed . . ."[43] Dying as Jesus had died was a privilege that Polycarp felt honored to receive.

Thus Wiesel's observation regarding how Jews and Christians assess the value of martyrdom, if it is a generalization, nonetheless touches on an important distinction. Jewish tradition does not valorize death in the same way that Christian tradition does. The difference perhaps can be found in the relation between the martyr's death and his or her life. Explains Eliezer Berkovits, "Continuing with 'the routine' of Jewish existence and ignoring the world that is bent on crushing the Jew is one of the marks of *Kiddush haShem.* Often it is practiced long before the hour of radical abandonment arrives."[44] Studying the death of Rabbi Akiva, what Berkovits finds most significant is not the rabbi's final moments themselves, but rather how those moments were of a piece with the rest of his life. The martyrdom was only one step in a lifelong commitment, and its significance comes from the context in which it occurred: "The defiant No with which a man meets a tyrant or a persecuting church or a humiliating falsehood is itself a supreme act of living self-affirmation. If it is done for the sake of God, in whose truth alone one finds self-fulfillment, it is a heroic act of *Kiddush haShem*."[45]

Again, by contrast, Christians have frequently looked to the death of Jesus as both ordained by God and as a good in itself. The entrance antiphon or *Introit* for the Holy Thursday Mass of the Lord's Supper proclaims, "We should glory in the cross of our Lord Jesus Christ, for he is our salvation, our life and our resurrection; through him we are saved and made free."[46] Here the death of Jesus is not simply the result of his defiant assertion of dignity in the face of tyranny. It is rather an event that saves the world and is the occasion for glorious celebration. Likewise, in a preface of the eucharistic prayer said at the Mass of the Lord's Supper, the presider prays, "He [Jesus] is the true and eternal priest who established this unending sacrifice. He offered himself as a victim for our deliverance and taught us to make this offering in his memory. As we eat his body which he gave for us, we grow in strength. As we drink his blood which he poured out for us, we are washed clean."[47] Jesus's bloody death nourishes, cleanses, and saves. It is a positive good rather than simply a heroic response to tragedy.

It is hard to reconcile that understanding of sacrifice with either the slaughter of the Passover lambs or the *Akedah*. In the story of Passover, God resorts to killing human beings only after having already visited nine plagues upon Egypt. The slaughter is a final resort, one last measure in the effort to free the Israelites. Moreover, the lambs killed on the eve of Passover are offered precisely as a way of lessening human bloodshed. Their sacrifice is not a joyous measure but an attempt to mitigate the terror that would sweep through Egypt that night. By interpreting Jesus's death as a good in itself, Catholic tradition has significantly altered the meaning of the Jewish texts in ways that may be neither necessary nor helpful to Jewish-Christian relations after the Holocaust.

There are some notable exceptions to the Catholic tradition of seeing Jesus's crucifixion as a positive event that was divinely ordained, and these will be discussed in Chapter Six. Those exceptions will, in fact, provide opportunities for rethinking the death of Jesus in ways that are both more constructive and more credible in a post-Auschwitz world. What we can conclude thus far is rather along the lines of the negative. If the traditions of Holy Thursday utilize the imagery of Passover, they cannot do so in ways that are simplistic or naive. More, they cannot do so in ways that are unthinkingly supersessionist, taking over the "Old Testament" celebration of Passover and replacing it with New Testament meanings. Judaism has a long tradition of wrestling with the notions of sacrifice, suffering, martyrdom, and vicarious atonement, a tradition that did not end in the first century with the advent of Christianity. That tradition is complex and ambivalent, and has become only more so since the Holocaust. If the Holy Thursday liturgy incorporates Passover imagery, it must do so in a way that takes into account how that festival has been affected by the centuries of Christian persecution of Jews that led to in the Holocaust.

II. Responsorial Psalm: Psalm 116:12–13, 15–16, 17–18

In the Mass of the Last Supper, the Responsorial Psalm that is sung between the reading from the Hebrew Bible and the Epistle (that is, between the first two readings) contains the following verses:

> How shall I make a return to the LORD
>   for all the good he has done for me?
> The cup of salvation I will take up,
>   and I will call upon the name of the LORD . . .
> Precious in the eyes of the LORD
>   is the death of his faithful ones.

The translation of that last line, verse 15 of the psalm, is both significant and problematic. Consider how three other sources render the text:

Precious in the sight of Yahweh / Is the faith/trust of
his devoted ones. (Michael Barré)[48]

The death of His faithful ones is grievous in the Lord's
sight. (Jewish Publication Society)

Too costly in the eyes of the Lord is the death of his
faithful. (New American Bible)

Obviously, translation makes an enormous difference in how
one reads the psalm. It also makes a difference in how one understands the death of Jesus.

The problem for interpreters of this verse lies in an apparent
contradiction within the psalm itself. Psalm 116 is a song of
thanksgiving that praises God for delivering the author from
death. In verse 6 the singer exults, "I was brought low and He
saved me." In verse 8, the psalmist says, "You [God] have delivered me from death, my eyes from tears, my feet from stum-
bling." It does not really make sense, then, that just a few lines
later the text would portray death as something with positive
value in the eyes of God. Rendering verse 15 as "Precious in the
eyes of the Lord is the death of his faithful ones" seems to contradict the basic thrust of the song.

Aware of this problem, scholars have turned to other possibilities for interpreting the verse. Michael Barré, who translates
the text as "Precious in the sight of Yahweh / Is the faith/trust of
his devoted ones," thinks that the problem is the result of scribal
error. He argues that the Hebrew word for death, *hamāwĕtāh*,
should instead be *hēmānûtāh*, or "trust, faith(fulness)."[49] It is the
trust of God's faithful ones, rather than their death, that is precious in the eyes of the Lord.

Other scholars approach the problem of the verse differently.
Unlike Barré, they accept that the noun in the text is "death"
rather than "trust." However, they disagree that the adjective
that describes the death of the faithful ones should be interpreted
as "precious." At issue for them is the meaning of the Hebrew
word *yāqār*. In many cases, *yāqār* does mean "precious." For
example, in the Jewish Publication Society (JPS) translation of
Proverbs, wisdom is described as "more precious (*yĕqārāh*) than
rubies" (3:15). The word also means "highly valued," as in

I Kings 5:31, where the king orders that huge blocks of "choice" (*yĕqārôt*) stone be quarried. Why then does the JPS opt for "grievous" when it comes to Psalm 116:15?

The answer, again, lies in the context of the psalm itself. It simply does not seem to make sense that after thanking God for sparing him from death, the psalmist would then say that death is "precious." The medieval Jewish scholar Rashi did not think so either. In his commentary on Psalm 116:15 he wrote, "IS GRIEVOUS IN THE LORD'S SIGHT. The Holy One Blessed be He showed me that it is a hard and serious matter in His sight to let His devotees die."[50]

J.A. Emerton notes that the Aramaic cognate of *yāqār* took on several meanings in the ancient world, including "difficult," "heavy," and "burdensome." He concludes, therefore, that "it is plausible to translate *yāqār* as 'grievous' in Ps. cxvi.5, even though that meaning is not clearly attested elsewhere in Biblical Hebrew."[51]

Likewise, the New American Bible translation picks up on the same connotations of the word and translates *yāqār* as "too costly." Significantly, this is the version that the United States Conference of Catholic Bishops (USCCB) has placed on its Web site. A footnote to the verse as it appears on the site explains that "the meaning is that the death of God's faithful is grievous to God, not that God is pleased with the death."[52]

And yet, in the Holy Thursday liturgy, the verse is translated as we saw above: "Precious in the eyes of the Lord is the death of his faithful ones." The reason for this is that the translation is derived from the Neo-Vulgate (*Nova Vulgata*), a Latin version of the Bible published under Pope John Paul II in 1979. In the Neo-Vulgate, Psalm 116:15 is rendered as "*Pretiosa in conspectu Domini mors sanctorum eius.*"[53] It is only natural, then, that the English version of this text, the version approved for liturgical use, translates *yāqār* in line with *pretiosa* and thus as "precious."[54]

Natural, but unfortunate. As it stands, the use of Psalm 116 as the Responsorial song in the Mass of the Lord's Supper on Holy Thursday reinforces the idea that the death of Jesus was a good willed by God. The problem is not simply that the liturgy translates *yāqār* as "precious." Neither is the problem simply that the liturgy takes a Jewish psalm and applies it to Jesus. The problem is rather the combination of those two elements, plus the placement of the psalm between the first and second readings. The first reading, recall, tells the story of the slaughter of the Passover lambs. The second reading, as we will see, tells the story of Jesus reflecting on his own impending death. Situating Psalm 116 between these two texts, the Holy Thursday liturgy's translation expresses the conviction that Jesus's death was a sacrifice required by God and approved by God. As Emerton points out, if death is precious, then "God regards the saints' death [sic] as valuable, which is most naturally understood to mean that he wants them to be killed . . . "[55] It is this concept of salvation through sacrifice that, as we have seen, has only limited resonance in Judaism. Nonetheless, it is a notion that is at the heart of the next reading of the Mass of the Lord's Supper.

III. The Eucharist: I Cor. 11:23–26

The second reading of the Holy Thursday liturgy is taken from Paul's First Letter to the Corinthians. In his letter Paul tells the community in Corinth,

> I received from the Lord what I also handed on to
>   you,
>   that the Lord Jesus, on the night he was handed
>   over,
>   took bread, and, after he had given thanks,
>   broke it and said, "This is my body that is for you."

Likewise, says Paul, after the meal Jesus took a cup and said,

> "This cup is the new covenant in my blood.
>   Do this, as often as you drink it, in remembrance of
>   me."

Paul concludes that every time the followers of Jesus eat the bread and drink from the cup, they "proclaim the death of the Lord until he comes."

Scholars disagree about whether or not Jesus actually said the words that Paul attributes to him. Indeed, they disagree about whether or not anything like a "Last Supper" happened at all. John Dominic Crossan, for example, concedes that Jesus and his followers would certainly have shared a meal that, in retrospect, turned out to have been their last. He argues, however, that the accounts of that meal as they are found in Paul's letter and in the Gospels of Mark, Matthew, and Luke do not derive from the historical Jesus.[56] He bases this claim in part on an analysis of an early Christian document known as the *Didache*. The *Didache*, says Crossan, contains two separate accounts of liturgies of the eucharist. The first account "indicates a eucharistic meal with no ritualization of bread and wine/cup, let alone anything else." The second, later account (which Crossan dates to the late first century) does have a ritualization of the cup and the bread, but there is still "absolutely no hint of Passover meal, Last Supper, or passion symbolism built into its origins or development." Crossan concludes that since these elements were not included in the *Didache*'s description of the eucharistic meal, they do not go back to "solemn, formal, and final institution by Jesus himself."[57] They are, in other words, an interpretation placed on Jesus's actions by the early church.

John Meier disagrees. His primary argument is that accounts of the Last Supper are found in several different sources and that they therefore enjoy the backing of multiple attestation. As do most experts, Meier believes that the authors of Matthew and Luke relied in part on the Gospel of Mark, and so their texts do not count as separate sources of information about the Last Supper. Nonetheless, Meier contends that the accounts of Paul, Mark, and John are good evidence that the memory of a Last Supper had a basis in fact. While John's gospel does not include an account of Jesus breaking bread and passing around a cup of wine, it does include Jesus's "bread of life" discourse, in which Meier sees hints of a eucharistic celebration.[58]

The question of the historical accuracy of the Last Supper cannot, of course, be settled here. But I raise the issue for two reasons. The first is to present the possibility that what Catholics have come to think of as Jesus's institution of the eucharist may have its origins rather in the life of the early church. If Crossan is correct, then some early Christians had no memory of a special injunction to eat the bread/body and to drink the wine/blood of Jesus. In addition, the eucharistic celebration of those early Christians made no mention at all of Jesus's death. The eucharist was simply what the word implies: a thanksgiving. The emphasis was not on death, but rather on gratitude for life. The *Didache* instructs, "At the Eucharist, offer the eucharistic prayer in this way. Begin with the chalice: 'We give thanks to thee, our Father, for the holy Vine of thy servant David, which thou hast made known to us through thy servant Jesus' . . . Then over the particles of bread: 'We give thanks to thee, our Father, for the life and knowledge thou hast made known to us through thy servant Jesus.'"[59] The prayer focuses not on the Passion but on the life of and knowledge passed on by Jesus.

The second reason I have included the issue here is to emphasize that even if one accepts Meier's argument that at his last meal with his friends, Jesus did perform a ritual in which he equated bread with his body, that ritual has undergone innumerable interpretations and reinterpretations ever since. Even Meier cautions that "we must appreciate that Last Supper and eucharist are not the same thing, pure and simple."[60] The Last Supper, he points out, took place in the presence of the earthly Jesus. The eucharist, by contrast, remembers the earthly Jesus but also celebrates the risen Jesus and looks forward to Jesus's second coming. It is by definition a later reflection on the events of the Last Supper.

Meier shows how difficult it is to peel back layers of tradition to arrive at what Jesus really said and did. He contends, for example, that Paul's use of the phrase "new covenant" may not go back to Jesus himself, but may rather reflect a later stage of Christian belief and practice.[61] Likewise, Paul's inclusion of the injunction, "Do this, as often as you drink it, in remembrance of me," was most likely not uttered by Jesus, but rather was added by early Christians.[62] Meier also notes that in the accounts of both Paul and Luke, Jesus's actions with the bread and with the cup are separated by the meal itself, while Mark, on the other hand, places the two actions side by side. Mark also explicitly connects the wine with Jesus's blood "which is poured out for many" (14:24). Both of these Markan features, Meier feels, were later developments not present in the earliest memories of the Last Supper.[63]

In sum, then, even if we can assert with some degree of certainty that Jesus celebrated a last meal with his friends that was in some way special or distinctive (a claim that, again, Crossan disputes), there is very little that we can say about that meal with any historical confidence. Meier offers a version of what he believes to have been the first eucharist narrative: "he [i.e., Jesus] took bread, and giving thanks [or: pronouncing a blessing], broke [it] and said: "This is my body." Likewise also the cup, after supper, saying: "This cup is the covenant in my blood.""[64] Everything else (and even this much, if Crossan is correct) comes from later strata of tradition.

The significance of this is that there is room within Catholic tradition for a theology of the eucharist that does not see the Last Supper as having initiated a new covenant that superseded the covenant with Israel. There is room for a theology that does not equate the spilling of Jesus's blood with the salvation of the world. There is certainly room for interpretations of Jesus's death that do not invoke the slaughter of the Passover lambs or the binding of Isaac.

Placed as it is after the reading from Exodus and after a translation of Psalm 116 that portrays the death of God's faithful ones as precious, the reading from Paul's letter to the Corinthians furthers a theology in which the shedding of Jesus's blood appears as both initiated and approved of by God. Paul, after all, urges the Christians in Corinth not simply to remember the death of Jesus as one might remember the tragic loss of a holy man, but indeed to *proclaim* it. The prayer over the offerings confirms the connection between blood and salvation: "Lord, make us worthy to celebrate these mysteries. Each time we offer this memorial sacrifice, the work of our redemption is accomplished."[65]

Following Elie Wiesel, what I have tried to show thus far is that the connection between death and salvation finds only limited resonance within Jewish tradition. Judaism, though it certainly has a history of valorizing its martyrs, has nonetheless for the most part seen the deaths of those martyrs as tragedies to be mourned. Catholicism, on the other hand, has exulted in the crucifixion of Jesus and in the deaths of Christian martyrs. The Holy Thursday liturgy uses texts written by Jewish authors (the Passover story from Exodus, Psalm 116, and Paul's letter to the Christians at Corinth) to present the shedding of Jesus's blood as a cause for joy. During the course of the Mass, the presider prays, "In union with the whole Church we celebrate

that day when Jesus Christ, our Lord, was betrayed for us."
This is a significant and, I believe, unnecessary alteration of the
meanings of the Jewish texts as Jews have read them.

IV. The Washing of the Feet: John 13:1–15, and the Ritual of Footwashing

Unlike the other three canonical gospels, the Gospel of John
contains no account of Jesus breaking bread and drinking wine
with his friends at the Last Supper. Instead, it offers a different
memory. As the portion read at the Mass of the Last Supper
recounts:

So, during supper . . .
>he [Jesus] rose from supper and took off his outer
>garments.
He took a towel and tied it around his waist.
Then he poured water into a basin
>and began to wash the disciples' feet
>and dry them with the towel around his waist . . .
So when he had washed their feet
>and put his garments back on and reclined at table again,
>he said to them, "Do you realize what I have done
>for you? . . .
I have given you a model to follow,
>so that as I have done for you, you should also do."

As might be expected, scholars disagree about whether or not
this account has any basis in history. The Jesus Seminar, a group
dedicated to the search for what it calls "the authentic Jesus,"
writes regarding John's story of the footwashing, "The narrative
setting is the product of the evangelist's imagination, and the
content of Jesus' instruction reflects the evangelist's theology, not
the vision of Jesus."[66] On the other hand, Raymond Brown offers
tentative support for the opposite conclusion. He notes that there
were two different interpretations of footwashing in the
Johannine church, and thus, "the tradition of the footwashing
must have been old." Perhaps, he implies, it was old enough to
have originated with Jesus. Furthermore, regarding the likeli-
hood of Jesus having performed such a clearly symbolic gesture,

Brown writes, "While such a prophetic action may seem implausible to modern eyes, one could point to much more bizarre actions by Jeremiah and Ezekiel predicting the fall of Jerusalem."[67]

Regardless of whether or not Jesus actually washed his disciples' feet, the story as told by John has given rise to numerous interpretations. The description of Jesus's gesture has been read as an example of humility, as a symbol of the eucharist, as a symbol of baptism, as an argument against baptism, as a sacrament in addition to eucharist and baptism, as a sign of forgiveness and cleansing, and as a sign of the salvation wrought by Jesus's death.[68] The text narrating the scene is complicated and fertile, and it continues to generate new speculation and insight.

If the meaning of the text is unclear, however, the meaning of the ritual that follows is less ambiguous. At the Mass of the Lord's Supper, it is customary for the presider physically to wash the feet of one or more of the faithful. The directions for this ritual are minimal. After those who have been chosen have been led to chairs prepared for them, "the priest (removing his chasuble if necessary) goes to each man. With the help of the ministers, he pours water over each one's feet and dries them."[69] In the United States, not just men but women also can participate in this ritual.[70]

The meaning of the ceremony is spelled out by the antiphons that are suggested by the *Sacramentary*. One verse quotes Jesus as saying, "If there is this love among you, all will know that you are my disciples." Another emphasizes the *mandatum* of Holy Thursday: "I give you a new commandment: love one another as I have loved you, says the Lord." Still another borrows a text from Paul's letter to the Corinthians: "Faith, hope, and love, let these endure among you; and the greatest of these is love."[71] The ritual is clearly interpreted as a symbol of Jesus's devotion for his followers and, therefore, the love that the followers ought to have for one another. Significantly, "love" here is identified by an action. If there is *this* love among you, Jesus says, that is, if you *serve* each other, then people will identify you as my followers.

Just as significantly, however, John's account of the footwashing emphasizes service only within the Christian community. As John Christopher Thomas has noted, "There is nothing in this to suggest that footwashing be extended beyond the limits of the disciples (i.e. the believers)."[72] And yet, perhaps this moment of the Mass of the Lord's Supper would be the perfect time to remind Catholics that their *mandatum* extends also to the poor, to the brokenhearted, to captives, and to prisoners, and indeed to all who mourn, as Isaiah proclaimed and as Jesus echoed. Perhaps Holy Thursday would be the perfect time to recall the not-so-distant past when Catholics were faced with the choice of whether to serve or whether to turn away from their Jewish brothers and sisters. Many served. Many, many, turned away.

V. Conclusion

Earlier, I said that Catholicism cannot use Passover imagery without taking into account how that imagery has changed since the Holocaust. But of course it can. It can dismiss such associations as irrelevant to the true meaning of the holiday, or it can brush them aside as relevant only to Jews. However, the basic assumption of this book is that the Holocaust is, as Wiesel claims, a Christian problem. Christians are faced with the question of how millions of Jews could be slaughtered in the heart of Christian Europe by people who had virtually all been raised as Christians. Many of those people continued to think of themselves as good Christians even during the Holocaust, and some went so far as to see what they were doing as their good Christian duty.[73]

Given these facts, it seems that the least that Catholic tradition can do is to examine itself to see how it may have contributed to the massacre, and a good place to start is with the way the tradition has appropriated and reinterpreted the central scriptures and festivals of Judaism. In the Passover Seder, Jews remind themselves that their liberation came at the expense of their cruel masters' suffering. They spill a few drops of wine in the memory of those masters. How much more should Catholicism remember not the time of its oppression, but the time when many of its members oppressed Jews to the point of death. A few drops of reflection do not seem too much to ask.

During the Mass of the Lord's Supper, the priest consecrates enough bread for the following days' liturgies. At the end of the service, accompanied by candles and incense, he then carries the Blessed Sacrament away from the altar and places it in a "place of reposition prepared in a chapel suitably decorated for the occasion." The altar is then stripped, and decorations, including crosses, are removed from the church or covered with cloths to hide them from sight. The focus for the next two days will be the suffering and death of Jesus. How that death might be interpreted after the Holocaust will be the subject of the next chapter.

CHAPTER 6

Good Friday

In November of 1942, a Polish teacher from Lukow recorded the following incident in his diary:

> On 5 November, I passed through the village of Siedliska. I went into the cooperative store. The peasants were buying scythes. The woman shopkeeper said, "They'll be useful for you in the round-up today." I asked, "What round-up?" "Of the Jews." I asked, "How much are they paying for every Jew caught?" An embarrassed silence fell. So I went on, "They paid thirty pieces of silver for Christ, so you should also ask for the same amount." Nobody answered. What the answer was I heard a little later. Going through the forest, I heard volleys of machine-gun fire. It was the round-up of the Jews hiding there.[1]

The teacher's reference to thirty pieces of silver evokes the story in the New Testament of how one of the disciples conspired to bring about the death of Jesus: "Then one of the twelve, who was called Judas Iscariot, went to the chief priests and said, 'What will you give me if I betray him to you?' They paid him thirty pieces of silver. And from that moment he began to look for an opportunity to betray him" (Matt. 26:14–16).

That Judas was paid thirty pieces of silver is mentioned only in Matthew. Neither Mark nor Luke mentions the amount the betrayer was given; both state only that the priests gave Judas a sum of money. John's gospel does not include a monetary exchange at all; likewise, the Acts of the Apostles, though it references Judas's betrayal, says only that Judas "acquired a field with the reward of his wickedness" (1:18). And yet the phrase "thirty pieces of silver" lives in the cultural imagination as shorthand for any despicable act of treachery, as does the name Judas itself. In the rock opera *Jesus Christ Superstar*, when Jesus cries "You liar—you Judas!," there is no worse epithet that he could hurl at his betrayer.

This chapter will begin by examining the story of Judas and how it functions in the Christian imagination. One of the reasons why Judas continues to play such a large role in the story of Jesus's death, I will suggest, is that he allows Christians to participate in a twofold dynamic. On the one hand, Christians are able to identify with Judas as they acknowledge their own sinfulness. At the same time, however, by vilifying Judas, they distance themselves from all who reject Jesus the Christ. This double dynamic is complicated by the fact that in the gospels, in literature, and in popular imagination, Judas has repeatedly been associated with Jews. Thus a vilification of Judas has often been at the same time a vilification of Jews.

This dual movement (i.e., identification and differentiation) plays itself out in several of the readings and responses in the Good Friday liturgy. Thus the remainder of this chapter examines these texts to identify how they might reinforce Christian supersessionist tendencies and how, alternatively, they might be used to counteract such interpretations.

YOU JUDAS!

Christian tradition says that because of his act of treason, Judas came to a very bad end. Accounts differ, though, regarding what exactly happened to the former friend of Jesus. According to the Acts of the Apostles, Judas fell headlong (or swelled up) in the field he had bought with his blood-money, and he burst open and his bowels gushed out. The field in which he died became known as "Hakeldama," or the Field of Blood (1:18–19). According to the second-century *Fragments of Papias*, on the other hand, Judas choked to death, but only after having become a grotesquerie:

> His body bloated to such an extent that, even where a wagon passes with ease, he was not able to pass; no, not even his bloated head by itself could do so . . . His private

part was larger and presented a more loathsome sight than has ever been witnessed; and through it there oozed from every part of the body a stream of pus and worms to his shame, even as he relieved nature.[2]

According to the Gospel of Matthew, Judas regretted his action and attempted to return the thirty pieces of silver to the chief priests and the elders, saying, "I have sinned by betraying inno-cent blood" (27:4). The leaders rebuffed his gesture, though, and so Judas threw the money into the Temple and went off to hang himself. The priests, not wanting to have blood money con-tributed to the Temple treasury, used the silver to purchase a field for the burial of foreigners. Matthew explains, "Then was ful-filled what had been spoken through the prophet Jeremiah, 'And they took the thirty pieces of silver, the price of the one on whom a price had been set, on whom some of the people of Israel had set a price, and they gave them for the potter's field, as the Lord commanded me'" (Matt. 27:9–10). (What Matthew seems to have in mind here is actually a mixture of elements from Zechariah 11:13 and Jeremiah 19:1–13.)[3]

Regardless of when, how, or even if Judas might have died, his story did not die with him. I say "if" because some writers speculate that the Judas of the biblical story is a fabrication. For example, Hyam Maccoby, in *Judas Iscariot and the Myth of Jewish Evil*, argues that "Judas Iscariot the Betrayer of Jesus never existed. He was a fictional character used to displace a real person of the same name who was not only loyal to Jesus, but was an honoured member of the Jerusalem Church and the pos-sible author of a canonical work revered by Christians to this day [the Epistle of Jude]."[4] According to Maccoby, through processes both conscious and unconscious, Judas came to be associated with Jews and was transformed in memory from a disciple into a betrayer.

If that is so, it is not the only transformation Judas under-went. By the Middle Ages, he had become a protagonist in his own right, and his narrative was embroidered with tales of his childhood and episodes from his married life. For example, in the thirteenth-century *Golden Legend*, Jacobus de Voragine recounted a tale which he said derived from "a certain admit-tedly apocryphal history."[5] According to the tale, Judas was born to parents by the names of Ruben and Cyborea. Before her child's birth, Cyborea dreamt that she would bear a son so wicked that he would be responsible for the ruin of "our whole people"— presumably the Jews, since Ruben is said to have been of the tribe of either Dan or Issachar. When Judas was born, his parents were unwilling to kill him outright, and so they put him in a basket and set him out to sea.

By chance, the queen of an island called Scariot found him and raised him as her own son. The child Judas was evil, however, and eventually his adoptive mother informed him of his origins. In a fury, Judas then killed his putative brother, the rightful heir to the throne. He fled to Jerusalem, where he was employed in the court of Pilate. Living next door to Pilate were none other than Ruben and Cyborea, but Judas of course did not recognize them. One day Judas went to pick some apples for Pilate in his neighbors' orchard, and when an argument broke out, Judas killed Ruben. As a reward for his efforts to obtain the fruit, Pilate gave to Judas both Ruben's estate and the widow Cyborea, whom Judas then married. It was only afterwards that the ill-fated man learned that his marriage was incestuous, and in repentance he turned to Jesus for forgiveness. From that day on he became one of Jesus's disciples, but his wicked nature led him finally to betray his Lord and master. The tale is obviously patched together from several other stories, including the biblical account of the birth of Moses and the tragic Greek drama about the life of Oedipus. This does not seem to have detracted from its popularity, however.

It is worth pondering why Judas has come to have such a prominent place in the western imagination. In his book *Judas: Images of the Lost Disciple*, Kim Paffenroth comments on numerous texts featuring Judas, ranging from Dante's *Divine Comedy* to the sermons of St. Vincent Ferrer to the theology of Karl Barth. And yet he points out that it is quite possible to tell the Passion narrative without any reference to Judas at all. Indeed, Paffenroth notes that "Paul, the earliest of the New Testament writers (ca. 50–60 C.E.), never mentions Judas by name. In fact, it is not clear that he even knows that there was a betrayer."[6] Of course, Paffenroth explains, Paul knew that Jesus was "handed over" to death and was crucified, but there is no sense in Paul's letters (see Rom. 4:25 and 8:32, Gal. 2:20, I Cor. 11:23) that this handing over was done by a betrayer. Rather, in Paul's mind, Jesus handed himself over, or he was handed over by God.[7]

And yet if the Good Friday story does not require Judas, it is certainly enriched by him, and this despite the possibility that he may never have actually existed as a historical person. Paffenroth remarks that the Passion without the betrayer "would be a story of much less power and vitality."[8] He does not, however, explain exactly why this is so. What is gained by Judas's presence in the narrative? What function does he perform that makes his role so memorable, so troubling, and, indeed, so haunting? Allow me to propose four answers.

1) First, of course, Judas gives the Passion story a kind of tragic quality because of his status as one of the apostles. As an intimate companion of Jesus, he is privy not only to the public preacher but also to the man himself in his private, unrecorded moments. He knows where the Master goes to pray, and he knows when he will be the most vulnerable. If Jesus had simply been struck down by one of his opponents, his story would have been sad and frustrating and angering, but it would not have had that peculiar poignant quality that comes with betrayal. Think of Samson's folly in sharing the secret of his strength with Delilah. Or Julius Caesar's plaintive "Et tu, Brute?" The victim falls prey to one whom he has trusted, and therefore his plight is all the more painful.

It is also more frightening. If friend can be betrayed by friend, then no one can be trusted and everything becomes uncertain. This is one aspect of tragedy: that the hero is overcome by forces beyond his or her control. But what makes tragedy so tragic is not simply that bad things happen, but that we can imagine the possibility of them *not* having happened. If only Oedipus had not flown into a rage and killed his father. If only Lincoln had stayed home instead of attending the theater that night. If only Jesus had not chosen Judas for his disciple. If only Judas had not betrayed him. What Judas lends to Good Friday is this sense of the inevitable that need not have been.

2) There is another function that Judas plays in the Passion story, one that has more to do with the trajectory of the narrative itself. Virtually the entire gospel story centers on the ministry and teaching of Jesus. Even the activities of "outsiders" such as the Pharisees and the centurions come into the picture only

as they intersect with Jesus. Judas, as both an insider and a soon-to-be outsider, provides a narrative link between the two groups. In all four accounts of the arrest of Jesus, he provides that link physically—he is present at the Last Supper and then accompanies the guards as they close in on the small band of Jesus and his friends.

3) This leads to a third reason why Judas seems so critical to the Passion story. He provides a mechanism by which the Jewish opponents of Jesus assume the foreground in the death of Jesus. Of course, historically, Romans crucified Jesus just as they had crucified thousands of Jews before him. Accounts of the cruel involvement of Romans in Jesus's death would have provoked only a weary sense of déjà vu among Jewish audiences. However, the gospels also convey a sense of outrage that Jewish leaders would have conspired with or at least acquiesced to Roman ruthlessness; more might have been expected of them, the texts seem to suggest. This anger, which originated in a particular historical context, is read by some later Christians as an indictment of all Jews for all time.

Gerard Sloyan attempts to explain, at least in part, why Christians developed and held on to the notion that Jews were responsible for Jesus's execution, despite the fact that as a colonized people, Jews did not crucify. He cites a need that Christians had to justify the separation between themselves and the larger body of Judaism: "Christianity's superiority to Judaism was," as he put it, "a demand of their logic," and accusing Jews of having killed Jesus provided the needed rationale. He writes,

> If the Jews had done extreme wrong by working violence on the one whom God had sent them in fulfillment of all prophecy, several things—including accounting for the sufferings of the Jews at Roman hands—would be achieved. That is what made the crucifixion of Jesus by the Jews a kind of theological necessity. His having been done to death by Roman authority, on the contrary, would have been a commonplace of pagan cruelty. There was no place for it in the scheme of prophecy and fulfillment.[9]

Thus the accusation that Jews had killed Jesus had its roots in theology, rather than in history.

Christians found further confirmation of their accusation, I am suggesting, in the role that Judas plays in the Passion story. Judas exacerbates the responsibility of the Jewish authorities by revealing the secret of Jesus's whereabouts to them rather than to Roman leaders. Judas could not have been expected to have had connections with Pilate or with the Roman guard. Any report of such a conversation would have stretched credibility. The only authorities to whom the Judas of the story could have turned were Jews, and it is Jews whom later Christians held responsible for crucifying Jesus. Judas thus provides corroboration for the charge of deicide that Christians have hurled against Jews for centuries.

The link between Judas and Jews went on to assume a life of its own in the Christian imagination. For example, John Chrysostom made an implicit connection between the two in one of his homilies on the Gospel of Matthew. Stressing the importance of stopping small sins from growing larger, he wrote, "So likewise in the instance of Judas, that great wickedness had its birth. For if it had not seemed to him a little thing to steal the money of the poor, he would not have been led on to this treachery. Unless it had seemed to the Jews a little thing to be taken captive by vainglory, they would not have run on the rock of becoming Christ's murderers."[10]

In another homily, the preacher made the connection between Judas and Jews even more explicit. The context for his remarks was the first chapter of the Acts of the Apostles, in which Peter makes a speech about the need to find a replacement for Judas so that the apostles will once again number twelve. Peter says, "For it is written in the book of Psalms, 'Let his homestead become desolate, and let there be no one to live in it'; and 'Let another take his position of overseer'" (1:20). Reflecting on this speech, John Chrysostom writes,

> God compelled them to call the field in Hebrew "Aceldama" [i.e., Hakeldama]. (Matt. xxvi. 24.) By this also the evils which were to come upon the Jews were declared: and Peter shows the prophecy to have been so far in part fulfilled, which says, "It had been good for that man if he had not been born." We may with propriety apply this same to the Jews likewise; for if he who was guide suffered thus, much

more they . . . [Referring to the desolation of the field of blood:] This desolation was the prelude to that of the Jews, as will appear on looking closely into the facts.[11]

For John Chrysostom, the entire history of the Jews was encapsulated in the history of Judas. Just as Judas had been offered salvation through Jesus, so had the Jews. Just as he had betrayed Jesus, so had the Jews. And just as Judas suffered horrible punishment, so too had they, in the destruction of Jerusalem, and so too would they, in the world to come.

John Chrysostom was not the only one to draw a connection between Judas and the Jews. By the Middle Ages the association had become commonplace. For example, in the sixteenth-century Alsfeld Passion Play, both Judas and Jews were portrayed as part of a devilish plot to bring an end to Jesus. Early in the drama, Satan says to Lucifer,

> O noble lord Lucifer, / I have carried out your wishes. / I have been in the midst of the Jews / and have ensnared them all—/ they have sworn to take Jesus' life! / That should please you well. / I will think on it early and late / how we might bring him unto death. / I will come into his disciple Judas, / the one who was chosen—/ and will quickly bring him to the point / where he shall betray his master / and sell his blood to the Jews![12]

The association is furthered by the fact that Judas is portrayed in a way that fits the stereotype of the business-savvy Jew, though admittedly his greed seems muted next to that of the priests. When he approaches the Jewish authorities to strike a deal regarding the betrayal of Jesus, Judas initially asks for thirty schillings; he settles, however, for thirty pence, boasting, "I will arrange this matter for you; / rather than let him live I would give him to you for one penny!" But if he is less money-hungry than the priests, he is nonetheless as cunning as they. As the High Priest Caiaphas counts out the coins,

> JUDAS says: This penny is bogus!
> CAIAPHAS says: It's good enough to buy meat and bread!
> JUDAS: This one is worthless!

CAIAPHAS: Judas, listen, what a good ring it has!

JUDAS: But this one is torn!

CAIAPHAS: Judas, take another and don't make a fool of yourself!

JUDAS: This one has a hole in it!. . . . This one has false markings! . . . But this one is black! . . . This crack is really long! This one is lead!

Only when Caiaphas asks, "Would you have the best of us today?" does Judas agree to resolve the matter: "Well, gentlemen, now I am satisfied! Now I will do as you wish."[13] He is no innocent dove as he bargains. He knows how to get what he wants, and only after considerable wrangling is he satisfied.

Moreover, Judas shares in the bloodthirstiness of the Jews of the Alsfeld script, promising that he will destroy Jesus: "I will bring about his death! Indeed I will cause him great anguish!" The Jews, for their part, are positively gleeful in their desire for torture, suggesting to the executioners that they drive nails not only through Jesus's hands but also his feet, and that Jesus be crucified in a way that will re-open the wounds he received from his scourging.[14] In short, Judas and Jews are alike in their wickedness. They will also be alike in their fate. After Judas hangs himself on stage, he is physically led to hell by an assembly of devils; the Jews, in similar fashion, are told that unless they put their faith in Jesus, they will be "damned to eternal death." A character named Ecclesia ("Church") promises that "pain and agony will ne'er more be lifted from you!"[15]

4) There is still a fourth reason, though, why Judas seems critical to the Passion story, or more precisely, to the telling of the Passion story. When Christians gather during Holy Week, they essentially re-live the last hours of Jesus's life as they are presented in the gospels. On Palm Sunday they carry fronds and cry "Hosanna!" as they imagine Jesus riding into Jerusalem. On Holy Thursday they watch as a priest, acting *in persona Christi*, echoes the words of Jesus at the Last Supper. And on Good Friday they remember with horror the crucifixion of the one whom they worship.

In fact, it is common practice on Good Friday, especially among Catholics, to participate in a ritual designed precisely to re-create Jesus's last hours. Known as the Way of the Cross, the devotion involves physically traversing a course of fourteen "stations," each one of which commemorates a moment in Jesus's Passion. Some stations are dedicated to events taken from the scriptures: for example, "Jesus Is Condemned to Death," and "Simon Helps Jesus to Carry His Cross." Others stem instead from extra-biblical traditions, such as Jesus falling three times on his way to Golgotha, or the disciple Veronica wiping the sweat and blood from Jesus's face as he strains under the weight of the cross.

It is important to notice that there is a double movement involved in this re-creation of the Passion. First, there is an identification with all those who tormented the savior. In "The Way of the Cross" as presented by Saint Alphonsus Liguori (d. 1787), for example, the faithful pray, "My Jesus, it was not Pilate, no, it was my sins that condemned You to die," and "My beloved Jesus, it is not the weight of the Cross, but my sins, which have made You suffer so much pain."[16] The physical agony that Jesus suffered becomes unimportant next to the contemporary outrages inflicted on him by his own faithful. Indeed, director Mel Gibson echoed this sentiment when he was asked if he believed that Jews caused the death of Jesus. Gibson answered that the crucifixion was caused by the sins of all humanity: "So it's not singling them [the Jews] out and saying, 'They did it.' That's not so. We're all culpable."[17] In *The Passion of the Christ*, the director made this point graphically by having his own hand drive the first nail into Jesus's body.[18]

Alongside this identification with the betrayers of Jesus, however, one finds in the Stations of the Cross a movement that both opposes and overrides it. For no matter how sinful Christians may be, they may still differentiate themselves from Judas. Judas, after all, squandered his chance to worship Jesus. Christians, on the other hand, acknowledge sinfulness precisely as an act of devotion. Liguori's "Way of the Cross" makes this clear. As worshipers make their way around the various stations, the prayers they offer become more affirmative: "O my dying Jesus, I kiss devoutly the Cross on which You died for love of me." "O mother of sorrow [Mary], for the love of this Son, accept me for your servant, and pray to Him for me." "Oh, my buried Jesus, I kiss the stone that encloses You."[19] In other words, I am sinful, but at least I am here, participating in this Way of the Cross as a public act of worship.

It is this dynamic of identification/distinction that I would like to suggest accounts for much of the importance of the Judas character in the Passion narrative. Judas allows the faithful to participate vicariously in the betrayal of Jesus and simultaneously to affirm their conviction not to do what he did. They are like him but better than he was. They are, after all, Christians, and not Judas. Given the historical associations outlined earlier, one might say: they are, after all, Christians, and not Jews.

Let us see how this dynamic plays itself out in the Good Friday liturgy.

GOOD FRIDAY:
THE CELEBRATION OF THE LORD'S PASSION

The instructions for the Good Friday liturgy begin by noting, "According to the Church's ancient tradition, the sacraments are not celebrated today or tomorrow."[20] In other words, the sacrifice of the Mass is not conducted on this day. Instead, Catholics gather for the Liturgy of the Word (readings from scripture), the veneration of the cross, and reception of holy communion from the store of consecrated bread that had been set aside the evening before at the Mass of the Lord's Supper. The *Sacramentary* advises, further, that at the Celebration of the Lord's Passion the altar should be completely bare, with all cloths and candles removed. The celebrants are to wear red vestments in remembrance of the blood shed by Jesus.

The liturgy itself begins as the priest reminds the faithful of the connection between Good Friday and Passover, saying in the opening prayer, "Lord, by shedding his blood for us, your Son, Jesus Christ, established the paschal mystery. In your goodness, make us holy and watch over us always."[21] Following this opening prayer, readings from the prophet Isaiah (52:13–53:12), from the Letter to the Hebrews (4:14–16, 5:7–9), and from the Gospel of John (18:1–19:42) are proclaimed.

I. Wounded for Our Sins (Isa. 52:13–53:12)

The first reading is taken from the Book of Isaiah. This scriptural portion, the "Song of the Suffering Servant," is the last of that book's four Servant Songs. It is found in what is often called

Deutero-Isaiah, or the section of Isaiah (chapters 40–55) thought to have been written years later than the earlier chapters. The reading begins:

> See, my servant shall prosper,
>> he shall be raised high and greatly exalted.
>
> Even as many were amazed at him—
>> so marred was his look beyond human semblance
>> and his appearance beyond that of the sons of
>>> man—
>
> so shall he startle many nations,
>> because of him kings shall stand speechless . . .

The text describes the servant as "spurned and avoided by people, / a man of suffering, accustomed to infirmity." It says that "there was in him no stately bearing to make us look at him, / nor appearance that would attract us to him," and that "we held him in no esteem."

The reading then introduces a new theme: that the servant suffered not merely on his own behalf but on behalf of others: "Yet it was our infirmities that he bore, / our sufferings that he endured / . . . But he was pierced for our offenses, crushed for our sins . . ." It concludes

> Therefore I will give him his portion among the great,
>> and he shall divide the spoils with the mighty,
>
> because he surrendered himself to death
>> and was counted among the wicked;
>
> and he shall take away the sins of many,
>> and win pardon for their offenses.[22]

It is difficult for a contemporary Christian to hear those passages and not to think of Jesus. The notion that Jesus was crucified so as to save people from their sins has become so much a part of Christian thinking that any reference to suffering on behalf of others is bound to bring that death to mind. Indeed, the contemporary Christian rock band "Stryper" takes its name from the passage in Isaiah 53:5 that proclaims that "by his stripes we are healed."[23]

And yet, it is not at all clear that this text from Isaiah lies beneath the original Christian proclamation that Jesus's death was salvific. Rudolf Bultmann argued in his *Theology of the New Testament* that one cannot find in Jesus's sayings any indication that Jesus thought of himself as the servant spoken of in Isaiah 53.[24] Likewise, in her influential book entitled *Jesus and the Servant*, Morna D. Hooker concluded that "we have found no indication that [Jesus] directly associated his sufferings—in which his followers also were to share—through which [his] vocation was to be largely achieved, with that prophet's concept of vicarious suffering."[25] Hooker went on to add that such a conclusion in no way diminished the aptness of the later Christian interpretation of Jesus as the Suffering Servant. That is, to say that Jesus did not think of himself in such terms is not to say that it is inappropriate for his followers to do so. In fact, in a later essay, Hooker raised the possibility that the connection between Isaiah's text and Jesus may have emerged as early as in the writings of Paul.[26]

Other scholars disagree, and in both directions. Some contend that Jesus himself thought of his mission in terms of Isaiah's Servant.[27] Gerard Sloyan, on the other hand, contends that neither Paul nor any of the gospel writers used the text as the paradigm for Jesus's expiatory death.[28] He points instead to the Temple practice of animal sacrifice as the basis for Paul's theology of salvation.[29]

In any case, it is undeniable that within a hundred years or so after his death, Jesus was being identified by his followers with the Servant spoken of in Isaiah. The text became a focal point for Christian claims about the messiah. (See, for example, Justin Martyr's "Dialogue with Trypho.") By contrast, there is hardly any attention paid to the Suffering Servant in rabbinic sources.[30] Most of those commentators who did write about the passage assumed that the Servant-language referred to a coming messiah. However, as early as the third century, some Jewish thinkers saw the Servant rather as a symbol of the Jewish people as a whole.[31] This interpretation gained prominence in the writings of the eleventh-century Jewish scholar Rabbi Solomon ben Isaac, better known as Rashi. Rashi, who is thought to have written his commentary after learning of the First Crusade in 1096, paid particular attention to Isaiah 52:13: "Indeed [*hīnēh*], my servant shall prosper." He rendered the text in this way: "*Behold* in the latter days *my servant* Jacob, i.e. the righteous who are in him, *will prosper.*"[32] The Servant, in other words, is the righteous people of Israel. Rashi continues:

> Israel suffered in order that by his sufferings atonement might be made for all other nations: the sickness which ought to have fallen upon us was carried by him. *We* indeed *thought* that he had been hated of God: but it was not so; he was wounded for our transgressions, and bruised for our iniquities . . . *All we like sheep have gone astray:* it is now revealed how all the Gentiles have erred . . . The prophet here publishes the glad tidings of Israel's release, representing the Gentiles as announcing it in the latter days when they see him *taken from* the *confinement* in which he had been kept by their hands, and *from* the *judgment* or sentence which he had hitherto borne . . . *He gave* himself over to whatever burial the wicked Gentiles might decree: for the Gentiles used to condemn the Israelites to be murdered and then buried like asses in the bellies of dogs.[33]

In this context, the Suffering Servant of God is the innocent Jew who is persecuted by Gentiles but who will one day be vindicated by God.

There is a profound irony at work here. Christians used the wretched death of Jesus to buttress their claim that Jesus was the messianic Servant spoken of by Isaiah. On the other hand, they used the "wretchedness" of Jews to buttress the claim that Jews were accursed of God, precisely because as Christ-killers they had caused the wretched death of Jesus. Rashi's commentary revives the sense that suffering is a mark of divine favor, but in his eyes that favor has been bestowed on Jews rather than on Gentiles.

Rashi's commentary on Isaiah 52–53 is only one of many interpretations and has been the subject of considerable debate. Many believe that the Servant in the text refers not to a people, but rather to an individual: Moses, one of the Jewish kings, one of the prophets, and Deutero-Isaiah himself have all been proposed.[34] Some scholars, however, have chosen to bracket the "Who?" question in order to consider other aspects of the text. They have set aside the issue of the Servant's identity in order to analyze the language and structure of the entire song. Patricia Tull Willey, for example, has compiled a literary analysis of the relation between the Servant Song and the Book of Lamentations. She considers the similarities between the man [ha-geber] who speaks in Lamentations 3 and the Servant of Isaiah 50–53, and she offers convincing evidence that the former served as one of the models for the latter.[35] She is not the first to have noticed a relation between the two texts. One rabbinic commentator contended that the Song of the Suffering Servant was the preemptive antidote to the bleak vision offered by the acrostic Book of Lamentations (thought to have been written by Jeremiah): "R. Nehemiah said, 'While Jeremiah brought curses following the alphabet in Lamentations, but Isaiah came first with healing verse by verse, down to "Let all their wickedness come before you" (Lam. 1:22).'"[36]

Though he does not concur with Rabbi Nehemiah that Isaiah preceded Lamentations, biblical scholar Tod Linafelt does agree that the Servant Song is an attempt to heal the devastation presented by the other book. He notes that much of Lamentations is simply an account of raw, engulfing pain. The book was written after the destruction of Jerusalem by the Babylonians in the sixth century B.C.E., and the horrors it narrates sound chillingly like descriptions of the Nazi campaign against Jews: "Our heritage has passed to aliens, / Our homes to strangers. / We have become orphans, fatherless; / . . . We get our bread at the peril of our lives, / . . . Our skin glows like an oven, / With the fever of famine. / . . . No respect has been shown to elders. / Young men must carry millstones, / And youths stagger under loads of wood" (5:2–13). Zion, weeping at the atrocities she has witnessed, cries, "On the day of the wrath of the LORD, / None survived or escaped; / Those whom I bore and reared / My foe has consumed" (2:22). Lamentations concludes with a plea for God's mercy, "For truly, / You have rejected us, / Bitterly raged against us. / Take us back, O LORD, to Yourself, / And let us come back; / Renew our days as of old!" (5:22).

Linafelt sees the Servant Song as an attempt to interpret and thus make bearable the anguish recorded in the earlier book. He writes, "Second Isaiah's antiphonal response to Lamentations may be taken as . . . an effort to dam up the torrent of rage (on the part of God), death (on the part of the children), and tears (on the part of Mother Zion) that 'pour out' from the book."[37] And yet, he points out, the language of the Servant cannot overcome the initial experience of loss. He observes, "The figure of Zion from Lamentations has been co-opted to serve a role in the ideology of Second Isaiah; but the figure of Zion has also set the terms for the imagined restoration. Her demand for the survival of her children has contributed as much to the poetry of Second Isaiah as has the ideology behind the exiles' return."[38] In other words, the original experience of devastation cannot be written away. It can be covered over, however, as interpreters attempt to discern the "meaning" of the suffering and thereby soften its effects.

Lamentations itself does this, primarily in its third chapter. As Linafelt notes, Christian commentators tend to disregard the cries of pain in the other chapters in order to focus instead on the speech of the figure who speaks in Lamentations 3. In his speeches, the *geber* offers a glimmer of hope that the destruction he is witness to will end: "For the Lord does not / Reject forever, / But first afflicts, then pardons / In His abundant kindness" (3:31–32). The speech of *ha-geber* fits nicely with the restoration offered by Isaiah 52–53.

The danger, however, is that in the move towards restoration, the original cries of the victims will be lost. Lamentations 3 attempts to redeem the suffering presented in the rest of the book, just as the Song of the Suffering Servant from Isaiah does. It contains that suffering by explaining it and by offering a *telos* in which the pain is only a small part of a larger plan. The anguish is muffled by the anticipation of happier days to come. There is a danger in this, however: that the initial cry of torment will be forgotten. This danger is particularly acute if that first voice is omitted entirely and only the second, reconciling voice is heard, as happens in the Good Friday service. On that day, the devastation of Lamentations is not read at all; instead, worshipers hear the Song of the Suffering Servant, in which the agony of the righteous has already been transformed into redemption.

Thus, the reading from Isaiah as it occurs in the Good Friday liturgy initiates the same dynamic that we identified in our examination of Judas: both identification and distinction. In hearing the laments of the Servant, participants are asked to empathize with the Servant's suffering. At the same time, however, they are assured that the suffering has been overcome and that healing has already taken place. On the other hand, the language of Lamentations, because it speaks of the devastation of entire cities and of an entire people, would present the kind of suffering that continues to plague the world and that appears night after night on our television sets. It evokes images of Iraq, and of Rwanda, and of Sudan, and of Bosnia, and of course of Auschwitz. For the most part it does not interpret that pain[39] but simply presents it, all the while crying for relief. An encounter with Lamentations might stir hearers to action in the present in a way that Isaiah, with its assurances that suffering has been overcome, might not.

II. Hebrews 4:14–16, 5:7–9

The second reading of the Good Friday liturgy comes from the Letter to the Hebrews. The letter draws on imagery taken from the Temple cult: "Since we have a great high priest who has passed through the heavens, Jesus, the Son of God, let us hold fast to our confession." Significantly, however, the portion read during the liturgy does not emphasize the death of Jesus, but rather his submission to the will of God:

> Son though he was, he learned obedience from what
> he suffered;
> and when he was made perfect,
> he became the source of eternal salvation for all
> who obey him.

This emphasis on submission is reinforced by the Gospel acclamation that immediately follows the second reading:

> Christ became obedient to the point of death,
> even death on a cross.
> Because of this, God greatly exalted him
> and bestowed on him the name which is above every
> other name (Phil. 2:8–9).

The choice of this particular portion of the Letter to the Hebrews is intriguing precisely because of what it does not say. Much of

Hebrews compares the death of Jesus to the sacrifice of animals as practiced in Jewish ritual. In portions of the letter not read on Good Friday, Hebrews describes how when the Israelites accepted the Law as it proclaimed by Moses, calves and goats were slaughtered, and the blood of the animals was then sprinkled on the assembly. In much the same way, Hebrews affirms, Jesus with his blood sealed a new relationship with God: "For this reason he is the mediator of a new covenant, so that those who are called may receive the promised eternal inheritance, because a death has occurred that redeems them from the transgressions under the first covenant" (9:15). The offering of Jesus effects atonement: "[H]e has appeared once for all at the end of the age to remove sin by the sacrifice of himself" (9:26).

The Letter to the Hebrews does not think of Jesus's death in itself as atoning. Richard D. Nelson explains that in the letter, "[T]he cross was neither the totality of Jesus's sacrificial work nor even its central focus. Rather, the cross was the first component in a larger sacrificial script. His death made entrance into the heavenly sanctuary possible and provided the blood needed to cleanse, as on the Day of Atonement."[40] Thus in Hebrews, death is not thought of as "payment" for sin. Rather, death is the precondition for the sacrificial offering by which atonement through the offering of blood could take place.

And yet, in the portion of the letter that is read on Good Friday, neither death nor sacrificial blood offering is the focus. The emphasis is rather on the obedience of Jesus, as well as on his solidarity with other human beings:

> For we do not have a high priest
>   who is unable to sympathize with our weaknesses,
>   but one who has similarly been tested in every way,
>   yet without sin.

Thus, as it stands, the reading actually lends itself to an interpretation in which atonement does not depend on crucifixion. The idea is not as strange as it might sound; on the contrary, it can be found in a variety of Christian texts.

For example, in his fourth-century treatise *On the Incarnation*, Athanasius explains that salvation comes primarily from Christ having taken on human form: "For the solidarity of mankind is such that, by virtue of the Word's indwelling in a single human body, the corruption which goes with death has lost its power over all."[41] This is not to say that Athanasius does not make reference to the crucifixion or say that Jesus's death had saving power. On the contrary, it was necessary for Jesus to die, Athanasius explains, because only then could he share fully in the human experience. As the Word of God Incarnate, Jesus's role was to restore God's image in human beings, and this could only be done if Jesus endured death as all humans endure death. Thus, explains Athanasius, "having proved His Godhead by His works, He might offer the sacrifice on behalf of all, surrendering His own temple to death in place of all, to settle man's account with death and free him from the primal transgression."[42]

However, the emphasis here is not on death itself, but rather on Jesus's complete identification with those whom he came to save. In fact, Athanasius has to go to great lengths to explain why Jesus had to die by crucifixion when it would have been much more seemly for him to have expired in private. The answers that he gives have nothing to do with suffering or blood; rather, they stem from very practical concerns. First, Jesus had to die publicly in order for the resurrection to be believed. After all, if Jesus showed up proclaiming that he had risen from the dead, but no one had seen him die, then he would have been dismissed as a "teller of tales." Second, if Jesus had died of a natural illness, it would have seemed that he was weak and simply like all other mortal men. Third, it was necessary for Jesus to be crucified in order to show that he could overcome any kind of death, no matter how painful or humiliating. Finally, it was fitting that Jesus died on a cross, "for it is only on the cross that a man dies with arms outstretched . . . that He might draw His ancient people with the one and the Gentiles with the other, and join both together in Himself."[43]

Athanasius's approach to the death of Jesus is very much in keeping with that of the Good Friday reading from Hebrews. Again, that reading proclaims that Jesus is able to sympathize with our weaknesses because, like us, he has also been tested. Because Jesus was human, like us, we can approach him for understanding and help, says the text; further, Jesus offers a model to emulate and obey, as he himself obeyed God. Salvation comes not through death per se but through faithfulness to God's demands.

This is a model of atonement that involves, as Dietrich Bonhoeffer would say, "costly grace." Bonhoeffer, a Lutheran theologian who was executed by the Nazis in 1945, contrasted the true gospel message with its ersatz version. With "cheap" grace, he said, we are free not to change anything about our selves or our lives. Satisfied that grace will accomplish whatever is necessary, we can be complacent about the world and our role in it. Costly grace, on the other hand, demands discipleship: "Such grace is *costly* because it calls us to follow, and it is *grace* because it calls us to follow *Jesus Christ*. It is costly because it costs a man his life, and it is grace because it gives a man the only true life."[44] The Letter to the Hebrews provides a message about costly grace: that Jesus is the source of salvation only for those who obey his call to feed the hungry and clothe the naked and to welcome the orphan and the stranger.

III. John 18:1–19:42 and the Reproaches

The Gospel reading for Good Friday tells the story of the Passion as recounted by John. As we have seen, this account is particularly troubling because it appears to indict an entire people for the crucifixion. When Pilate shows reluctance to execute Jesus, he is urged on by a group described by Mark as a crowd that has been stirred up by the priests, by Matthew as a crowd that has been stirred up by the priests and the elders, and by Luke as "the chief priests and the rulers and the people" (23:13). In John 19:14, those urging that Jesus be killed are simply "the Jews." Though, as we saw in Chapter Three, that term should be understood as referring to "Jewish authorities" rather than to Jews as a whole, to most listeners this distinction would not be apparent.

The Gospel reading ends with the burial of Jesus:

> Now in the place where he had been crucified there
>   was a garden,
>   and in the garden a new tomb, in which no one
>   had yet been buried.
> So they laid Jesus there because of the Jewish
>   preparation day;
>   for the tomb was close by.

However, that this is not the end of the story has already been made clear from the verse that is recited immediately before the Gospel reading, from Philippians 2:8–9. That verse affirmed that though Jesus had died, God had exalted him and had given him a name of highest honor.

Following the Gospel reading and an optional homily, the General Intercessions are offered. This is the portion of the Good Friday liturgy that in the past was notorious for its urging that God lift the veil of unbelief from the hearts of the "perfidious Jews." The Roman Missal from 1928, for example, includes the following: "Almighty and everlasting God, who drivest from thy mercy not even the perfidious Jews, hear the prayers which we offer for the blindness of that people; that, acknowledging the light of thy truth, which is Christ, they may be delivered from their darkness."[45] The current liturgy prays simply "for the Jewish people, the first to hear the word of God, that they may continue to grow in the love of his name and in faithfulness to his covenant." Though it adds, "Listen to your Church as we pray that the people you first made your own may arrive at the fullness of redemption,"[46] as we saw in Chapter One, redemption is not to be equated with conversion.

After the intercessory portion of the liturgy comes a ritual that to outsiders may seem puzzling. Norms for the liturgy stipulate that during that day's worship service, a cross be displayed and that the priest and congregation "make a simple genuflection or perform some other appropriate sign of reverence according to local custom, for example, kissing the cross."[47] Older manuals suggested that the faithful remove their shoes and then "creep" to the cross by prostrating themselves before it in procession, and that they then kiss the feet of the crucified Jesus.[48] During the reverencing of the cross, a chant known as the "Reproaches" may be sung. In the Reproaches, God asks,

> My people, what have I done to you?
> How have I offended you? Answer me!
>
> I led from slavery to freedom
> and drowned your captors in the sea,
> but you handed me over to your high priests . . .

I opened the sea before you,
but you opened my side with a spear . . .

I led you on your way in a pillar of cloud,
but you led me to Pilate's court . . .

I gave you a royal scepter, but you gave me a crown
    of thorns . . .

I raised you to the height of majesty,
but you have raised me high on a cross.

My people, what have I done to you?
How have I offended you? Answer me![49]

Of course, according to the Gospel of John read earlier in the service, it was Roman soldiers (and not the Jews, whom God had freed from slavery) who crucified Jesus. Moreover, it was a Roman soldier (and not the Jews, whom God had led through the desert) who pierced his side with a lance.

Why then have these Reproaches (for that is the title of the chant) been included in the Catholic liturgy? Two possibilities come to mind. On the one hand, they allow Christians to identify themselves with the Jews whom God brought out of Egypt and into the Promised Land. Christians, even as they accept blame for sins of the past, are thus affirmed as the rightful children of Abraham and the proper heirs of God's covenant. The chant reinforces, in other words, what Franklin Littell has called the myth of Christian supersession, or the idea that God is finished with the Jews and that Christians are now the site of God's activity.[50] It should be noted that Littell holds Christian supersessionism responsible at least in part for the horrors of the Holocaust.

The other effect of the Reproaches is to allow Christians to accuse themselves of sin, but in a derivative way. Christians are asked to recognize the sinfulness in themselves by looking at the sins of people whom God clearly (at least according to the chant) finds odious: something along the lines of, "Yes, God, I am as bad as those Jews who killed you were."

It is difficult to see how reciting the Reproaches can do anything but exacerbate tensions between Christians and Jews. For several years, Catholics have had the option of not including this text in the service, and one liturgist has estimated that more than half of them exercise that option.[51] It would seem to be the wisest choice.

Conclusion

The Christian celebration of Good Friday has historically been a source of great suffering for Jews. Accusations of deicide have provided the incentive for Christian contempt of Jews, as well as Christian violence against them. And yet the day can also be understood precisely as an exhortation for such violence to cease. If the cries of Mother Zion can still be heard beneath the assurances of the Suffering Servant, and if the call to obedience in Hebrews can remind us that grace is a pearl of great price, then celebrating the death of Jesus can be a source of repentance and transformation.

As a final note, and for a contemporary example of how sacrifice might be understood, we can turn to the rituals that followed the death of Emmett Till, an African-American boy from Chicago who was murdered in 1955. Till was fourteen years old when he was killed in Mississippi after he allegedly whistled at a white woman. His mother, a young widow when Emmett was killed, refused to allow her son to be hidden away in a closed coffin. Instead, Mamie Till Bradley insisted that the boy's body be brought back to Chicago and placed in an open coffin for all to see. Emmett's ear and all but two of his teeth were missing, and one of his eyes was detached. His face and body were so swollen that they were unrecognizable; his mother could identify him only by the ring he was wearing. And yet thousands of mourners came to pay their respects to the boy and to his mother, who, before her own death in 2003, stated, "I have not spent one minute hating."[52]

The mourners who came to view Emmett Till came with a sense of outrage at injustice, and Till's funeral became a galvanizing force in the civil rights movement. Emmett's mother once commented, "When people saw what had happened to my son, men stood up who had never stood up before. People became vocal who had never vocalized before . . . Emmett's death was the opening of the Civil Rights movement. He was the sacrificial lamb of the movement."[53] He was a sacrificial lamb. Not a payment. Not a payback. Just a boy whose battered body somehow became a sign that moved people to weep and stand and speak for a future that they could just barely imagine. Perhaps venerating the broken and bloody body of Jesus every Good Friday might help bring about that future.

CHAPTER 7

Tenebrae

When Primo Levi arrived at the Auschwitz work camp in 1944, he quickly learned that his fellow prisoners could be divided into two groups whom he called "the saved" and "the drowned." The saved he described as adaptable, savvy, and strong, and able to find ways of avoiding the hardest work or of gaining an extra ounce of bread. The drowned, on the other hand, were the great mass who, "through basic incapacity, or by misfortune, or through some banal incident" found themselves overcome by the conditions of the camp. Of these latter, Levi wrote,

> Their life is short, but their number is endless; they, the *Muselmänner*, the drowned, form the backbone of the camp, an anonymous mass, continually renewed and always identical, of non-men who march and labour in silence, the divine spark dead within them, already too empty to really suffer. One hesitates to call them living: one hesitates to call their death death, in the face of which they have no fear, as they are too tired to understand.[1]

No one seems to know the origin of this term—the *Muselmänner* —used in the camps for the anonymous masses whom Levi described. Levi himself says only that the word "was used by the old ones of the camp to describe the weak, the inept, those doomed to selection."[2] Some have speculated that the word, which is German for "Muslims," was used because the *Muselmänner* of the camp were thought to resemble Muslims prostrating themselves in prayer.[3] In any case, looking back on his experiences at Auschwitz, Levi wrote of the *Muselmänner*, "They crowd my memory with their faceless presences, and if I could enclose all the evil of our time in one image, I would choose this image which is familiar to me: an emaciated man, with head dropped and shoulders curved, on whose face and in whose eyes not a trace of a thought is to be seen."[4]

If the *Muselmänner* of the Holocaust represent all the evil of our time, they also represent a horrifying potential within each one of us: namely, the ability for human nature to dissolve into something less than human, and indeed something not recognizable as ever having *been* human. It is commonplace for us to speak of "human nature" as if we know what it is, and as if we know precisely what distinguishes us from other life forms. And yet we are also aware that at the edges of human nature lie ambiguities often too disturbing to contemplate.

In both Jewish and Christian traditions, our having been made in the image and likeness of God is believed to be the essence of our humanity. The first creation story of the Book of Genesis says that after God had created the sky, the earth, the waters, and the stars, then, on the sixth day, God said, "Let us make man ['*adam*] in our image, after our likeness. They shall rule the fish of the sea, the birds of the sky, the cattle, the whole earth, and all the creeping things that creep on earth" (1:26). And then God did make people. God made people "in His image, in the image of God He created him; male and female He created them" (1:27).

What exactly does it mean to have been made in the image and likeness of God? Interpretations vary. For Judaism, the idea that humans were created *b'tzelem Elohim* is foundational both for individual anthropology and for communal morality. In terms of the individual, some rabbinic traditions say that the image of God is nothing other than the human soul.[5] For these interpreters, the soul was fashioned with particular care by God: "The soul of man was created on the first day, for it is the spirit of God moving upon the face of the waters. Thus, instead of being the last, man is really the first work of creation."[6] According to one tradition, God breathed the soul into the first human's nostrils: "[A]s they discern the unclean and reject it, and take in the fragrant, so the pious will shun sin, and will cleave to the words of the Torah."[7]

Other commentators have focused more on humans' ability to reason. The medieval Jewish scholar Rashi (d. 1105), for example, identified the likeness of God with "the power to comprehend and to discern."[8] Likewise, in his *Guide for the Perplexed*, the philosopher Maimonides (d. 1204) argued that because Adam was created in the form and the likeness of God, his intellect was able to distinguish between the true and the false. Thus, when Adam was still in a state of innocence, he was guided solely by reflection and reason. After he had eaten from the forbidden tree, however, he lost part of that intellectual faculty, though he gained the ability to perceive the difference between good and bad.[9]

The claim that the first person was formed in the image and likeness of God also has had social implications. The mystical *Zohar Hadash* used an analogy to explain Genesis 1:26: just as a king builds a city but then installs a prince as governor, says the text, so God made the world and appointed people as God's ministers. "For that reason, *in the image of God created He him*; yea, *God created man in His own image*, to promote the well-being of the world and care for its needs, even as *He* had done hitherto."[10] Being made in the image of God is, in this instance, not a quality inherent in individual humans, so much as it is an expression of the obligations people have toward each other and toward other living creatures.

The ancient rabbis also saw significance in the fact that God initially created only one person, and that all others are descended from that common ancestor. In a discussion of the serious nature of serving as a witness in a capital case, the Talmud's Tractate *Sanhedrin* explains,

> For this reason was man created alone, to teach thee that whosoever destroys a single soul of Israel, Scripture imputes (guilt) to him as though he had destroyed a complete world; and whosoever preserves a single soul of Israel, Scripture ascribes (merit) to him as though he had preserved a complete world. Furthermore, (he was created alone) for the sake of peace among men, that one might not say to his fellow, "My father was greater than thine . . . [T]he supreme King of kings, the Holy One, blessed be He, fashioned every man in the stamp of the first man, and yet not one of them resembles his fellow. Therefore every single person is obliged to say: The world was created for my sake. (Sanhedrin 37a)

There is a twofold significance to the theme of every person having been fashioned after the image of the first person (who was fashioned after the image of God). First, everyone shares a common ancestry, and so all are equal in the eyes of God. Second, each person is as important as the first person. Each person contains the world within himself or herself, and injury to one is injury to all.

The notion that human beings were made in *imago dei* has played as large a role in Christian tradition as it has in Judaism.[11] For example, for Augustine, the image of God could be found in the intellect: "After all, the authority of the apostle as well as plain reason assures us that man was not made to the image of God as regards the shape of his body, but as regards his rational mind."[12] In the thirteenth century, Thomas Aquinas concurred: "The image of God, in its principal signification, namely the intellectual nature, is found both in man and in woman."[13]

Christians, like Jews, have also interpreted Genesis 1:26 as having not just an individual but also a social significance. Though he affirmed that both men and women were made in the *imago Dei* in that both had an intellectual nature, Aquinas also reasoned that women were naturally subject to men because in man "the discretion of reason predominates."[14] Moreover, Aquinas pointed out that in a secondary sense, men were the image of God while women were not, "for man is the beginning and end of woman; as God is the beginning and end of every creature."[15]

Aquinas did argue that the subjection of woman to man should not become a form of slavery but should instead be the natural recognition of superiority and inferiority. Slavery, which involves the forced surrender of a person's freedom, did not exist in the Garden of Eden and is the result of sin, said Aquinas. That sentiment was echoed in the nineteenth century by abolitionists such as Methodist clergyman Charles Elliott, who decried American slavery as an attempt to destroy the image of God in man and thus as an attack on God himself.[16]

The recent *Catechism of the Catholic Church* understands the image of God to be the human soul, or "the *spiritual principle*," or "that which is of greatest value" in us.[17] The *Catechism* emphasizes that because all were created in the image of God, all share an equal dignity.[18] It affirms, citing the Vatican II document *Gaudium et Spes*, that excessive economic disparity in the world "militates against social justice, equity, human dignity, as well as social and international peace."[19] Again, the *imago Dei* is not simply a quality inherent in humans, but is also a mandate that people be treated with respect.

For the *Catechism*, as for most of Christian tradition, human beings can never be understood apart from the Christ, who is understood as the image of God *par excellence*. Thus, "The vocation of humanity is to show forth the image of God and to be transformed into the image of the Father's only Son."[20] The connection between Genesis 1:26 and proclamations about Jesus goes back nearly to the inception of Christianity. For example, in a letter to the followers of Jesus at Corinth, Paul explained why not all were able to discern the importance of Jesus: "In their case the god of this world has blinded the minds of the unbelievers, to keep them from seeing the light of the gospel of the glory of Christ, who is the image of God" (II Cor. 4:4). If they were not blinded, those who encountered Christ would see not just the divine image as it appears in all humans, but that image in perfection. In his Letter to the Philippians, Paul included a hymn that is believed to have been in use among early followers of Jesus: "Let the same mind be in you that was in Christ Jesus, who, though he was in the form of God, did not regard equality with God as something to be exploited, but emptied himself, taking the form of a slave, being born in human likeness" (2:5–7). Here Jesus is contrasted with Adam, who, though made in the image of God, wanted more and so ate from the forbidden tree. Jesus is the new Adam who is obedient to God and so brings salvation for all.

Taking their cues from Paul, as well as from a variety of other early writers, since at least the second century most Christians have professed that Jesus was not only a perfect man, sinless and blameless, but also that he shared in the nature of God in a way that was both unprecedented and never repeated. Jesus, in the words of the fifth-century Council of Chalcedon, which shaped virtually all orthodox thinking about Jesus ever since, was "at once complete in Godhead and complete in manhood, truly God and truly man, consisting also of a reasonable soul and body; of one substance [*homoousios*] with the Father as regards his Godhead, and at the same time of one substance with us as regards his manhood; like us in all respects, apart from sin." Christ's two natures, his humanity and his divinity, said

Chalcedon, were "Without confusion, without change, without division, without separation; the distinction of natures being in no way annulled by the union, but rather the characteristics of each nature being preserved and coming together to form one person and subsistence."[21]

Three things should be noted immediately about the Chalcedonian formulation. First, the Council's decision came about only as the result of a long struggle involving not only theological considerations but a considerable amount of political maneuvering as well. Second, even after the Council, there were groups of Christians who refused to recognize its authority. Some, called Nestorians, agreed that Christ had two natures, but believed these to be separate from one another. They felt that it did not make sense to say that God had died on the cross or that the human Jesus had saved the world. Others, called Monophysite Christians, disliked the notion of there being two natures in Christ, and believed him to have only one unified nature instead.

The third thing to be noted about the Chalcedonian definition is that it leaves open the question of what exactly it means to have a divine nature or a human nature. What is divinity? And what is humanness? And how is it possible for one person to be both at once? These christological questions have been the stuff of theology for centuries, but they become particularly acute as we consider the twentieth century and its Holocaust. What did it mean to be a human at Auschwitz? What did it mean, if anything, to have been made in the image of God? Toward the end of his life, Treblinka *Kommandant* Franz Stangl remembered how he had looked at pits filled with the men, women, and children whom his fellow Nazis had murdered and refused to believe that what he was seeing was human: "It had nothing to do with humanity—it couldn't have; it was a mass—a mass of rotting flesh. [Christian] Wirth said, 'What shall we do with this garbage?' I think unconsciously that started me thinking of them as cargo."[22]

Human beings as cargo. Human beings as garbage. Human beings reduced to shells of themselves with no spark of life or identity to call their own. Is that who we are? Is that what "human nature" is? And, if so, then what are the implications of that fact for the one human whom Christians call the Christ, the messiah, the savior of the world? What was his human nature like, and what would it have been like at Auschwitz? Or, as Jewish philosopher Emil Fackenheim puts the question, "*Could Jesus of Nazareth have been made into a* Muselmann?"[23]

If one is a Christian, one's first instinct might be to cry out "No! Of course Jesus could not have become such an empty shell of a being! Of course he could not have lost the spark that makes people human and that made him divine!"

This is a valuable instinct, and it may in fact be the basis of Easter faith itself—the sheer refusal to accord death the last word. And yet if we return to the question more slowly, gently probing assumptions and examining their implications, we may find answers that satisfy not only the demands of faith but also the demands thrust upon us by the twentieth century. Fackenheim's question places us directly at the intersection of Christian claims about the messiah and the insistent challenges of recent history.

"ONE HESITATES TO CALL THEIR DEATH DEATH"

The earliest Christian kerygma (proclamation) seems to have been something along the lines of "He is risen!" The one who had died, in other words, is alive. As we will see in the following chapter, this claim seems to have emerged separately from both stories about Jesus's post-death appearances to his followers as well as stories about his empty tomb. Easter faith, oddly enough, does not seem to have its roots either in ghostly apparitions or in the disappearance of a corpse.

The resurrection kerygma was just one reaction that developed in the wake of Jesus's death. It did not take very long for alternative theories about Jesus's fate to develop. First, there were those who denied the resurrection and, as part of that denial, asserted that Jesus's body had simply been stolen by his disciples. According to the Gospel of Matthew, soldiers who were guarding Jesus's tomb witnessed an angel descending from heaven and rolling back the stone that sealed the grave. This angel proclaimed that Jesus had been raised, at which point the soldiers, who "shook and became like dead men" because they were so frightened, went to the chief priests to report what they had seen. The priests, in response, bribed the soldiers to lie: "You must say, 'His disciples came by night and stole him away while we were asleep.'" The gospel concludes, "So they took the money and did as they were directed. And this story is still told among the Jews to this day" (28:2–15). Matthew's inclusion of the story shows an awareness of claims running counter to the Easter proclamation about Jesus, and it seeks both to offer an explanation for those claims and to discredit them at the same time.

Other reactions moved in the opposite direction, not by denying that Jesus had been raised, but by asserting that he had never died in the first place. Docetism, for example, was an early Christian position that denied that Jesus had been truly human. Jesus had appeared to be human, the Docetists held, but the appearance had been an illusion. And, they continued, if he had not been truly human, then he had not been subject to the humiliation of mortality.

For example, an early Docetic document called *The Second Treatise of the Great Seth* depicted Jesus as mocking those who thought they were tormenting him in the crucifixion. Jesus says:

> I *visited* a bodily dwelling. I cast out the one who was in it first, and I went in . . . And I am the one who was in it, not resembling him who was in it first. For he was an earthly man, but I, I am from above the heavens . . . They struck me with the reed; it was another, Simon, who bore the cross on his shoulder. It was another upon whom they placed the crown of thorns . . . And I was laughing at their ignorance.[24]

In this scenario, Jesus could not really have suffered because he had no flesh with which to feel pain. He was merely visiting another's body, himself immune to the tortures of the cross.

Perhaps in part to counter such claims, in the fourth century, Christian creeds began to assert that after his death Jesus had "descended to the underworld."[25] This is not to say that the belief was invented at this relatively late date. On the contrary, this theme seems to have emerged earlier in Christian tradition, as a probable reference to it appears in I Peter (ca. 70–90 C.E.):

> For Christ . . . was put to death in the flesh, but made alive in the spirit, in which also he went and made a proclamation to the spirits in prison, who in former times did not obey, when God waited patiently in the days of Noah, dur-

ing the building of the ark, in which a few, that is, eight persons, were saved through water. And baptism, which this prefigured, now saves you . . . (3:18–21)

Belief in Jesus's descent to the underworld is also mentioned in the writings of Ignatius, Polycarp, Irenaeus, Tertullian, and other early Church fathers.[26] It is expressed in particularly vivid fashion in an ancient homily that is also read during the Holy Saturday Liturgy of the Hours. The homily, often (though probably mistakenly[27]) attributed to Epiphanius, depicts Jesus arriving in Hades and freeing Adam and Eve. Jesus assures Adam, "I slept on the cross and a sword pierced my side for you who slept in paradise and brought forth Eve from your side. My side has healed the pain in yours."[28] The homily appears to draw from the apocryphal Gospel of Nicodemus, which was written sometime between the fourth and sixth centuries.[29]

Thus when creedal statements began to include an affirmation that Jesus had traveled to the underworld, they were not offering an innovation, but rather spelling out something that was taken for granted by many Christians.

The import of belief in Jesus's descent into the underworld seems to have been twofold. First, it affirmed that Jesus had indeed truly died on the cross. Patristics scholar J.N.D. Kelly suggests that the descent was simply "the natural corollary of the Lord's death" and that this "probably explains why it was so often passed over in silence in creed-expositions."[30] The second implication of the descent was that no one was excluded from the good news of salvation: that even the dead were included in its sweep.

Regarding this second point, liturgical scholar Martin F. Connell points out that the emphasis on Jesus's outreach to the dead was lost when Christians began to replace the formula "descended to the underworld" with "descended into hell." That is, early creeds claimed that Jesus had descended *ad inferos*, or to the lower world—to the place of the dead. However, fourth-century believers changed the formula to *ad inferna*, or to "hell."[31] This shift in vocabulary moved the focus away from God's presence to the dead and put the emphasis instead on Christ's offer of salvation to sinners. As Connell observes, the result was that "the descent became just another narrative about God's reconciling sinful humanity. Yet God's love for the dead, beyond the limits of time, had no alternative narrative or theological metaphor outside the descent. Without it God's love for the dead is not given voice or expression."[32]

And it is precisely that presence of God to those who have died that might be useful in thinking about Fackenheim's question: Could Jesus have become a *Muselmann*? For surely there is no death more complete than actual death. Primo Levi described the *Muselmann* as an emaciated man on whose face and in whose eyes not a trace of a thought was to be seen. Death itself, actual death, is this image in the extreme. The emaciated man becomes merely bones; eyes and thoughts disperse into dust.

The claim that Jesus the Christ truly descended into death, therefore, entails a claim that there is no human condition outside the concern of God. Even the concentration camp slave, who is seen by his masters as merely "garbage" or "cargo," and in whom, as Levi put it, the divine spark is to all appearances dead, matters to God.

In other words, the phrase "image of God" can have a third implication in addition to the two that we have already identified. We have seen how Genesis 1:26 functions as a claim about the nature of the individual: that each person has a soul or a spiritual nature or a rational intellect. We have also seen how it functions as a moral injunction to treat all people with respect and dignity. A third meaning of the phrase, however, might be added: that even when people seem to have lost their soul or their spirit or their rational intellect, when they are too depleted even to register the outrages and insults that are heaped upon them, when they have become nothing more than lifeless shells, even then, and even in the indignity of death, people are nonetheless the image of God, because this is how God sees them.[33]

This is a faith claim, of course, the sort of statement that can be neither verified nor disproved. It is, as I hope to show in the final chapter, the content of Easter faith. It is faith that no one and no thing is beyond the redemptive power of God.

It is also an answer to Fackenheim's question. The answer is that Yes, Jesus could have become a *Muselmann*, but the good news is that even this could not make him, or any of us, less than the image of God.

TENEBRAE

At the close of the Good Friday liturgy, Catholic churches strip their altars bare. From the end of Good Friday until the Easter Vigil, no Mass may be celebrated, and only the sick may receive the Eucharist. The day before Easter, known as Holy Saturday, marks a solemn time of mourning and lamentation, and its liturgies are likewise stark and somber.

One of these liturgies is Tenebrae, celebrated in the West since the eighth century. Tenebrae (Latin for "darkness") is the collective name for three prayer services associated with the last three days of Holy Week. The term probably came into use because during Tenebrae services, candles on the altar and on a nearby stand are extinguished one by one, so that by the time the last psalm has been sung the congregation is in darkness.

In contemporary Catholic practice, Tenebrae services are not widely celebrated. In a 1988 document entitled "Circular Letter Concerning the Preparation and Celebration of the Easter Feasts," however, the Sacred Congregation for Divine Worship recommended that churches hold communal celebrations of the Office of Readings and Morning Prayer on the two days preceding Easter. The document explicitly compared such services to the Tenebrae services held before the reforms brought about by Vatican II.[34] Such services may take a variety of forms: a traditional service, one adapted to the contemporary Liturgy of the Hours, or a para-liturgy in which the Palm Sunday narrative of the Passion is read along with psalms.[35]

If the traditional rite is observed, a large candelabra should be set up in front of the altar with fifteen candles lit, and another six candles should be lit on the altar. As the nine psalms of Matins and the five psalms of Lauds are sung, the candles in the candelabra should be extinguished one by one, leaving only one candle still burning. As the "Benedictus" (Luke 1:68–79) is sung during Lauds, one altar candle should be extinguished as each of the last six verses of the canticle are recited. Thus just one candle should be left burning at the close of the service.[36] The ceremony may conclude with the *strepitus*, a loud noise that symbolizes the earthquake that, according to the Gospel of Matthew, occurred when Jesus died.[37]

As noted above, the name Tenebrae was probably assigned to these services because the church is left in relative darkness at the end of them. There is another nuance to the term, however, that deserves our attention. Though Tenebrae was originally observed during the late night/early morning hours designated for the monastic prayers known as Matins and Lauds, it gradually came to be celebrated more often as an "anticipated" rite. In other words, it was observed on the evening before the day to which it belonged.[38] Explaining this custom, Pope Benedict XIV in the eighteenth century wrote, "On the three days before Easter, Lauds follow immediately on Matins, which in this occasion terminate with the close of day, in order to signify the setting of the Sun of Justice and the darkness of the Jewish people [*tenebrae Judaici populi*] who knew not our Lord and condemned Him to the gibbet of the cross."[39] The "darkness" of Tenebrae thus refers, at least according to Benedict, not only to the darkness of night and the darkness of death but also to the supposed moral and spiritual darkness of Jews.

It is in this context that we should read Jewish writer Paul Celan's haunting poem called "Tenebrae."[40] Celan was born in 1920, and during the Holocaust he was imprisoned in Nazi labor camps. Though he survived, both of his parents were murdered by the Nazi regime. Celan wrote "Tenebrae" in 1957 shortly after having translated the narration for the Holocaust documentary *Night and Fog*, and he described the poem as one of his favorites.[41]

Near are we, Lord,
near and graspable . . .

Wind-skewed we went there,
went there, to bend
over pit and crater.

Went to the water-trough, Lord.

It was blood, it was
what you shed, Lord.

It shined.

It cast your image into our eyes, Lord.
Eyes and mouth stand so open and void, Lord.
We have drunk, Lord.
The blood and the image that was in the blood, Lord.

Pray, Lord.
We are near.[42]

Celan evokes not only the horrors of the Holocaust, the mass graves and the vacant faces of the dead. He also evokes with bitter irony the role that Christianity played in those horrors. His text recalls the words placed in the mouths of Jews at the trial of Jesus by the Gospel of Matthew: "His blood be on us and on our children!" (27:25). According to Celan's poem, it is the image of Jesus that shimmers in the blood that the victims must drink. It is the image of Jesus that is cast into the victims' eyes. The image of Jesus torments them even as they bend over the pits into which their bullet-ridden bodies will fall.

This explains why the poem twice demands that *Jesus* pray to the *victims:* "Pray, Lord, / pray to us, / we are near." "Pray, Lord. / We are near." In a devastating reversal, the Lord of the Christians is now indebted to the victims of the Christians. In an ironic twist, those who are nearest to Jesus are not his Christian followers but his fellow Jews, who are, as the poem says, "near and graspable. / Grasped already, Lord, / clawed into each other, as if / each of our bodies were / your body, Lord."

In an essay about his translation of Celan's poem, John Felstiner points out that in writing the poem, Celan was inspired in part by an eighteenth-century cantata written for Tenebrae services, which set the words of Lamentations to music.[43] Here there is no softening of the victims' cries as we saw in the Song of the Suffering Servant, the Bible's response to Lamentations. Celan does not conclude his poem by promising better days to come or by explaining that suffering will end in redemption. Here there are only pits dug for bodies so tightly packed together that they are "clawed into each other." Indeed, Felstiner points out that shortly before Celan wrote his poem, a history of the Holocaust was published in which those precise words were used to describe a pile of bodies found in a gas chamber, pressed against the door in a final hope for air.[44]

We find ourselves then at the heart of what philosopher John Caputo has called the "undecidability" of our human situation. Undecidability, as Caputo understands it, characterizes not only texts (though it surely does that), but also our very lives. Texts are undecidable because they must always be interpreted, and interpretations are notoriously unstable. But life too is unsteady, says Caputo. To be alive is to have "a brush with the deep undecidability in things, with the wavering instability in things, with . . . the silence of God that we cannot avoid even as it elicits a choice from us."[45]

That silence, ritualized in the empty dark waiting of Holy Saturday, has terrifying consequences. That silence raises the deeply frightening, deeply troubling possibility that the meaning we think we find in life is simply *one* meaning, one meaning among thousands of other potential meanings. It raises the possibility that in the end there is really no meaning at all. It raises the possibility that, if we are honest with ourselves, we have no way of knowing if the grave is the final word or if there is reason to hope that even there we are of concern to God. We simply do not know.

And yet that is not all that there is to say. The Christian story did not end at a tomb, and our own stories have not ended there yet either. Like it or not, we continue to have the question of "what's next" thrust upon us. We have the task of interpreting graves, of making choices about what they mean and how we will live until we end up in one. As Caputo reminds us, "Undecidability is a condition of choice, not an excuse for staying on the sidelines."[46] If there are only interpretations to hazard and decisions to live with, then our responsibilities become all the more urgent. Which brings us, at last, to Easter.

CHAPTER 8

Easter and Beyond

On Thursday, September 25, 1941, the Jews of Eishyshok, Lithuania, learned that they would be slaughtered before nightfall. A German *Einsatzgruppe* unit, accompanied by Lithuanians, used guns and clubs to drive the men of Eishyshok away from the town and out to the Old Cemetery. There they ordered the Jews to undress and to stand next to large trenches that had originally been dug to keep cattle away from the burial site; now the trenches themselves served as mass graves. Zvi Michalowski stood next to his father and held the older man's hand. Then shots rang out, and Zvi's mortally wounded father fell on top of his son, pushing him into the grave. The teenager lay in the trench for a long time, but as darkness fell, he managed to crawl out from among the bodies and to look for help. At each house he approached, Zvi was told, "Jew, go back to the grave where you belong." Shivering and desperate, he tried one last farmhouse, and, when the woman who answered the door tried to send him away, he told her that he was Jesus Christ and that he had just come down off the cross on an earthly mission. The woman let the young man into the house, and she gave him food and clothed him. Zvi Michalowski survived the war.[1]

Who can guess what was going on in the mind and heart of that peasant woman who took the Jewish boy into her home? Did she truly believe that Zvi was the risen-but-still-bloody Jesus? Or did the boy's words just remind her of her duties as a Christian? Or, perhaps the woman simply found that the longer she looked at the spectre at her door, listening to his voice and seeing his sorrowful state, the more she was moved to pity. What exactly did she see when she looked at the naked, gore-covered boy who had just returned from the grave?

The story of Zvi Michalowski is oddly reminiscent of other tales that haunt Christian history. For nearly two thousand years, stories have been told of unlikely strangers who turn out to be Jesus himself. One of the most famous concerns Saint Martin of Tours, a young man who lived in the fourth century and who was forced to follow in his father's footsteps as a soldier. According to legend, one winter's day, Martin, who had been studying to be a Christian but who had not yet been baptized, passed a beggar at the city gates. Taking pity on the man who was trembling with the cold, Martin took out his sword and cut his own cloak in two, wrapping half of it around the wretched creature's shoulders. That night Jesus appeared to the soldier in a dream, wearing the cloak that Martin had given away; he said to him, "Martin, yet a catechumen, has covered me with this garment." Martin was baptized soon after.[2] Similar stories can be found in the legends of Blessed Alvarez of Cordova, Saint Marcian of Constantinople, Saint Catherine of Siena, and Saint John the Almsgiver.

Perhaps these legends were the impetus for Leo Tolstoy's short tale, "Where Love Is, There God Is Also." According to Tolstoy's story, a shoemaker named Martyn Avdyeich dreamed one night that Jesus would visit him the next day. Hoping that the dream would come true, when he awoke, the shoemaker readied himself to receive the Lord. Instead, his day was filled with visits from only ordinary people. When an old man appeared outside his window, Martyn invited him in for tea; when a shivering woman and her baby stopped outside his door, he gave them soup and bread and money; when an apple-seller became angry with a little boy who tried to steal her wares, Martyn pacified her by offering to pay for the apple and by speaking to her of forgiveness. In the evening, Martyn had a vision in which all of the people whom he had helped revealed themselves as Jesus: "And Avdyeich understood that his dream had not deceived him, that the Saviour had really come to him that day, and that he had received Him."[3]

Of course, all of these stories were preceded by similar texts found in the gospels themselves. The Gospel of Matthew, for example, contains a speech made by Jesus shortly before his death, in which he speaks of a time in the future when the Son of Man will come in glory to claim his throne. According to Jesus, all the nations will gather before the king to be judged. To those on his right, the king will say,

> "Come, you that are blessed by my Father, inherit the kingdom prepared for you from the foundation of the world; for I was hungry and you gave me food, I was thirsty and you gave me something to drink, I was a stranger and you welcomed me, I was naked and you gave me clothing, I was sick and you took care of me, I was in prison and you visited me . . . Truly I tell you, just as you did it to one of the least of these who are members of my family, you did it to me." (25:34–35, 40)

In this text, Jesus manifests himself in what Mother Teresa has called "the distressing disguise of the poor."[4]

In the Gospel of Luke one finds a strange account of Jesus's appearance to two of his disciples as the pair make their way to Emmaus, a village just a few miles from Jerusalem. The appearance takes place on the first day of the week following Jesus's crucifixion, and as the disciples are walking along they discuss everything that has happened since that terrible day. They are joined on their journey by Jesus, but, as the gospel says, "their eyes were kept from recognizing him" (24:16). The stranger asks the disciples what they have been discussing, and they reply that they had hoped that their teacher was to be the redeemer of Israel, but that he had been handed over to death instead. Moreover, they continue, some of their fellow followers were now reporting that Jesus's body was missing from its tomb and that angels were proclaiming that Jesus was alive. At this point the stranger remonstrates with the disciples, asking, "Was it not necessary that the Messiah should suffer these things and then enter into his glory?" (24:26). He reaches back through salvation history, back to the time of Moses and the prophets, and he explains to them how everything in the scriptures pertained to him.

According to Luke's gospel, the stranger at this point prepares to leave the pair of disciples at the village, but they plead with him to stay on with them. The stranger agrees, and the three sit down to dinner. The stranger then takes bread, blesses it and breaks it, and he gives it to the disciples. "Then their eyes were opened, and they recognized him; and he vanished from their sight" (24:31). Astonished, the two returned to Jerusalem that very night, and they told the eleven apostles how they had met the Lord on the road.

John's gospel contains an even stranger account. According to his text, early on the first day of the week after the crucifixion, one of Jesus's friends, Mary Magdalene, went to the tomb and saw that the stone seal had been removed. She ran and alerted two of the apostles, and the three of them ran back together, only to find the tomb empty except for Jesus's burial shroud. At that point the two apostles, Peter and the one whom Jesus loved, returned to their homes; Mary Magdalene, however, stayed on, weeping outside the tomb. Two angels in white heard her tears and asked, "Woman, why are you weeping?" (20:13). Mary explained that she was upset because Jesus's body had been taken away and she did not know now where to find him. After saying this, she turned around and saw a man whom she supposed to be a gardener. She said to him, "Sir, if you have carried him away, tell me where you have laid him, and I will take him away" (20:15). Then the man said her name, and she recognized him as her teacher. Jesus then said to her, "Don't cling to me. Since I have not yet ascended to the Father, go to my brothers and tell them I am ascending to my Father and your Father and my God and your God'" (20:17).[5] Then Mary went and told the disciples that she had seen the Lord.

One element stands out immediately about these stories: they take place after the death of Jesus. That point may sound obvious, but we should recognize that there are no stories in the New Testament of Jesus disguising himself during his earthly lifetime, or of him appearing and disappearing in the manner in which he does after the crucifixion. These stories are told rather of the resurrected Lord, of the one who went into the grave but did not stay there.

THE EASTER LITURGY

Which brings us to Easter. The Catholic Easter liturgy begins during the night of Holy Saturday with the service known as the Easter Vigil. Easter has its roots in the silence of Jesus's tomb: in the silence of uncertainty. According to two of the gospels in the New Testament, when Jesus was arrested, his followers fled in fear (Mark 14:50, Matt. 26:56). According to all four, while Jesus was being interrogated, Jesus's stalwart friend Peter denied ever knowing him (Matt. 26:75, Mark 14:72, Luke 22:61–62, John 18:27). According to John, when Joseph of Arimathea asked Pilate for permission to take away the body of Jesus and bury it, he had to do so secretly (19:38). The hours following Jesus's death seem to have been filled with fear and bewilderment.

Thus Easter begins in the darkness of undecidability. Philosopher John Caputo (to whose work I have already made reference and to whose thought I will have occasion to return shortly) writes, "Undecidability is the place in which faith takes place, the night in which faith is conceived, for night is its element."[6] It seems appropriate, then, that the Vigil begins quite literally in the dark; the liturgical guidelines state that at the beginning of the service, "All the lights in the church are put out."[7] As soon as the lights are extinguished, however, a large fire is lit outside the church, and the people gather around it as the priest lights the Easter candle from its flames. The congregation then processes inside, and the lights in the church are turned on.

Next the priest (or a deacon) sings the Easter Proclamation. The prayer includes these verses: "For Christ has ransomed us with his blood, and paid for us the price of Adam's sin to our eternal Father! This is our passover feast, when Christ, the true Lamb, is slain, whose blood consecrates the homes of all believers."[8] Two distinct models of atonement are evident here.

The first model uses the image of hostages who are freed by virtue of the price paid by Jesus: "Christ has ransomed us with his blood." It is an ancient theme, one found as early as Paul's Letter to the Romans: "For there is no distinction, since all have sinned and fall short of the glory of God; they are now justified by his grace as a gift, through the redemption that is in Christ Jesus, whom God put forward as a sacrifice of atonement by his blood, effective through faith" (3:22–25). There has been considerable debate throughout Christian history concerning who, precisely, received the ransom paid by Jesus.

As we saw in Chapter Four, the New Testament's Letter to the Hebrews portrays Jesus's death as a sacrifice offered to God, along the lines of the Temple sacrifices. However, not all Christians agreed that Jesus's offering was made to his Father. In the third-century writings of Origen, for example, Jesus's ransom was paid to Satan instead, because "undoubtedly we were bought from someone whose slaves we were, who also demanded the price he wanted so that he might release from his authority those whom he was holding. Now it was the devil who was holding us, to whom we had been dragged off by our sins. Therefore he demanded the blood of Christ as the price for us."[9] In Origen's understanding, humans had indebted themselves to Satan by their sin. Therefore, the ransom of Jesus's blood had to be paid to the devil in order to win our release.

Why point this out? Because the ransom model of atonement is not as simple as it might seem. The proclamation that Christ has ransomed us with his blood can sound as if a simple transaction has taken place: blood for souls. And yet neither Paul nor Origen seems to have had such a transaction in mind. According to Paul, if we join ourselves to Jesus through faith, then Jesus's offering becomes ours as well. The death of Jesus does not placate a God thirsty for blood, but it is a manifestation of total self-giving on the part of the Son of God and on behalf of those who count themselves his disciples.

Even in Origen's writings, the emphasis is placed not on a transaction sealed with blood, but rather on the salvific nature of the incarnation. Explains Gerard Sloyan, "In all the christological disputes of the third through the fifth century and beyond, the church fathers of East and West assumed that the redemption was already accomplished through the incarnation of the Son of God. The cross and resurrection made it manifest."[10] Salvation comes through God's restoring God's image in humankind, which is demonstrated in God's willingness to endure humanness even unto death, and which is ratified in God's raising up of Jesus the Christ. This incarnational basis for salvation is muted in the Easter Vigil prayer, however, which focuses more on blood as a payment.

The second model of atonement in the prayer is drawn from the Passover story in Exodus: "This is our passover feast, when Christ, the true Lamb, is slain, whose blood consecrates the homes of all believers." As we saw in Chapter Four, this use of the Jewish festival is troubling not least because it lends itself to a Christian supersessionism in which Passover is merely a foreshadowing of the Passion. Here, for example, Jesus is referred to here as the "true" lamb, presumably because he is the fulfillment of a redemption only hinted at in Passover itself. Such references to the Passover story can cause misunderstandings about the continuing vibrance of the Jewish celebration of Passover.

THE LITURGY OF THE WORD

Following the Easter proclamation, nine scriptural portions are read. These texts proclaim the following events and themes in salvation history: the creation of the world (Gen. 1:1–2:2), Abraham's sacrifice (Gen. 22:1–18), the passage through the Red Sea (Exod. 14:15–15:1), the new Jerusalem (Isa. 54:5–14), God's offer of salvation (Isa. 55:1–11), God's fountain of wisdom (Bar. 3:9–15, 32–4:4), a new heart and a new spirit (Ezek. 36:16–17a, 18–28), baptism (Rom. 6:3–11), and the resurrection of Jesus (Matt. 28:1–10, or Mark 16:1–7, or Luke 24:1–12, according to a three-year cycle). Separating the readings are psalms and prayers, including the Alleluia which is proclaimed before the Gospel reading.[11]

Some of these texts we have already explored in some detail, including God's creation of human beings in the image of God, the *Akedah*, and the Passover. A careful examination of the other readings, psalms, and prayers would, unfortunately, require a separate volume. The same can be said for the ritual of baptism that follows the priest's homily. According to the *Sacramentary*, "If there are candidates to be baptized, they are called forward and presented by their godparents. If they are children, the parents and godparents bring them forward in front of the congregation."[12]

Following the rite of baptism, the members of the congregation are asked to stand and to renew their own baptismal promises. Among the first questions the priest asks the congregation are, "Do you reject sin, so as to live in the freedom of God's children?" and "Do you reject the glamor of evil, and refuse to be mastered by sin?"[13] These are not questions of belief, as are the questions that follow (for example, "Do you believe in God, the Father Almighty, creator of heaven and earth?"). The first questions the faithful are asked concern what John Caputo calls "doing the truth" (*facere veritatem*) or, better, "making the truth."[14] Followers of Jesus are asked to put themselves on the line, to commit themselves freely and without reservation to a life in which sin and evil hold no sway. They commit themselves to the unimaginable future that is the Kingdom of God. As Caputo says, "Having faith means testifying (which is what the Greek *martyreo* means) to the love of God, doing something, a deed, making justice flow like water over the land, not getting a proposition right."[15]

In his essay entitled "Holy Hermeneutics versus Devilish Hermeneutics," Caputo cites Catholic theologian Edward Schillebeeckx and his theology of the resurrection of Jesus and Jesus's subsequent conversations with the disciples. Schillebeeckx argues that, strangely enough, Easter faith actually emerged independently of both stories about the empty tomb and accounts of Jesus's post-resurrection appearances.[16] This is counterintuitive. As the gospels tell the Easter story, the empty tomb comes first, then Jesus appears to the disciples, and then Easter faith is born. Schillebeeckx (and others as well) conclude that historically, the order was reversed: first Easter faith, and then stories about an empty tomb and about appearances of the risen Jesus.

What happened to convince the disciples to proclaim, "He is risen!"? For Schillebeeckx, the origin of the Easter kerygma is the conversion experience that the disciples underwent after the disastrous events of Good Friday. On that terrible day, Jesus was executed, and the disciples not only betrayed him but also scattered in fear for their lives. And yet something brought them back together. Contends Schillebeeckx, "The reassembly of the disciples is precisely what has to be explained. Appearance stories and accounts of the empty tomb assume the fact of the reassembled community and its Christological *kerygma*."[17]

In answer to his own question, Schillebeeckx asserts that the Easter experience is, most properly, the renewed offer of grace and forgiveness that the disciples experienced after the death of Jesus: "A dead man does not proffer forgiveness. A present fellowship with Jesus is thus restored."[18] In other words, what the disciples underwent was some sort of experience in which the meaning of their lives was once again found in Jesus, the same Jesus with whom they had worked and eaten, and who now, mysteriously, despite his death, was continuing to reconcile them to himself. That experience was then expressed not only in terms of Jesus having been raised from the dead, but also in such proclamations as "I have seen the Lord!" and "The tomb is empty!"

Significantly, Easter itself seems originally to have been tied up with an expectation of the imminent establishment of the Kingdom of God about which Jesus had preached: "The Easter experience was initially an experience of Jesus as the One about to come; it was assuring men of the imminent Parousia, confirming God's coming rule, the substance of Jesus's preaching."[19] As the years following the death of Jesus progressed, however, Christians had to ask themselves if perhaps Jesus had been mistaken. Perhaps the arrival of the Kingdom of God was not imminent after all. Or, worse, perhaps Jesus had been wrong about the whole thing.

The conclusion that they came to, says Schillebeeckx, was that Jesus was himself the definitive promise of the Kingdom to come. His life was ratified by God when God raised him up from the grave—as we saw before, in the earliest proclamations, Jesus did not rise from the grave but was raised up by God. God, in other words, put God's seal of approval on the life and the person of Jesus the Christ. Thus the resurrection was the foretaste of what Schillebeeckx calls "eschatological humanity," or "God's corrective triumph over the negativity of death and man's history of suffering."[20] Easter faith is not justified by an empty tomb. On the contrary, the empty tomb is another way of expressing the gut-level Easter conviction that life is not merely a tale told by an idiot, full of sound and fury and signifying nothing.

What then does justify the Easter promises made by the faithful as they renew their own baptismal vows? Why reject sin and evil? Why profess belief in God? Why profess belief that Jesus, son of Mary, "rose from the dead, and is now seated at the right hand of the Father"?[21] Is there any good reason to do so? Schillebeeckx asserts that "our faith in the resurrection is itself still a prophecy and a promise for this world—*qua* prophecy unsheltered and unprotected, defenceless and vulnerable. And so the life of the Christian is not visibly 'justified' by the facts of history."[22] But is this really the case? What about that empty tomb? And what about those post-crucifixion appearances? Are they not "protection" for faith in the resurrection?

By itself, an empty tomb is not evidence of anything other than the fact that a body is missing. As we saw, the Gospel of Matthew is aware of one non-faith-filled explanation for the missing Jesus: that his body was simply stolen by the disciples. It is no great trick to empty a grave.

On the other hand, stories about post-resurrection appearances of Jesus can be explained less easily. Are they not evidence that the resurrection really took place? After all, seeing a dead man walking and talking would seem like a solid basis for faith in the resurrection.

And yet the matter is not quite so simple. If Schillebeeckx is correct, then the appearance stories are articulations of a conversion experience already undergone by the disciples. This means that one only "sees" the risen Jesus when one has faith in the risen Jesus. In other words, it is not merely a question of visual, sensory input. It is rather a question of identifying the one whom one sees as precisely Jesus of Nazareth, the risen Christ.

This helps explain those odd stories in the gospels in which disciples of Jesus visually see him but do not recognize him. Mary Magdalene on Easter morning sees one whom she mistakes as a gardener. The disciples on the road to Emmaus see one whom they think to be a stranger. Those visual experiences in themselves are not resurrection appearances. It is only when the stranger is recognized in faith as the Christ that we can speak of an Easter narrative. It is only when we understand that the sorrowful, the wayfarer, the hungry, the thirsty, the prisoner, and the sick are really and truly Jesus that we truly can speak of resurrection.

Easter faith, then, isn't the assurance of things unseen but is rather the unhinged, unjustifiable claim that the panhandler, the homeless on the street corner, and the Jewish boy covered with the slime of the grave are manifestations of Jesus and are honored members of the Kingdom of God. Easter faith says that Jesus appears in the poor, the lame, and the dying, and that if we can't see him there, then we shouldn't expect to see him anywhere else.

What is too often lost in the interpretation of Easter, though, is precisely the sense of risk. Somehow, in the hermeneutics of salvation, Easter becomes the happy ending to a well-worn tale that is enjoyable precisely and only because it all happened far away and long ago, and no one need be too concerned about it anymore. Worse, Easter at times becomes an excuse for inaction. Easter Sunday's proclamation that what the world longs for has already in fact been accomplished can have the effect of muting the ongoing sufferings of men and women.

Alexander Donat makes this point in chilling fashion. Donat, who was rounded up in the last days of the Warsaw Ghetto and was imprisoned in Majdanek, entitled his memoir *The Holocaust Kingdom*—a telling contrast to the Kingdom of God. In early April of 1943, Donat and his wife entrusted their child to Christian friends. They then hid themselves in an attic until fire forced them to surrender to the attacking German soldiers. From his hiding place, the former newspaper publisher watched the devastation taking place around him:

> Then came Easter Sunday. Church bells rang out that bright April morning as the God-fearing Poles of Warsaw, dressed in their finest, crowded into their lovely churches to hear once again the glad tidings—so often repeated, yet always joyfully anticipated—that he who had died on the cross for the love of man was risen from the dead . . . My five-year-old son was among them, perhaps, his tiny treble joining the choral response of the Easter service: *Kyrie Eleison!* He Is Risen!
>
> Mass over, the holiday crowds poured out into the sun-drenched streets. Hearts filled with Christian love, people went to look at the new unprecedented attraction that lay halfway across the city to the north, on the other side of the ghetto wall, where Christ's Jewish brethren suffered a new and terrible Calvary not by crucifixion but by fire. What a unique spectacle! Bemused, the crowds stared at the hanging curtains of flame, listened to the roar of the conflagration, and whispered to one another, "But the Jews—they're being roasted alive!" There was awe and relief that not they, but the others had attracted the fury and the vengeance of the conqueror. There was also satisfaction.[23]

Donat's words are harsh, though with good reason. After the war, his small son, who had survived because he had been placed in a Catholic orphanage, informed his parents, "All Jews are thieves and swindlers. They killed the Lord Jesus and now they kill Christian children to mix their blood in the matzos."[24]

Of course, the boy's beliefs represented only one strand of Catholicism, one that his Jewish mother described as "a medieval distortion of Christianity, a fanatic version of Catholicism impregnated with hatred for his own people."[25] And yet there is within Christianity an undeniable tendency to skip quickly from suffering to resurrection, from apparent defeat to sure triumph. Christ is risen and reigns triumphantly with God. If there is still suffering in this world, then that is unfortunate, but surely it, like the suffering of Jesus, has a purpose and serves the greater will of God.

There is one more festival in the Catholic cycle that we need to consider, a feast so strange that no one quite seems to know what to do with it. It is the Feast of the Ascension, the day in the liturgical year that celebrates the departure of Jesus from the earth to his throne in heaven. It is a feast that, I will suggest, re-situates us in Caputo's undecidability. It reminds us that, as Caputo says, "We are the *ecclesia* [community] of those who come too late for the Origin and too early for the *parousia* [fulfillment, or, lit.: 'presence']."[26]

Jesus, Who Has Been Taken from You

In the New Testament, there are different accounts of Jesus's ascension. The most elaborate is found in the Acts of the Apostles, and says that for forty days after his resurrection, Jesus met with his followers and spoke with them about the Kingdom of God. Then, Jesus "was lifted up, and a cloud took him out of their sight." Suddenly two men dressed in white appeared and said to the apostles, "Men of Galilee, why do you stand looking up toward heaven? This Jesus, who has been taken up from you into heaven, will come in the same way as you saw him go into heaven" (1:9-11).

The idea that Jesus was lifted up many weeks after his resurrection is found only in Acts. The Gospel of Luke, thought to have been written by the same author as Acts, seems to indicate that Jesus's ascension took place on the same day as his resurrection. Early versions of the Gospel of Mark did not include an ascension scene at all, and actually ended with the apostles finding the empty tomb and fleeing in terror and saying nothing, "for they were afraid" (16:8). Later, a new ending was appended to Mark that included a short narrative in which Jesus appeared to the apostles as they were seated at table. He spoke with them, and then he "was taken up into heaven and sat down at the right hand of God" (16:19). Several other texts in the New Testament allude to or presume an ascension, but do not describe it explicitly. Among these are Hebrews 4:14, I Peter 3:22, Romans 10:6–8, Ephesians 4:7–11, and John 20:17.[27]

Over the years, there has been considerable debate about how to interpret Jesus's ascension into heaven. Christianity from its inception has used spatial categories to differentiate the realm of God from the realm of humans, but in recent centuries these categories have been interpreted less and less as actual descriptions of cosmic locations. Ever since Copernicus and Galileo revolutionized our conceptions of the cosmos, it has been difficult to continue to think of heaven as in the sky, and hell as underground. The revolution in thought demanded by relativity theory has made such designations even more complex, as there is no fixed point in the universe by which one might measure "above" or "below."

The advent of space travel has also challenged conceptions of heaven, as one of the cosmonauts is said to have remarked sarcastically that he couldn't see God out of his spaceship window. True, many Christians continue to preach that heaven is, as the Reverend Billy Graham once put it, "as real as Los Angeles, London, Algiers or Boston," a place that is "1,600 miles long, 1,600 miles wide and 1,600 miles high."[28] Moreover, a *Time*/CNN poll taken in 1997 found that sixty-seven percent of Americans who believe in heaven think of it as "something that is 'up there.'"[29]

And yet, increasingly, Christian leaders and theologians interpret heaven as a state of being, rather than a physical location. In 1999, Pope John Paul II set off something of a firestorm when he reflected, "In the context of Revelation, we know that the 'heaven' or 'happiness' in which we will find ourselves is neither an abstraction nor a physical place in the clouds, but a living, personal relationship with the Holy Trinity."[30] An uproar ensued in which some preachers accused the pope of watering down revelation. Still, even the recently published Catholic *Catechism* explains that Jesus's ascension was not a physical journey upwards, but rather the "irreversible entry of his humanity into divine glory, *symbolized* by the cloud and by heaven, where he is seated from that time forward at God's right hand."[31]

Such interpretations of heaven and Jesus's entry into it are able to accommodate a contemporary cosmology in which the universe appears as an expanding complex of matter, energy, and empty space with no divine being in sight. They make claims about the ascension of Jesus palatable to people steeped in a scientific world view. And yet, they leave a number of questions unanswered.

First, they blur the distinction between resurrection and ascension. The *Catechism*, for example, describes the ascension as the irreversible entry of Jesus's humanity into divine glory, but speaks of the resurrection in the same way: "At Jesus' Resurrection his body is filled with the power of the Holy Spirit: he shares the divine life in his glorious state, so that St. Paul can say that Christ is 'the man of heaven.'"[32] If Jesus is already glorified and is already a "man of heaven" at the resurrection, then of what particular significance is the ascension? Why maintain the two as separate dogmas and, indeed, separate feasts in the liturgical calendar? Some theologians state explicitly that there really is no difference between the two. For example, Laurence Hull Stookey explains that "we must affirm above all that the ascension is an integral part of the resurrection, not something distinct from it. The ascension is observed separately for the sake of closer contemplation, not because it provides an independent set of meanings."[33]

In a somewhat different vein, Edward Schillebeeckx contends that the ascension is "distinct from the resurrection according to its redemptive significance,"[34] but it is unclear how precisely this is so. Schillebeeckx notes that in the writings of Luke, the ascension is significant because it marks the last time Jesus is in immediate contact with the apostles: "Thus after the last appearance, a new period of salvation begins, in which the Lord guides the Church not directly, visibly, but in the virtue of His Spirit via the visible organ of the apostolic college."[35] As he points out, however, the situation is somewhat different in the Gospel of John, wherein Jesus appears to the twelve and breathes the Spirit upon them some time after he has already ascended.

Schillebeeckx sees the significance of the ascension as its establishment of Jesus as Lord.[36] It is the basis for Pentecost, in which Jesus sends the Holy Spirit upon the disciples. According to Schillebeeckx, Jesus cannot bestow the Spirit when he is "not with" the Father during his earthly life: "He will only be able to send us the Holy Spirit when His sonship is completely realized in human form, and therefore utterly given over in love to the Father who answers this gift in the resurrection."[37] However, if Jesus's sonship is confirmed by God in the resurrection, it is not at all clear what the ascension adds to this. How is Jesus "more" glorified or exalted in the ascension than in the resurrection? Likewise, Joseph Fitzmyer asserts that Jesus's ascension is "nothing more than *the* appearance from glory in which Christ took his final leave from the community of his followers—his last visible leave-taking from the assembled followers."[38] And yet he also says that there is little difference between the appearances of the risen Jesus to Peter and the ten other apostles, and his appearance later (that is, post-ascension) to Paul (see I Cor. 15:5–6).[39] If Jesus has made his final leave-taking, then it's difficult to see why he appears to Paul in the same way that he had to the apostles.

One can find the conflation of resurrection and ascension even in the popular media. In 1997, thirty-nine members of the Heaven's Gate community in California killed themselves in an effort to enter what they called the "Kingdom Level Above Human." In a statement posted on its Web site some time earlier, the group had explained, "We fully desire, expect, and look forward to boarding a spacecraft from the Next Level very soon (in our physical bodies)." Members believed that the spacecraft they were waiting for was traveling in the wake of the Hale-Bopp comet then visible in the sky. For reasons that remain unclear, on March 26th the group decided not to wait any longer to board the spacecraft with their bodies, and they chose to board it without them instead.[40]

The Heaven's Gate members were far from the first to believe that human destiny lies not in the ground but rather in the sky. The group was unusual not because of their belief in ascension, but because of their willingness to act on it. What is interesting for our purposes is how the *New York Times* editorialized about the event a few days after the suicides were discovered: "Resurrection, the meaninglessness of the flesh, the primacy of the spirit, the conversion from the physical to the heavenly plane are features of several faiths. But the crucial safety brake in most theologies is that the believer himself cannot choose the moment of ascension. Only the central deity can do that."[41] Here resurrection is understood to be the same as ascension, and both are portrayed as the negation of fleshly, earthly existence.

In contrast, I think, the Christian claim about Jesus's resurrection and ascension must take very seriously both the notion that it was his human body (different from, but continuous with, his earthly body) that was resurrected, and also the claim that after the resurrection, that human body disappeared.

A second problem with many contemporary theologies of ascension arises as a consequence of the first. If resurrection and ascension are collapsed together, then the meaning of the parousia, or the second coming of Jesus, is vitiated. Stories of the resurrection, after all, are stories about the ongoing presence of Jesus. Jesus was raised from the dead, and then he appeared to his followers in various guises, and, depending on which account one reads, for varying periods of time. The ascension of Jesus, on the other hand, is about loss. At the ascension, the apostles are left gazing up at the sky, looking for something that they can no longer see. At the same time, however, they are promised (at least in Acts) that what they long for will be fulfilled one day, when the Son of Man comes in glory.

This element of loss is muted if resurrection and ascension are conflated into the one single theme of the glorification/exaltation of Jesus. But it is precisely this sense of loss that, I believe, can provide a starting point for Christians to re-think faith after the Holocaust.

One of the most prominent Catholic theologians of the twentieth century, the German Jesuit Karl Rahner, described the Feast of the Ascension as "the festival of holy pain."[42] On Good Friday, Jesus died, an event of catastrophic proportions for his followers. Then, miraculously, amazingly, just when all hope had been lost, those followers found their lives transformed. Their despair changed to a sense that they had been forgiven. They began to believe that the time that they had spent with Jesus, and all the effort that they had put into living as he had taught, made sense after all. And then, when they least expected it, they began to encounter Jesus in strange and unpredictable places. Scarcely able to contain their joy, they started to proclaim that he had been raised from the dead. They shared in his table fellowship once again, and they took to heart his words.

And then the rug was pulled out from under them. Then the one whom they had loved and followed and sacrificed for left them alone. Reflecting on this, Rahner writes, "He has departed from us. It is frightening that we feel so little pain about this . . . we should be inconsolable at the fact of his remoteness from us."[43]

Having said this, however, Rahner immediately turns his attention to the consolation offered to the community by the Holy Spirit, which was given to the followers of Jesus soon after the ascension. According to the Acts of the Apostles (2:1–47), on the Jewish festival of Pentecost (*Shavuot*), after Jesus had been taken up, the disciples were assembled together. Suddenly a sound like a violent wind came from heaven, accompanied by strange fiery lights that settled on each one of those gathered. Then the disciples were filled with the spirit of God, and they began to speak in other languages. Onlookers scoffed, accusing the group of having drunk too much wine. In defense, Peter then rose and made a speech in which he explained the behavior of his fellows by recalling the words of the prophet Joel. Joel, he said, had promised that God's spirit would flow forth, and that sons and daughters would prophesy and young men would see visions (see Joel 2:28). Because Jesus had been exalted by God and had received from God the promise of the Holy Spirit, he had now poured out that Spirit upon his followers.

For Rahner, this sending of the Holy Spirit on Pentecost is immediate consolation for the loss of Jesus in the ascension, as "the separation implicit in this festival is simply another way of expressing the nearness of the Lord in his Spirit, which has been imparted to us through his death and resurrection."[44] Jesus is not really gone, in other words, but he is near to us in his Spirit. What is the purpose of the ascension, then? Rahner answers, "It is because he wants to give us an opportunity to live *his* life; in order that when he returns he may find in us that which he brings with him to us of himself: a human life which belongs to God."[45] Jesus's life is ongoing in those who live in his Spirit, his Church, his words, and his sacraments.

What I would like to suggest is that post-Auschwitz, it might be more credible to emphasize the absence of Jesus rather than his presence. We live in a world quite different from the one described by Isaiah (61:1–4), the same one evoked by Jesus as he began his ministry (Luke 4:18–19). There are far too many people oppressed and brokenhearted, living as captives, mourning in ruin and devastation. The poor are still with us in great numbers. Many of the lame, whether their limbs have been ravaged by disease or land mines or bullets, cannot walk. Many of the blind cannot see. And millions of children starve to death every year. This does not make the words or the life of Jesus any less meaningful. Indeed, those words and that life become ever more urgent calls. We live, as John Caputo put it, in the time of undecidability, between the beginning and the end, and that very undecidability is a condition of choice, not an excuse for staying on the sidelines.[46]

In one of the very few full-length treatises on the ascension of Jesus published in recent years, Douglas Farrow re-thinks the meaning of Christianity by taking seriously the departure of Jesus. He criticizes theologies such as Rahner's that de-emphasize the loss undergone by the followers of Jesus in the ascension. Writes Farrow, "For Pentecost does not *resolve* the problem of the presence and the absence. It *creates* it, by adding a presence which discloses the absence."[47] For Farrow, and, I am suggesting, for an adequate post-Holocaust theology, it is precisely the absence of Jesus that must be reckoned with. If that absence is forgotten, then we might confuse our own projects with the projects of God, substituting the first for the second. The "still to come" of the parousia holds everything we do against an eschatological horizon, comparing it to the last days when the sheep will be separated from the goats, and when God will ask if we have fed the hungry, visited the sick, and welcomed strangers.

In the first chapter of this book, I invoked the words of the Jewish philosopher Emmanuel Levinas, whose essay "Loving the Torah More Than God" criticized Christianity for what it called its "sentimental communion within the love of a God made flesh." This communion, Levinas felt, led to a complacency that made few demands on its followers. In that same essay, Levinas concluded, "Man's true humanity and his powerful gentleness make their entrance into the world in the severe words of a demanding God; the spiritual does not impart itself in anything of substance; it is an absence. God manifests Himself not by incarnation but by absence."[48] Perhaps, though, we need not choose between incarnation and absence. The Christian liturgical cycle incorporates both: Christmas and then Good Friday, Easter Sunday and then the Feast of the Ascension. This dynamic of presence and loss should make us uneasy. It should remind us constantly that the world as we know it is unstable, and that much hangs in the balance. It should be a call to action, forcing us from the sidelines and into the tormented, waiting, longing, God-starved world.

CHAPTER 9

Conclusion

At the beginning of this book, I explored the issue of the cross at Auschwitz and why it was perceived so differently by Christians and Jews. Many Christians saw the cross as a symbol of God's victory over death. Many Jews saw it as an expression of Christian triumphalism that erased the Jewish significance of the Holocaust. The turmoil that the cross provoked indicates that the *Shoah* is an ongoing source of pain.

What I have tried to show is how contemporary Catholic celebrations of Holy Week both contribute to that pain and offer ways of mitigating it. Liturgies contribute to this pain largely in two ways: first, by perpetuating the myth that Jews killed Jesus, and second, by offering supersessionist interpretations of Judaism, in which Judaism is seen as no longer relevant since it has been replaced and surpassed by Christianity.

On the other hand, the celebration of Holy Week can be a way of atoning for Christian antisemitism and at the same time mitigating its future effects. The Ash Wednesday liturgy, for example, could serve as a powerful caution against humanity's propensity to inflict mass death. Clear and consistent teaching during the Palm Sunday liturgy about the Roman Empire's responsibility for the death of Jesus could eliminate Christian accusations that Jews were or are "Christ-killers." (Eliminating the "Reproaches" from the Good Friday liturgy is already a good start in this direction.) Re-thinking models of Christian ministry could lessen supersessionist tendencies that see the Jewish Temple and its priesthood as null and void in light of Jesus. Education about contemporary Jewish celebrations of Passover could remind Christians that Judaism is not a "fossil" religion whose symbols and rituals can be appropriated without consequence. The recognition that if Jesus had lived in Europe in 1942, he would have been sent to a death camp, could force Christians to confront the Jewishness of Jesus. And understanding that Easter Sunday is followed by the departure of Jesus from the earth, that the Kingdom promised by Jesus has not yet come to fulfillment, and that all of us wait for the time when God's will will be done "on earth as it is in heaven," can remind Christians of the obligation to work toward that Kingdom with all their heart and all their strength.

The liturgies of Holy Week, and of the days that precede it and follow it, are festivals of holy pain. They are celebrations of a vision that has not yet come to fruition. They are reminders of what God requires, even as they mark the failure of all of us to live up to God's demands.

NOTES FOR THE FUTURE

Post-Holocaust Jewish theologian Richard L. Rubenstein has used the psychological theory of "cognitive dissonance" to explain, at least in part, Christians' historical animosity toward Jews. Cognitive dissonance describes the uncomfortable experience of holding at the same time two beliefs that are psychologically inconsistent. For example, Rubenstein describes a child who believes that his mother is loving and caring. When the mother acts abusively, the child must find a way to reconcile irreconcilable pieces of information: mother is loving; mother is cruel. So, the child may deny that the mother has acted harshly, or he may interpret her actions as a punishment justified by the child's own (perhaps real, perhaps imaginary) misbehavior.[1] In either case, the dissonance is reduced, and the child is able to achieve some measure of psychological equilibrium.

Rubenstein theorizes that one of the most significant functions of theology is to bring about precisely such equilibrium in the minds of religious communities.[2] Theologians, for example, construct theodicies to explain how God is good despite the evils in the world. Or, they devise explanations for why the apocalypse has not yet arrived despite predictions that it would. Or, they reassure communities that their revered leader really is the messiah, despite the messiah's apostasy or ignoble death. In each case, believers are asked to hold together two apparently contradictory beliefs of equal psychological import.

Once such a tenuous balance is reached, maintaining it becomes crucial to the psychological well-being of the individual or community. If the solution to the dissonance is challenged by outsiders, either directly or indirectly, some sort of repression must then take place. One can either repress one's own doubts and refuse to acknowledge the force of the other's critique, or one can repress those who dare to call the equilibrium into question. Or, one can do both: repress one's own doubts precisely by repressing those who voice them.

Just this choice is faced by Christians. Rubenstein points to the rival claims made by Christians and Jews about the significance of Jesus, and he asks, "[W]ould not a situation of potential cognitive dissonance arise from the presence within Christian Europe of a rival community of the same background as that of the historical figure whom the Christian churches assert to be humanity's sole hope for eternal salvation, a community that nevertheless flatly rejected Christian claims about the Savior?"[3] In other words, Jews' refusal to believe that Jesus was the messiah could be perceived by Christians as an ongoing and painful challenge to the central claim of their religion. Rubenstein continues,

> Could not the violence of the defamations [against Jews] be seen as related to the degree to which the potentially disconfirming information was perceived as threatening a value or an institution of overwhelming importance? Would this not help to explain the violent anti-Jewish animus of some of Christianity's most saintly personalities?[4]

Cognitive dissonance is a powerful psychological motivation. It is akin to hunger in its ability to motivate, and yet it is unlike hunger in that it is more difficult to assuage.[5] Its dynamic is such that in order for one group to erase self-doubts about its own rightness, it must show that another group is wrong. And the best way to confirm the second group's wrongness is to persecute it for entertaining the very doubts that the first group, in principle, refuses to entertain.

Precisely this dynamic has been observed by some scholars as playing a role in the long tradition of Christian animosity towards Jews. Historian Gavin I. Langmuir, for example, points to the Catholic theology of the eucharist as one place where he sees this dynamic clearly in evidence. When Catholics turned what (in Langmuir's assessment) was a symbolic utterance (i.e., "This is my body") into a claim about the physical reality of the bread and wine, "they confused metaphor with empirical proposition, and introduced a latent conflict between their non-rational and rational thinking about bread and wine."[6] This conflict came to a head in the Middle Ages, when dogmatic teaching made it incumbent upon Catholics to believe in transubstantiation, or the belief that the bread and wine cease to be what they are and become instead the body and blood of Jesus. The claim that what looks like bread and wine is not really bread and wine was a challenge to rational thought. However, doubt about the dogma was not permitted. To reduce cognitive dissonance, concludes Langmuir, Catholics "defended their beliefs by imagining that the threats to their faith were external. They attributed cosmic evil to other human beings—heretics, sorcerers, witches, and Jews."[7]

Likewise, says Langmuir, Christians used persecution of Jews to mask their own ongoing doubts about the divinity of Jesus: "The deicide accusation camouflaged Christian awareness that the continued existence of Jewish disbelief challenged Christian belief. The accusation enabled Christians to repress doubts about Jesus' resurrection by imagining that no one who was not blind could have encountered Jesus without perceiving he was God."[8] Again, in order to reduce the dissonance caused by one's own doubt, anyone who raised questions about a teaching or, worse, who was perceived to be the very embodiment of unbelief, had to be repressed.

This is why, according to Langmuir, medieval Catholics reacted with such fury upon discovering the existence of the Talmud. Developed and written in the first few centuries of the common era, the Talmud is, after all, evidence that Judaism did not cease with the coming of Jesus, but continued to be a vital, vibrant religion despite Christian beliefs to the contrary. As Langmuir puts it, "Christians had long taken for granted that the religion of Jews was what Christians, relying on their own interpretation of the Old Testament, thought it was. But they were wrong."[9] In the minds of some Christians, Jews might be forgiven for adhering to the "Old Testament." At least then they were living according to the Bible. But to hold as authoritative another book, a book with which Christians were not familiar and in which the Bible was read in ways not authorized by Christians, was unforgivable. Rosemary Ruether makes much the same point when she writes, "The 'wrath upon the Jews,' poured out by Christianity, represents this ever-unsatisfied need of the Church to prove that it has the true content of the Jewish Scriptures by finally making 'the Jews' (Jewish teaching authority) 'admit' that this is the true interpretation."[10] When in the thirteenth century the existence of the Talmud came to the attention of Church authorities, they reacted (at least in some cases) by ordering that all copies of it be burnt. It was intolerable that Jews should be allowed to interpret the Bible on their own terms, rather than in the terms that had been set down by Christians.

This dynamic can be disrupted, however, if one does not envision Judaism and Christianity as competing with one another. Is it possible to imagine that the two traditions are not "disconfirming others," as Richard Rubenstein has called them?[11] Need Judaism and Christianity be seen as disconfirming each other any more than a poem by Robert Frost disconfirms a sonnet by Shakespeare?

The American bishops took a step in this direction when they discouraged Catholics from attempting to convert Jews. The bishops stated that the Church's task of evangelization "no longer includes the wish to absorb the Jewish faith into Christianity and so end the distinctive witness of Jews to God in human history." They wrote that the Church now recognizes that the witness of Jews to the Kingdom of God "must not be curtailed by seeking the conversion of the Jewish people to Christianity."[12]

If the voice of the bishops were taken seriously, then the task of ending Christian antisemitism would be made immeasurably easier. Catholics would no longer feel a need to prove themselves right by proving Jews wrong. And they would no longer see it as necessary to claim that Christianity has superseded Judaism and thus rendered it insignificant.

In his landmark statement entitled "We Remember: A Reflection on the *Shoah*," Pope John Paul II wrote,

> We pray that our sorrow for the tragedy which the Jewish people has suffered in our century will lead to a new relationship with the Jewish people. We wish to turn awareness

of past sins into a firm resolve to build a new future in which there will be no more anti-Judaism among Christians or anti-Christian sentiment among Jews, but rather a shared mutual respect, as befits those who adore the one Creator and Lord and have a common father in faith, Abraham.[13]

The pope concluded the document with these words:

The victims from their graves, and the survivors through the vivid testimony of what they have suffered, have become a loud voice calling the attention of all of humanity. To remember this terrible experience is to become fully conscious of the salutary warning it entails: the spoiled seeds of anti-Judaism and anti-Semitism must never again be allowed to take root in any human heart.[14]

Careful attention to the celebration of Holy Week, this book has argued, can be one step towards this goal.

Notes

Preface

1. Pope John Paul II, "We Remember: A Reflection on the *Shoah*," 16 March 1998, par. II.
2. Karl Rahner, "The Festival of the Future of the World," in *Theological Investigations*, Vol. 7, *Further Theology of the Spiritual Life 1*, trans. David Bourke (New York: Crossroad, 1971), p. 182.
3. Simon Wiesenthal, *The Sunflower* (New York: Schocken Books, 1976), p. 99.
4. Cynthia Ozick, "Notes Toward a Meditation on 'Forgiveness,'" in Wiesenthal, *Sunflower*, pp. 184–5.
5. Alan Cooperman, "Ideas About Christ's Death Surveyed; Growing Minority: Jews Responsible," *Washington Post*, 3 April 2004, sec. A, p. 3.
6. Adam Dylewski, *Where the Tailor Was a Poet . . .*, trans. Wojciech Graniczewski and Ramon Shindler (Bielsko-Biala: Pascal, 2002), p. 274.

1. The Convent and the Cross

1. The height of this cross has variously been reported as twenty-two, twenty-four, or twenty-six feet tall.
2. The title of one of Cargas's books is *Reflections of a Post-Auschwitz Christian* (Detroit: Wayne State University Press, 1989).
3. Wladyslaw T. Bartoszewski, *The Convent at Auschwitz* (New York: George Braziller, 1990), p. 34. See also Kazimierz Smolen, *Auschwitz Birkenau Guide Book*, trans. Stephen Lee (Oswiecim: State Museum in Oswiecim, 2003), map on front flyleaf.
4. Carol Rittner and John K. Roth, "Introduction: Memory Offended," in *Memory Offended: The Auschwitz Convent Controversy*, eds. Carol Rittner and John K. Roth (New York: Praeger, 1991), p. 2.
5. There is some discrepancy regarding the number and identity of the second group of prisoners. The guidebook published by the Auschwitz museum refers to them as "250 of the sick from the camp hospital." A sign at the site itself identifies them as "250 sick Polish prisoners." Martin Gilbert identifies the victims as three hundred Jews. See Gilbert's *The Holocaust* (New York: Henry Holt, 1985), p. 239.
6. Bartoszewski, *Convent at Auschwitz*, p. 7.

7. Ibid., p. 8. See also Judith Hershcopf Banki, "Historical Memories in Conflict," in *Memory Offended*, eds. Rittner and Roth, p. 158.

8. Emma Klein, *The Battle for Auschwitz* (Portland, Oregon: Vallentine Mitchell, 2001), p. 5.

9. Francis A. Winiarz, "We're Not Moving a Single Inch," in *Memory Offended*, eds. Rittner and Roth, p. 261.

10. *Nostra Aetate* or "Declaration on the Relationship of the Church to Non-Christian Religions," in *The Documents of Vatican II*, ed. Walter Abbott (New York: America Press, 1966), no. 4, pp. 664–6.

11. Consultation of the National Council of Synagogues and the Bishops Committee for Ecumenical and Interreligious Affairs, United States Conference of Catholic Bishops, "Reflections on Covenant and Mission," August 12, 2002. This text is available through the Boston College Center for Christian-Jewish Learning at http://www.bc.edu/ research/cjl/meta-elements/texts/cjrelations/resources/documents/interreligious/ncs_usccb120802.htm.

12. Karl Rahner, "Christianity and the Non-Christian Religions," in *Theological Investigations*, volume 5, *Later Writings*, trans. Karl-H. Kruger (New York: Crossroad, 1966), pp. 123–4.

13. Daniel Jonah Goldhagen, *A Moral Reckoning: The Role of the Catholic Church in the Holocaust and Its Unfulfilled Duty of Repair* (New York: Alfred A. Knopf, 2002), p. 260.

14. Ibid., p. 259.

15. Order of Christian Funerals, n. 175a, in *The Rites of the Catholic Church*, trans. International Committee on English in the Liturgy, vol. 1 (Collegeville, Minnesota: Liturgical Press, 1990), p. 983.

16. Stanislaw Krajewski, "The Controversy Over Carmel at Auschwitz: A Personal Polish-Jewish Chronology," in *Memory Offended*, eds. Rittner and Roth, p. 123.

17. Pope John Paul II, Homily, Sunday, 11 October 1998, par. 4b. This text is available at http://www.vatican.va/holy_father/john_paul_ii/homilies/1998/documents/hf_ jp-ii _ hom _ 11101998_stein_en.html.

18. Ibid., par. 4c.

19. Abraham H. Foxman and Leon Klenicki, "An Unnecessary Saint," *Jerusalem Post*, 20 October 1998, p. 10.

20. See Friedrich Georg Friedmann, "Not Like That! On the Beatification of Edith Stein," in *Never Forget: Christian and Jewish Perspectives on Edith Stein*, ed. Waltraud Herbstrith, trans. Susanne Batzdorff (Washington, DC: ICS Publications, 1998), p. 112.

21. Elie Wiesel, *A Jew Today*, trans. Marion Wiesel (New York: Vintage Books, 1978), p. 220.

22. David Patterson, "Prayers of Victims, Victims of Prayer," in *The Continuing Agony: From the Carmelite Convent to the Crosses at Auschwitz*, ed. Alan L. Berger et al., American Studies in the History of Judaism (Binghamton, New York: Global Publications, 2002), p. 247.

23. Teresa of Avila, *The Collected Works of Saint Teresa of Avila*, vol. 1, *The Book of Her Life, Spiritual Testimonies, Soliloquies*, trans. Kieran Kavanaugh and Otilio Rodriguez, 2nd ed. (Washington, DC: ICS Publications, 1987), p. 96.

24. John of the Cross, *Dark Night of the Soul*, I.1.1, trans. and ed. E. Allison Peers (New York: Image Books, 1959), p. 37.
25. Patterson, "Prayers of Victims," p. 239.
26. Ibid., p. 240.
27. John of the Cross, *Ascent of Mount Carmel*, III.27.5, trans. and ed. E. Allison Peers (New York: Triumph Books, 1935, 1953, 1983), p. 275.
28. Ibid., III.27.2, p. 273.
29. Ibid., III.27.4, p. 274.
30. Ibid., pp. 274–5.
31. Ibid., p. 275.
32. Teresa of Avila, *The Interior Castle*, trans. Kieran Kavanaugh and Otilio Rodriguez, The Classics of Western Spirituality (New York: Paulist Press, 1979), p. 190.
33. Ibid., p. 194.
34. Marguerite Porete, *The Mirror of Simple Souls*, trans. Ellen L. Babinsky, The Classics of Western Spirituality (New York: Paulist Press, 1993), p. 190.
35. Ibid., p. 193.
36. The reasons for her condemnation remain unclear. See Ellen L. Babinksy, "Introduction" to Porete, *The Mirror of Simple Souls*, especially pp. 20–26.
37. Zvi Kolitz, *Yosl Rakover Talks to God*, trans. Carol Brown Janeway (New York: Vintage, 1999), p. 3.
38. Ibid., pp. 17, 20, 17–18.
39. Emmanuel Levinas, "Loving the Torah More Than God," in Kolitz, *Yosl Rakover*, p. 84. The French original can be found in "Aimer La Thora Plus Que Dieu," in *Difficile Liberté*, 3rd ed. (Paris: Albin Michel, 1976), p. 192.
40. Klein, *Battle for Auschwitz*, p. 5.
41. Ibid., p. 60.
42. Franciszek Piper, "The Number of Victims," in *Auschwitz: Nazi Death Camp*, ed. Franciszek Piper and Teresa Swiebocka (Oswiecim: Auschwitz-Birkenau State Museum, 2002), pp. 190, 195. Estimates of the number of victims at Auschwitz vary widely.
43. Ibid., p. 195.
44. John Chrysostom, "Discourse VI," in *Discourses Against Judaizing Christians*, The Fathers of the Church, Vol. 68, trans. Paul W. Harkins (Washington, DC: The Catholic University of America Press, 1979), p. 154.
45. John Tagliabue, "Amid Convent Dispute, Cardinal Cancels U.S. Trip," *New York Times*, 10 September 1989, sec. 1, part 1, p. 18, col. 4.
46. Roger Cohen, "Poles and Jews Feud About Crosses at Auschwitz," *New York Times*, 20 December 1998, sec. 1, p. 3, col. 1.
47. "300 Crosses Are Removed at Auschwitz," *New York Times*, 29 May 1999, sec. A, p. 8, col. 6.
48. The number of dead at each site are taken from the United States Holocaust Memorial Museum Web site, www.ushmm.org. The number of survivors is taken from Gilbert, *The Holocaust*, p. 287.
49. Piper, "The Number of Victims," pp. 194–5.

50. Alan Berger of Florida Atlantic University first brought this question to my attention.

51. Henryk Muszynski, "The Cross as the Symbol of the Highest Love of Man," in *The Continuing Agony*, ed. Berger et al., p. 117.

52. Alan L. Berger, "Interview with Elie Wiesel, 28 October 1998," in *The Continuing Agony*, ed. Berger et al., pp. 279–80.

53. Jacob Neusner, "Crosses in Auschwitz: Crisis and Turning," in *The Continuing Agony*, ed. Berger et al., p. 57.

54. Solomon bar Simson, "The Chronicle of Solomon bar Simson," in *The Jews and the Crusaders*, trans. and ed. Shlomo Eidelberg (Hoboken: KTAV, 1996), p. 25.

55. Andrzej Bryk, "The Struggles for Poland," in *Polin: A Journal of Polish-Jewish Studies*, vol. 4, ed. Antony Polonsky (Oxford: Basil Blackwell, 1989), p. 378.

56. See Jan T. Gross, *Neighbors: The Destruction of the Jewish Community in Jedwabne, Poland* (New York: Penguin, 2001), p. 38.

57. Helena Szereszewska, *Memoirs from Occupied Warsaw 1940–1945*, trans. Anna Marianska (Portland, Oregon: Vallentine Mitchell, 1997), p. 316.

58. "Ein Wort zur Judenfrage, der Reichsbruderrat der Evangelischen Kirche in Deutschland," 8 April 1948, in *Der Ungekündigte Bund*, ed. Goldschmidt and Kraus, pp. 251–4. Cited by Richard Rubenstein and John K. Roth, *Approaches to Auschwitz* (Atlanta: John Knox, 1987), p. 309.

59. *Nostra Aetate*, no. 4, p. 666.

60. Stanislaw Musial, "The Cross at the Gravel Heap at the Oswiecim Camp," in *The Continuing Agony*, ed. Berger et al., p. 53.

61. The actual site of Kolbe's death was the basement of Block 11.

62. Musial, "The Cross," in *The Continuing Agony*, ed. Berger et al., p. 53.

63. *Maly Dziennik*, 22 September 1935 and 9 October 1938. Cited by Ronald Modras, *The Catholic Church and Anti-Semitism: Poland, 1933–39* (Switzerland: Harwood, 1994), pp. 145, 182.

64. *Maly Dziennik*, 31 July 1937. Cited by Modras, *Catholic Church*, p. 176.

2. ASH WEDNESDAY

1. Gitta Sereny, *Into That Darkness: An Examination of Conscience* (New York: Vintage, 1974), p. 116.

2. Martin Gilbert, *The Holocaust* (New York: Henry Holt, 1985), p. 17.

3. Raul Hilberg, *The Destruction of the European Jews*, student ed. (New York: Holmes and Meier, 1985), p. 99.

4. Ibid., pp. 133, 137.

5. Sereny, *Into That Darkness*, p. 112.

6. Hilberg, *Destruction of the European Jews*, p. 152.

7. Rudolf Höss, *Autobiography of Rudolf Höss*, trans. Constantine

FitzGibbon, in Höss et al., *KL Auschwitz Seen by the SS* (Oswiecim: Auschwitz-Birkenau State Museum, 2002), p. 86.

8. *"Wo ist Mengele?,"* Friedmann Archive, Haifa, Joshua Rosenblum transcript, 5. Cited by Robert Jay Lifton, *The Nazi Doctors* (New York: Basic Books, 1986, 2000), p. 171.

9. Franciszek Piper, "Gas Chambers and Crematoria," in *Anatomy of the Auschwitz Death Camp*, eds. Yisrael Gutman and Michael Berenbaum (Bloomington: Indiana University Press, 1994), pp. 165–66. According to Richard Rubenstein and John K. Roth, estimates of the crematoria capacity range from twelve thousand to twenty thousand a day. See *Approaches to Auschwitz* (Atlanta: John Knox, 1987), p. 155.

10. Piper, "Gas Chambers and Crematoria," p. 171.

11. Jean-Claude Pressac and Robert-Jan Van Pelt, "The Machinery of Mass Murder at Auschwitz," in *Anatomy of the Auschwitz Death Camp*, eds. Gutman and Berenbaum, p. 238.

12. Testimony of Severina Shmaglevskaya, 27 February 1946, in *Trial of the Major War Criminals Before the International Military Tribunal, Nuremberg, 14 November 1945–1 October 1946*, vol. 8, *Sixty-Third Day–Seventy-Fourth Day*, 318. This testimony can be accessed via the Avalon Project at Yale Law School at http://www.yale.edu/lawweb/avalon/ imt/ proc/02-27-46.htm#shmaglevskaya1.

13. Irving Greenberg, "Cloud of Smoke, Pillar of Fire: Judaism, Christianity, and Modernity After the Holocaust," in *Auschwitz: Beginning of a New Era?*, ed. Eva Fleischner (New York: KTAV, 1977), p. 23.

14. United States Catholic Conference, Committee on Pastoral Practices, National Conference of Catholic Bishops, "Penitential Practices for Today's Catholics" (Brochure), 9–10. Available at http://www.usccb.org/dpp/ brochure.pdf. See also Canons 1249–53 of the *Code of Canon Law* (Rome: Libreria Editrice Vaticana, 1983).

15. Aelfric, Abbot of Eynsham, *Aelfric's Lives of Saints*, ed. Walter W. Skeat (London: Early English Text Society, 1881–1900), p. 263.

16. Adolf Adam, *The Liturgical Year*, trans. Matthew J. O'Connell (New York: Pueblo, 1981), p. 98.

17. Emile Durkheim, *The Elementary Forms of the Religious Life*, trans. Joseph Ward Swain (New York: Free Press, 1915), p. 455.

18. The readings for Ash Wednesday can be found in the *Lectionary for Mass, Second Typical Edition, Approved for Use in the Dioceses of the United States of America*, trans. Confraternity of Christian Doctrine, International Committee on English in the Liturgy (Collegeville, Minnesota: Liturgical Press, 2001), vol. II, *Proper of Seasons for Weekdays, Year I*, pp. 145–8, and vol. III, *Proper of Seasons for Weekdays, Year II*, pp. 145–8.

19. Jacques Derrida, *The Gift of Death*, trans. David Wills (Chicago: University of Chicago Press, 1995), p. 107.

20. Richard Rubenstein, *After Auschwitz*, 2nd ed. (Baltimore: Johns Hopkins University Press, 1966, 1992), p. 10.

21. Sereny, *Into That Darkness*, p. 364.

22. Hilberg, *Destruction of the European Jews*, p. 31.

23. Emil Fackenheim, *God's Presence in History* (New York: Harper and Row, 1970), p. 73.

24. Richard Rubenstein, "Some Perspectives on Religious Faith After Auschwitz," in *The German Church Struggle and the Holocaust*, eds. Franklin H. Littell and Hubert G. Locke (Detroit: Wayne State University Press, 1974), p. 262.

25. International Commission on English in the Liturgy, *The Roman Missal: The Sacramentary* (New York: Catholic Book Publishing, 1985), pp. 77–8.

26. Aelfric, *Aelfric's Lives of Saints*, pp. 265, 267.

27. Eliezer Berkovits, *Faith After the Holocaust* (New York: KTAV, 1973), p. 135.

28. Elie Wiesel, "Talking and Writing and Keeping Silent," in *The German Church Struggle and the Holocaust*, eds. Littell and Locke, p. 271.

29. The other is "Turn away from sin and be faithful to the gospel." See *The Sacramentary*, p. 77.

30. Apocalypse of Moses 14:2. The text can be found in *The Old Testament Pseudepigrapha*, ed. James H. Charlesworth, vol. 2 (New York: Doubleday, 1985), p. 277.

31. Louis Ginzberg, *The Legends of the Jews*, vol. 1, *From the Creation to Jacob* (Baltimore: Johns Hopkins University Press, 1909, 1937), pp. 79–80.

32. 3 Baruch (Slavonic text) 9:5–7. The text can be found in *The Old Testament Pseudepigrapha*, ed. James H. Charlesworth, vol. 1 (New York: Doubleday, 1983), p. 672.

33. Bereshit Rabah 20.10.4B, in Jacob Neusner, *Genesis Rabbah*, vol. 1, Brown Judaic Studies vol. 104 (Atlanta: Scholars Press, 1985), p. 224. The text from Genesis reads, "By the sweat of your brow shall you get bread to eat" (3:19).

34. Ginzberg, *The Legends of the Jews*, vol. 1, p. 81.

35. Apocalypse of Moses 29:4–5. The text can be found in *Old Testament Pseudepigrapha*, ed. Charlesworth, vol. 2, p. 285.

36. Ibid., 41:2–3, vol. 2, p. 293.

37. Ibid., 40:6, vol. 2, p. 293.

38. Augustine, *Opus Imperfectum Contra Julianum*, 6, 27. Cited by and trans. Elaine Pagels, *Adam, Eve, and the Serpent* (New York: Random House, 1988), p. 139.

39. *The Church Teaches: Documents of the Church in English Translation* (St. Louis: B. Herder, 1955), p. 158.

40. *Catechism of the Catholic Church*, 2nd ed. (New York: Doubleday, 2003), no. 1008 and no. 1006.

41. Karl Rahner, "The Sin of Adam," in *Theological Investigations*, vol. 11, *Confrontations 1*, trans. David Bourke (New York: Crossroad, 1982), p. 252.

42. Karl Rahner, "Christian Dying," in *Theological Investigations*, vol. 18, *God and Revelation*, trans. Edward Quinn (New York: Crossroad, 1983), pp. 236, 241.

43. Ibid., p. 251.

44. These transliterations are in accordance with the "Academic Style" of the *SBL [Society of Biblical Literature] Handbook of Style* (Massachusetts: Hendrickson, 1999), 26. For other texts on dust and ashes, see also Sirach 10:9—"How can dust and ashes be proud? Even in life the human body decays"; 17:32—"He marshals the host of the height of heaven; but all human beings are dust and ashes"; and 40:3—"From the one who sits on a splendid throne to the one who grovels in dust and ashes"; and 2 Esdras 13:11—". . . nothing was seen of the innumerable multitude but only the dust of ashes and the smell of smoke." All quotations are from the NRSV, *HarperCollins Study Bible* (New York: HarperCollins, 1993).

45. Edwin M. Good, *In Turns of Tempest: A Reading of Job* (Stanford, California: Stanford University Press, 1990), p. 131.

46. In this transliteration, I have used the SBL academic style, except that the *hêt* has been transliterated as *kh*, according to the "general purpose" style. See the *SBL Handbook of Style*, 28.

47. Good, *In Turns of Tempest*, p. 25.

48. John Briggs Curtis, "On Job's Response to Yahweh," *Journal of Biblical Literature* 98, no. 4 (1979): 505. In the original, the phrase "toward you, O God" is placed in brackets.

49. Jack Miles, *God: A Biography* (New York: Vintage, 1995), p. 325.

50. Good, *In Turns of Tempest*, p. 171.

51. Curtis, "On Job's Response to Yahweh," p. 504.

52. In the original, brackets are used rather than parentheses.

53. Miles, *God: A Biography*, p. 427 n. 324.

54. Good, *In Turns of Tempest*, p. 377.

55. Ibid.

56. Elie Wiesel, *Messengers of God* (New York: Summit Books, 1976), pp. 231–2.

57. Ibid., pp. 233–4.

58. Ibid., p. 235.

59. For this insight I am grateful to Tod Linafelt of Georgetown University.

60. Good, *In Turns of Tempest*, p. 396.

61. Ibid., p. 397.

62. Edith Wyschogrod, *Spirit in Ashes: Hegel, Heidegger, and Man-Made Mass Death* (New Haven, Connecticut: Yale University Press, 1985), p. 2.

63. Ibid., p. 34.

64. Rainer Maria Rilke, *Duino Elegies*, trans. J. B. Leishman and Stephen Spender (New York: Norton, 1939), p. 24. Cited by Wyschogrod, *Spirit in Ashes*, p. 11.

65. Wyschogrod, *Spirit in Ashes*, p. 12.

66. Ibid., p. 14.

67. On ashes being used as fertilizer, see Piper, "Gas Chambers and Crematoria," p. 171. On hair being used for mattresses, see Yehuda Bauer, *A History of the Holocaust* (New York: Franklin Watts, 2002), p. 239.

68. Wyschogrod, *Spirit in Ashes*, p. x.

69. Ibid., pp. 41–46.

70. Diary entry February 18, 1942, in Joseph Goebbels, *The Goebbels Diaries 1942–1943*, ed. Louis P. Lochner (New York: Doubleday, 1948), p. 92.
71. Wyschogrod, *Spirit in Ashes*, p. 38.
72. Salmen Gradowski, "Letter," in *Amidst a Nightmare of Crime: Manuscripts of Prisoners in Crematorium Squads Found at Auschwitz*, eds. Jadwiga Bezwinska and Danuta Czech, trans. Krystyna Michalik (New York: Howard Fertig, 1992), pp. 75–76.
73. Adam, *The Liturgical Year*, p. 98.

3. PALM SUNDAY

1. Adolph Hitler, *Hitler's Secret Conversations, 1941–1944*, trans. Norman Cameron and R.H. Stevens (New York: Signet, 1953), entry from the evening of 5 July 1942, p. 526.
2. For a tragic litany of Christian measures against Jews, see Raul Hilberg, *The Destruction of the European Jews*, student ed. (New York: Holmes and Meier, 1985), pp. 10–11.
3. Léon Poliakov, *The History of Anti-Semitism*, vol. 1, trans. Richard Howard (New York: Vanguard, 1965), p. 130 n. 4.
4. Gerard S. Sloyan, *The Crucifixion of Jesus* (Minneapolis: Fortress, 1995), p. 29.
5. International Commission on English in the Liturgy, *The Roman Missal: The Sacramentary* (New York: Catholic Book Publishing, 1985), p. 122.
6. Ibid., p. 126.
7. Raymond E. Brown, *The Virginal Conception and Bodily Resurrection of Jesus* (New York: Paulist, 1973), pp. 78–80.
8. *Sacramentary*, p. 124.
9. *Lectionary for Mass*, vol. 1, *Sundays, Solemnities, Feasts of the Lord and the Saints*, study ed. (Collegeville, Minnesota: Liturgical Press, 1998), p. 242. The readings themselves can be found on pp. 242–4.
10. *New Saint Joseph Sunday Missal*, trans. International Committee on English in the Liturgy (New Jersey: Catholic Book Publishing, 1999), pp. 1171, 309, 310.
11. Ibid., p. 1166.
12. W. Barnes Tatum, *Jesus at the Movies* (California: Polebridge, 1997), p. 9.
13. Mihail Sebastian, *Journal 1935–1944*, trans. Patrick Camiller (Chicago: Ivan R. Dee, 2000), p. 41.
14. Ibid., p. 120.
15. Ibid., p. 155.
16. Ibid., pp. 155–6.
17. Leonard Swidler and Gerard S. Sloyan, *A Commentary on the Oberammergau Passionsspiel in Regard to Its Image of Jews and Judaism* (New York: Anti-Defamation League of B'nai B'rith, 1978), p. 2.
18. Interview by Peter J. Boyer, "The Jesus War," *New Yorker*, 15 September 2003, p. 67.

19. *Providentissimus Deus: Encyclical of Pope Leo XIII on the Study of Holy Scripture* (1893), par. 17. Available on the Vatican Web site, http://www.vatican.va/holy_ father/leo_xiii/encyclicals/documents/hf_l-xiii_enc_18111893_providentissimus-deus_en.html.

20. Joseph Alois Daisenberger, rev. Otto Huber and Christian Stückl, *Oberammergau Passion Play 2000*, trans. Ingrid Shafer (Benediktbeuern: Gemeinde Oberammergau, 2000), p. 5. James Shapiro casts doubt onto this story of the play's origins in *Oberammergau: The Troubling Story of the World's Most Famous Passion Play* (New York: Pantheon, 2000), pp. 104–5.

21. Saul S. Friedman, *The Oberammergau Passion Play: A Lance Against Civilization* (Carbondale: Southern Illinois University Press, 1984), p. 50. For a photograph of the High Priest's costume as revised in 2000, see Shapiro, *Oberammergau*, Illustration 20.

22. Joseph Alois Daisenberger, *The Passion Play at Oberammergau*, official text for 1934 (Munich: J.C. Huber, 1934), p. 57. Cited by Friedman, *Oberammergau Passion Play*, pp. 89–90.

23. Joseph Alois Daisenberger, *The Passion Play at Oberammergau*, official text for 1960 (Munich: Zauner-Verlag, 1960), p. 111.

24. Swidler and Sloyan, *Commentary on the Oberammergau Passionsspiel*, pp. 6–7.

25. Ibid., pp. 6, 5, 8.

26. *Nostra Aetate* or "Declaration on the Relationship of the Church to Non-Christian Religions," in *The Documents of Vatican II*, ed. Walter Abbott (New York: America Press, 1966), no. 4, p. 666.

27. Daisenberger, rev. Huber and Stückl, *Oberammergau Passion Play 2000*, p. 44.

28. Ibid., p. 7.

29. John Dominic Crossan, "The Passion After the Holocaust," in *A Shadow of Glory: Reading the New Testament After the Holocaust*, ed. Tod Linafelt (New York: Routledge, 2002), pp. 173–74.

30. Jonathan Broder, "Oberammergau Cleans Up Its Act," *The Jerusalem Report*, 8 May 2000, p. 38.

31. Correspondence dated 6 April 2003.

32. Paula Fredriksen, "Mad Mel: The Gospel According to Gibson," *The New Republic*, 28 July 2003–4 August 2003, p. 25, par. 22.

33. Mary C. Boys et al., "Report of the Ad Hoc Scholars Group Reviewing the Script of *The Passion*," (2003), p. 5. A copy of this report can be found on the Boston College Center for Christian-Jewish Learning Web site, http://www.bc.edu/research/cjl/meta-elements/texts/cjrelations/resources/reviews/Passion_adhoc_report_2May.pdf.

34. Ibid.

35. Ibid., pp. 3–4.

36. Fredriksen, "Mad Mel," par. 4.

37. Boyer, "The Jesus War," p. 64.

38. Ibid., p. 65.

39. Interview with Bill O'Reilly, "The O'Reilly Factor" (Fox News), 25 February 2004. Available at http://www.foxnews.com/story/0,2933,112436,00.html.

40. Boyer, "The Jesus War," p. 67.

41. Amy-Jill Levine, "The Real Problem with 'Passion,'" (2005), available at http://www.beliefnet.com/story/130/story_13051_1.html, par. 15.

42. Amy-Jill Levine, "Mel Gibson, the Scribes, and the Pharisees," in Re-Viewing the Passion, ed. S. Brent Plate (New York: Palgrave Macmillan, 2004), p. 146.

43. Raymond E. Brown, for example, says that Matthew is "dramatizing theology," explaining, "I think that this episode represents a Matthean composition on the basis of a popular tradition reflecting on the theme of Jesus' innocent blood and the responsibility it created." See The Death of the Messiah, vol. 1 (New York: Doubleday, 1994), pp. 832–3.

44. Boyer, "The Jesus War," p. 61.

45. Levine, "Mel Gibson, the Scribes, and the Pharisees," p. 146.

46. Leo XIII, Providentissimus Deus, par. 17.

47. Ibid., par. 23. On this point, see Raymond E. Brown, Biblical Exegesis and Church Doctrine (New York: Paulist, 1985), p. 11.

48. Ibid., par. 18.

49. Pius X, Pascendi Dominici Gregis, no. 34. Available on the Vatican Web site, http://www.vatican.va/holy_father/pius_x/encyclicals/documents/hf_p-x_enc_19070908_pascendi-dominici-gregis_en.html.

50. Ibid.

51. Pius XII, Divino Afflante Spiritu, no. 33. Available on the Vatican Web site, http://www.vatican.va/holy_father/pius_xii/encyclicals/documents/hf_p-xii_enc_30091943_divino-afflante-spiritu_en.html.

52. For a description of these various forms of biblical study, see Daniel J. Harrington, "The Bible in Catholic Life," in The Catholic Study Bible: The New American Bible (New York: Oxford, 1990), especially pp. RG 20–22.

53. Paul VI, Dei Verbum, no. 13. Available on the Vatican Web site, http://www.vatican.va/archive/hist_councils/ii_vatican_council/documents/vat-ii_const_19651118_dei-verbum_en.html.

54. National Conference of Catholic Bishops, Bishops' Committee for Ecumenical and Interreligious Affairs, "Criteria for the Evaluation of Dramatizations of the Passion," 1988, par. C1c. The text is available at http://www.bc.edu/bc_org/research/ cjl/Documents/Passion%20Plays.htm.

55. Ibid., par. C2a.

56. Ibid., Conclusion.

57. Leonard Swidler with Gerard Sloyan, "The Passion of the Jew Jesus: Recommended Changes in the Oberammergau Passion Play After 1984," Recommendations par. 7. Available at http://ecumene.org/SHOAH/oberammer.htm.

58. "Mel Gibson's Great Passion," NewsMax Wires, 10 March 2003, pars. 8, 10. Available at http://www.newsmax.com/archives/articles/2003/3/9/14907.shtml.

59. Interview with David Neff and Jane Johnson Struck, "'Dude, That Was Graphic,': Mel Gibson Talks About The Passion of the Christ," pars. 10–11. Posted 23 February 2004, at http://www.christianitytoday.com/movies/interviews/melgibson.html.

60. John Dominic Crossan, *Who Killed Jesus?* (San Francisco: Harper SanFrancisco, 1995), p. 34.

61. Boyer, "The Jesus War," p. 71.

62. *Pascendi Dominici Gregis*, no. 28.

63. Ibid., no. 1.

64. Avery Dulles, *Models of Revelation* (Maryknoll, New York: Orbis, 1992), pp. 98–99, 199.

65. This quote first appeared in the *New York Times*, 27 March 1994. It is cited by Crossan, *Who Killed Jesus?*, p. 1.

66. Brown, *The Death of the Messiah*, vol. 1, p. 4. Italics omitted.

67. Ibid., p. 22.

68. Ibid., p. 17.

69. Crossan, *Who Killed Jesus?*, p. 22.

70. Ibid., p. 10.

71. Brown, *The Death of the Messiah*, vol. 1, p. 17.

72. Ibid., p. 382.

73. Ibid.

74. Ibid., pp. 395–6.

75. Raymond E. Brown, *The Death of the Messiah*, vol. 2 (New York: Doubleday, 1994), pp. 1334–5.

76. John Dominic Crossan, *The Cross That Spoke* (San Francisco: Harper and Row, 1988), pp. 405–6.

77. Crossan, *Who Killed Jesus?*, p. 25.

78. Brown, *The Death of the Messiah*, vol. 1, p. 14.

79. Crossan cites 18:60–62, which tells of an incident in which tens of thousands of Jews assembled to protest a decision by Pilate. Pilate signaled his soldiers to attack, and a great number of the unarmed people were slain. See Crossan, *Who Killed Jesus?*, p. 150.

80. Crossan, *Who Killed Jesus?*, 152.

81. Ibid., p. 35.

82. See, for example, John Meier, *A Marginal Jew: Rethinking the Historical Jesus*, vol. 1, *The Roots of the Problem and the Person* (New York: Doubleday, 1991), pp. 116–8.

83. Meier refers to Frans Neirynck, C.K. Barrett, W. Klaiber, and K. Kleinknecht as defenders of the position that John is dependent on Mark. He himself disagrees. See Meier, *A Marginal Jew*, pp. 44, 52, nn. 16 and 17.

84. Helmut Koester, *Ancient Christian Gospels: Their History and Development* (Philadelphia: Trinity Press International, 1990), p. 224.

85. Crossan, *Who Killed Jesus?*, p. 35.

4. HOLY THURSDAY, THE CHRISM MASS

1. Betty Jean Lifton, *The King of Children: A Biography of Janusz Korczak* (New York: Farrar, Straus and Giroux, 1988), p. 262.

2. Ibid., pp. 323–4.

3. Ibid., p. 323.

4. Janusz Korczak, *Ghetto Diary* (New York: Holocaust Library, 1978), p. 188. Ellipses in the original.

5. Lifton, *The King of Children*, p. 345.

6. Korczak, *Ghetto Diary*, p. 176.

7. Lifton, *The King of Children*, p. 345.

8. International Commission on English in the Liturgy, *The Roman Missal: The Sacramentary* (New York: Catholic Book Publishing, 1985), p. 132.

9. The readings for the Chrism Mass can be found in the *Lectionary for Mass, Second Typical Edition, Approved for Use in the Dioceses of the United States of America*, trans. Confraternity of Christian Doctrine, International Committee on English in the Liturgy, vol. 1, *Sundays, Solemnities, Feasts of the Lord and the Saints*, study ed. (Collegeville, Minnesota: Liturgical Press, 1998), pp. 1085–8.

10. Elisabeth Schüssler Fiorenza, "Redemption as Liberation: Apoc 1:5f. and 5:9f.," *Catholic Biblical Quarterly* 36 (April 1974): 232.

11. *Sacramentary*, p. 131.

12. Ibid., p. 413, italics added.

13. Edward Schillebeeckx, *The Church with a Human Face* (New York: Crossroad, 1985), pp. 119–20.

14. Ibid., p. 145.

15. Ibid., p. 143.

16. Ibid., p. 144.

17. Ibid.

18. Schüssler Fiorenza, "Redemption as Liberation," p. 220.

5. HOLY THURSDAY, THE MASS OF THE LAST SUPPER

1. Raul Hilberg, *The Destruction of the European Jews*, student ed. (New York: Holmes and Meier, 1985), p. 193.

2. Tuvia Borzykowski, *Between Tumbling Walls* (Tel Aviv, 1972, reprinted 1976), pp. 57–58. Cited by Martin Gilbert, *The Holocaust* (New York: Henry Holt, 1985), p. 559.

3. Hilberg, *Destruction of the European Jews*, pp. 209–10.

4. Irving Greenberg, *The Jewish Way* (New York: Summit, 1988), pp. 338–9.

5. On this point, see John Meier, *A Marginal Jew*, vol. 1 (New York: Doubleday, 1991), pp. 386–401.

6. International Commission on English in the Liturgy, *The Roman Missal: The Sacramentary* (New York: Catholic Book Publishing, 1985), p. 545.

7. Franklin Littell, *The Crucifixion of the Jews* (Macon, Georgia: Mercer University Press, 1986), p. 30.

8. Elie Wiesel, *A Passover Haggadah* (New York: Simon and Schuster, 1993), p. 94.

9. Marc Saperstein, *Moments of Crisis in Jewish-Christian Relations* (London: SCM Press, 1989), p. 19.

10. According to Robert Jay Lifton, "Mengele identified himself as a

Catholic on all his official forms, rather than using the more favored Nazi category of 'believer in God.'" See Robert Jay Lifton, *The Nazi Doctors* (New York: Basic Books, 2000), p. 339.

11. The readings for the Evening Mass of the Lord's Supper can be found in the *Lectionary for Mass, Second Typical Edition, Approved for Use in the Dioceses of the United States of America*, trans. Confraternity of Christian Doctrine, International Committee on English in the Liturgy, vol. 1, *Sundays, Solemnities, Feasts of the Lord and the Saints*, study ed. (Collegeville, Minnesota: Liturgical Press, 1998), pp. 293–7. The text of the first reading is from Exodus 12:1–8, 11–14.

12. Rabbi Ephraim of Bonn, *Sefer Zekhirah, or The Book of Remembrance*, in *The Jews and the Crusaders: The Hebrew Chronicles of the First and Second Crusades*, ed. and trans. Shlomo Eidelberg (New Jersey: KTAV, 1977), p. 132.

13. Akiva ben Eliezer, *The Book of Tears* (in Hebrew), ed. Simon Bernfeld (Berlin, 1924), ii, 154. Cited by David J. Malkiel, "Infanticide in Passover Iconography," *Journal of the Warburg and Courtauld Institutes* 56 (1993): 94.

14. Yosef Dov Sheinson, *A Survivors' Haggadah*, ed. Saul Touster (Philadelphia: Jewish Publication Society, 2000), p. 63.

15. Ibid.

16. Gubkin's paper, entitled "As If You Were There: Knowledge and Identity in *The Devil's Arithmetic*," was presented at the 2003 Annual Meeting of the American Academy of Religion.

17. Wiesel, *A Passover Haggadah*, pp. 68–69.

18. Piska 49.3, in William G. Braude, trans., *Pesikta Rabbati: Discourses for Feasts, Fasts, and Special Sabbaths*, vol. 2 (New Haven: Yale University Press, 1968), p. 833.

19. Greenberg, *The Jewish Way*, pp. 53–54, 58.

20. Wiesel, *A Passover Haggadah*, p. 6.

21. Shalom Spiegel, *The Last Trial*, trans. Judah Goldin (New York: Pantheon, 1967), p. 56.

22. P.R. Davies and B.D. Chilton, "The Aqedah: A Revised Tradition History," *Catholic Biblical Quarterly* 40 (1978): 536.

23. In Menahem M. Kasher, *Encyclopedia of Biblical Interpretation*, vol. 8: *Exodus*, trans. Harry Freedman (New York: American Biblical Encyclopedia Society, 1970), p. 47.

24. Pisha VII.III.8D, *Mekhilta According to Rabbi Ishmael*, vol. 1, trans. Jacob Neusner (Atlanta: Scholars Press, 1988), p. 45.

25. Louis Ginzberg, *The Legends of the Jews*, vol. 1, *From the Creation to Jacob* (Baltimore: Johns Hopkins University Press, 1937), pp. 284–5. The material in Ginzberg is largely derived from *Midrash Bereshit Rabah* 56.9–10. See Jacob Neusner, *Genesis Rabbah*, vol. 2 (Atlanta: Scholars Press, 1985), pp. 284–6.

26. Rabbi Ephraim ben Jacob of Bonn, *Akedah*, in Spiegel, *The Last Trial*, pp. 148–52.

27. Solomon bar Simson, "The Chronicle of Solomon bar Simson," in *The Jews and the Crusaders: The Hebrew Chronicles of the First and Second Crusades*, ed. and trans. Eidelberg, p. 33.

28. Ibid.

29. Jacob Glatstein, "My Father Isaac," in *Modern Poems of the Bible*, ed. David Curzon (Philadelphia: Jewish Publication Society, 1994), pp. 143–4.

30. Carol Delaney, *Abraham on Trial* (Princeton: Princeton University Press, 1998), pp. 120, 144.

31. Clement of Alexandria, *Christ the Educator*, trans. Simon P. Wood, The Fathers of the Church: A New Translation, vol. 23 (New York: Fathers of the Church, 1954), p. 23.

32. Elie Wiesel, *Messengers of God* (New York: Summit Books, 1976), p. 76.

33. Davies and Chilton, "The Aqedah," pp. 537–40.

34. Daniel Boyarin, *Dying for God* (Stanford, California: Stanford University Press, 1999), p. 118.

35. Ibid., p. 114.

36. Ibid., p. 106. The passage Boyarin cites is from Berakhot 61b.

37. Ibid., p. 56.

38. Solomon bar Simson, "Chronicle of Solomon bar Simson," p. 68.

39. Moses Maimonides, "The Epistle on Martyrdom," in *Epistles of Maimonides*, trans. Abraham Halkin (Philadelphia: Jewish Publication Society of America, 1985), p. 30. Avi Patt brought this passage to my attention.

40. Rabbi Ephraim Oshry, *Responsa from the Holocaust*, trans. Y. Leiman (New York: Judaica Press, 1983), p. 110.

41. Ibid., p. 124.

42. Ibid., p. 208.

43. *The Martyrdom of Polycarp*, in *Early Christian Writings*, trans. Maxwell Staniforth (New York: Penguin, 1968), pp. 157, 160–1.

44. Eliezer Berkovits, *Faith After the Holocaust* (New York: KTAV, 1973), p. 83.

45. Ibid., p. 81.

46. *Sacramentary*, p. 135.

47. Ibid., p. 467.

48. Michael L. Barré, "Psalm 116: Its Structure and Its Enigmas," *Journal of Biblical Literature* 109/1 (1990): 72.

49. Ibid. These transliterations are in accordance with the "Academic Style" of the *SBL* [Society of Biblical Literature] *Handbook of Style* (Massachusetts: Hendrickson, 1999), 26.

50. Rabbi Solomon ben Isaac (Rashi), in *Rashi's Commentary on Psalms*, ed. Mayer I. Gruber, Brill Reference Library of Judaism, vol. 18 (Boston: Brill, 2004), p. 666.

51. J.A. Emerton, "How Does the Lord Regard the Death of His Saints in Psalm cxvi.15?" *Journal of Theological Studies* 34 (April 1983): 153–4.

52. See http://www.nccbuscc.org/nab/bible/psalms/psalm116.htm.

53. See *Lectionary for Mass*, vol. 1, p. viii. See also http://www.vatican.va/ archive/bible/nova_vulgata/documents/nova-vulgata_vt_psalmo-rum_lt.html# PSALMUS%20116.

54. The current (1998) *Lectionary for Mass* employs the 1986 edition of the New American Bible's Revised New Testament and the 1970 edition

of the Old Testament, including the Psalms. The New American Bible's translation of the Psalms was updated in 1991, but this did not affect the text of the Lectionary. See the February–March 1998 newsletter of the United States Conference of Catholic Bishops' Committee on the Liturgy at http://www.usccb.org/ liturgy/innews/298.shtml. See also http://www. usccb.org/ nab/faq.htm. It may be important to note that the Vulgate also translated the phrase as *pretiosa in conspectu Domini mors sanctorum eius.*

55. Emerton, "How Does the Lord Regard the Death of His Saints?," p. 150.

56. John Dominic Crossan, *The Historical Jesus* (San Francisco: HarperSanFrancisco, 1991), p. 360.

57. Ibid., p. 364.

58. John P. Meier, "The Eucharist at the Last Supper: Did It Happen?" *Theology Digest* 42, no. 4 (Winter, 1995): 338, 343–4.

59. *The Didache,* in *Early Christian Writings,* trans. Staniforth, no. 9, p. 231.

60. Meier, "The Eucharist at the Last Supper," p. 348.

61. Ibid., p. 346.

62. Ibid., p. 345.

63. Ibid., p. 346.

64. Ibid., p. 347. Brackets appear in the original.

65. *Sacramentary,* p. 138.

66. Robert W. Funk et al., *The Acts of Jesus* (San Francisco: Harper SanFrancisco, 1998), p. 419.

67. Raymond E. Brown, *The Gospel According to John* (xiii–xxi), Anchor Bible (New York: Doubleday, 1970), p. 568.

68. John Christopher Thomas, *Footwashing in John 13 and the Johannine Community,* Journal for the Study of the New Testament Supplement series 61 (Sheffield, England: Sheffield Academic Press, 1991), pp. 11–17.

69. *Sacramentary,* p. 136.

70. See http://www.usccb.org/liturgy/q&a/general/feet.shtml.

71. *Sacramentary,* p. 137.

72. Thomas, *Footwashing in John 13,* p. 109.

73. On this topic, see historian Kevin Spicer's forthcoming work on "brown" (i.e., Nazi) priests.

6. GOOD FRIDAY

1. Quoted in Emmanuel Ringelblum, *Polish-Jewish Relations During the Second World War,* eds. Joseph Kermish and Shmuel Krakowski, trans. Dafna Allon et al. (New York: Howard Fertig, 1976), p. 138 n. 25.

2. Papias, "The Fragments of Papias," Fragment 3.2, in *The Didache, The Epistle of Barnabas, The Epistles and the Martyrdom of St. Polycarp, The Fragments of Papias, The Epistle to Diognetus,* trans. James Kleist, Ancient Christian Writers no. 6 (Maryland: Newman Press, 1948), p. 119.

3. Kim Paffenroth, *Judas: Images of the Lost Disciple* (Louisville: Westminster John Knox, 2001), pp. 116–7.

4. Hyam Maccoby, *Judas Iscariot and the Myth of Jewish Evil* (New York: Free Press, 1992), p. 153.

5. Jacobus de Voragine, *The Golden Legend*, trans. William Granger Ryan, vol. 1 (Princeton: Princeton University Press, 1993), p. 167.

6. Paffenroth, *Judas*, p. 1.

7. Ibid., p. 2. The NRSV translation of I Cor. 11:23 says that "the Lord Jesus on the night when he *was betrayed* took a loaf of bread..." However, it is also possible to translate the passage to say simply that Jesus "was delivered up."

8. Ibid.

9. Gerard S. Sloyan, *The Crucifixion of Jesus* (Minneapolis: Fortress, 1995), p. 92.

10. John Chrysostom, "Homily 86," in *Chrysostom: Homilies on the Gospel of Saint Matthew*, Nicene and Post-Nicene Fathers, vol. 10, ed. Philip Schaff, trans. George Prevost (Massachusetts: Hendrickson, 1888, reprinted 1995), p. 514.

11. John Chrysostom, "Homily 3," in *Chrysostom: Homilies on the Acts of the Apostles and the Epistle to the Romans*, Nicene and Post-Nicene Fathers, vol. 11:, ed. Philip Schaff, trans. J. Walker et al. (Massachusetts: Hendrickson, 1889, reprinted 1995), p. 21.

12. Larry E. West, trans., *The Alsfeld Passion Play*, Studies in German Language and Literature vol. 17 (Lewiston, New York: Edwin Mellen, 1997), lines 183–95, pp. 15–17.

13. Ibid., lines 3176–7, p. 251, and lines 3212–29, pp. 253–5.

14. Ibid., lines 3230–1, p. 255, lines 5632–4, p. 443, and lines 5580–7, p. 439.

15. Ibid., lines 3666–9, p. 293, line 4640, p. 371, and lines 4669–70, p. 373.

16. Alphonsus Liguori, "The Way of the Cross" (New York: Catholic Book Publishing, 1974–1969), pp. 5, 7.

17. Jon Meacham, "Who Killed Jesus?" *Newsweek*, 16 February 2004, par. 8.

18. Amy-Jill Levine, "Mel Gibson, the Scribes, and the Pharisees," in *Re-Viewing the Passion*, ed. S. Brent Plate (New York: Palgrave Macmillan, 2004), p. 146.

19. Alphonsus Liguori, "The Way of the Cross," pp. 16–18.

20. International Commission on English in the Liturgy, *The Roman Missal: The Sacramentary* (New York: Catholic Book Publishing, 1985), p. 140.

21. Ibid.

22. The readings for Good Friday can be found in the *Lectionary for Mass, Second Typical Edition, Approved for Use in the Dioceses of the United States of America*, trans. Confraternity of Christian Doctrine, International Commission on English in the Liturgy, vol. 1, *Sundays, Solemnities, Feasts of the Lord and the Saints*, study ed. (Collegeville, Minnesota: Liturgical Press, 1998), pp. 298–310.

23. http://www.stryper.com/history_stryperstory.html.

24. Rudolf Bultmann, *Theology of the New Testament*, vol. 1 (New York: Charles Scribner's Sons, 1951), p. 31.

25. Morna D. Hooker, *Jesus and the Servant* (London: SPCK, 1959), p. 163.

26. Morna D. Hooker, "Did the Use of Isaiah 53 to Interpret His Mission Begin with Jesus?" in *Jesus and the Suffering Servant*, eds. William H. Bellinger and William R. Farmer (Harrisburg: Trinity Press International, 1998), p. 103.

27. See, for example, Otto Betz, "Jesus and Isaiah 53," in *Jesus and the Suffering Servant*, eds. Bellinger and Farmer, pp. 70–87.

28. Sloyan, *The Crucifixion of Jesus*, p. 63.

29. Ibid., p. 67.

30. Joel E. Rembaum, "The Development of a Jewish Exegetical Tradition Regarding Isaiah 53," *Harvard Theological Review* 75 (July 1982): 290–1.

31. Ralph Loewe, "Prolegomenon," in *The Fifty-Third Chapter of Isaiah According to the Jewish Interpreters*, vol. 2: *Translations*, eds. S.R. Driver and A. Neubauer (New York: KTAV, 1969), pp. 22–23.

32. R. Sh'lomoh Yizhaqi (Rashi), in *Fifty-Third Chapter of Isaiah*, eds. Driver and Neubauer, p. 37.

33. Ibid., p. 38.

34. *Anchor Bible Dictionary*, s.v. "Isaiah, Book of (Second Isaiah): The Message of Second Isaiah, 'The Servant,'" vol. 3, p. 499.

35. Patricia Tull Willey, *Remember the Former Things: The Recollection of Previous Texts in Second Isaiah*, SBL Dissertation Series 161 (Atlanta: Scholars Press, 1997), p. 220.

36. Jacob Neusner, trans., *Lamentations Rabbah: An Analytical Translation* (Atlanta: Scholars Press, 1989), p. 125.

37. Tod Linafelt, *Surviving Lamentations* (Chicago: University of Chicago Press, 2000).

38. Ibid., p. 79.

39. Ibid., pp. 43–49.

40. Richard D. Nelson, "He Offered Himself: Sacrifice in Hebrews," *Interpretation* 57, no. 3 (July 2003): 254.

41. Athanasius, *On the Incarnation*, trans. and ed. Penelope Lawson (New York: Macmillan, 1946), p. 15.

42. Ibid., p. 32.

43. Ibid., p. 39. See also pp. 34–38.

44. Dietrich Bonhoeffer, *The Cost of Discipleship*, trans. R.H. Fuller and Irmgard Booth (New York: Macmillan, 1959), p. 47.

45. *The Missal: Compiled by Lawful Authority from the Missale Romanum* (London: Burns, Oates &Washbourne, 1928), p. 299.

46. *Sacramentary*, p. 153.

47. *Sacramentary*, p. 158.

48. Adrian Fortescue, *The Ceremonies of the Roman Rite Described* (London: Burns, Oates and Washbourne, 1930), pp. 323–4.

49. *Sacramentary*, pp. 163–4.

50. Franklin Littell, *The Crucifixion of the Jews* (Macon, Georgia: Mercer University Press, 1986), p. 30.

51. John L. Allen, "Good Friday's Can of Worms," *National Catholic Reporter*, 17 March 2000.

52. Alicia C. Shepard, "A Mother's Courage," *The Washington Post*, 11 January 2003, sec. A, p. 21.

53. Esther Iverem, "'Murder of Emmett Till' Still Haunts," posted 18 January 2003, available at http://www.bet.com/Entertainment/Archives/ BET.com+-+_Murder+of+ Emmett+Till_+Still+Haunts+178.htm.

7. TENEBRAE

1. Primo Levi, *Survival in Auschwitz*, trans. Stuart Woolf (New York: Collier, 1959), p. 82.

2. Ibid., p. 80 n. 1.

3. Israel Gutman, "Muselmann," in *Encyclopedia of the Holocaust*, vol. 3, ed. Israel Gutman (New York: Macmillan, 1990), p. 1010.

4. Levi, *Survival in Auschwitz*, p. 82.

5. Berakot 10a: "Just as the Holy One, blessed be He, fills the whole world, so the soul fills the body. Just as the Holy One . . . sees, but is not seen, so the soul sees but is not itself seen. Just as the Holy One . . . feeds the whole world, so the soul feeds the whole body. Just as the Holy One . . . abides in the innermost precincts, so the soul abides in the innermost precincts." See also Louis Ginzberg, *The Legends of the Jews*, vol. 1, *From the Creation to Jacob*, trans. Henrietta Szold (Baltimore: Johns Hopkins University Press, 1937), p. 60.

6. Ginzberg, *Legends of the Jews*, vol. 1, p. 56. Ginzberg is here paraphrasing R. Simeon b. Laqish: "'And the spirit of God hovered over the face of the deep' (Gen 1:2) refers to the spirit of the first man." See *Genesis Rabbah* VIII.I.6D, ed. Jacob Neusner, vol. 1 (Atlanta: Scholars Press, 1985), p. 74.

7. Ginzberg, *Legends of the Jews*, vol. 1, p. 60.

8. Rashi, *Pentateuch with Targum Onkelos, Haphtaroth and Rashi's Commentary*, trans. M. Rosenbaum and A.M. Silbermann (New York: Hebrew Publishing, 1946), p. 7.

9. Maimonides, *The Guide for the Perplexed*, trans. M. Friedlander, 2nd ed. (New York: Dover, 1956), p. 15.

10. *Zohar Hadash 5*, in Menahem M. Kasher, *Encyclopedia of Biblical Interpretation*, vol. 1, *Genesis* (New York: American Biblical Encyclopedia Society, 1953), p. 65.

11. For a history of the concept "image of God" in Christian thinking, see Anthony O. Erhueh, *Vatican II: Image of God in Man* (Rome: Urbaniana University Press, 1987), especially Chapter 1.

12. Augustine, *The Trinity*, XII.12, trans. Edmund Hill (New York: New City Press, 1991), pp. 328–9. In my book *Celluloid Saints: Images of Sanctity in Film*, I asserted that Augustine did not think women were made in the image of God, unless considered in conjunction with their husbands. This

was incorrect. For an insightful analysis of Augustine, women, and the image of God, see Kari Elisabeth Børresen, "God's Image, Man's Image? Patristic Interpretation of Gen. 1,27 and I Cor. 11,7," in Kari Elisabeth Børresen, ed., *The Image of God: Gender Models in Judaeo-Christian Tradition* (Minneapolis: Fortress Press, 1995), pp. 187–209.

13. Thomas Aquinas, *Summa Theologica*, Part I, q. 93, art. 4, ad. 1, trans. Fathers of the English Dominican Province (New York: Benziger, 1947), vol. 1, p. 472.

14. Ibid., Part I, q. 92., art. 1, ad. 2; vol. 1, p. 467.

15. Ibid., Part I, q. 93, art. 4, ad. 1; vol. 1, p. 472.

16. Charles Elliott, *Sinfulness of American Slavery*, in *Eve and Adam: Jewish, Christian, and Muslim Readings on Genesis and Gender*, ed. Kristen E. Kvam et al. (Bloomington: Indiana University Press, 1999), p. 335.

17. *Catechism of the Catholic Church*, 2nd ed. (New York: Doubleday, 2003), no. 363.

18. Ibid., no. 1934.

19. Ibid., no. 1938 (citation is from *Gaudium et Spes* 29.3).

20. Ibid., no. 1877.

21. "The Definition of Chalcedon," in *Documents of the Christian Church*, ed. Henry Bettenson, 2nd ed. (New York: Oxford University Press, 1963), p. 51. In Bettenson, some of the words of the quote are printed in all capital letters.

22. Gitta Sereny, *Into That Darkness* (New York: Vintage, 1974), p. 201.

23. Emil L. Fackenheim, *To Mend the World* (New York: Schocken Books, 1982), p. 286.

24. *The Second Treatise of the Great Seth*, in *The Other Bible*, ed. Willis Barnstone (San Francisco: Harper & Row, 1984), pp. 117, 119. Emphasis added.

25. J.N.D. Kelly, *Early Christian Creeds*, 3rd ed. (New York: David McKay, 1972), p. 378.

26. Ibid., p. 379.

27. On this point, see J. A. MacCulloch, *The Harrowing of Hell* (Edinburgh: T&T Clark, 1930), p. 192.

28. *Christian Prayer: The Liturgy of the Hours*, trans. International Committee on English in the Liturgy (Boston: Daughters of Saint Paul, 1976), p. 1676.

29. On the dating of the text, see Alan E. Bernstein, *The Formation of Hell* (Ithaca: Cornell University Press, 1993), p. 274.

30. Kelly, *Early Christian Creeds*, p. 381, and p. 381 n. 9.

31. Martin F. Connell, "*Descensus Christi ad Inferos*: Christ's Descent to the Dead," *Theological Studies* 62 (2001): 266.

32. Ibid., p. 267.

33. Biblical scholar Claus Westermann comes to a similar though slightly different conclusion when, following the insights of Karl Barth, he writes that "the text is speaking about an action of God, and not about the nature of humanity." Westermann's point is that the significance of the text in which God creates human beings in God's image and likeness is "in determining

further the nature of the act of creation which enables an event to take place between God and humans; it is not a question of a quality in human beings." See *Genesis 1–11: A Commentary*, trans. John J. Scullion (Minneapolis: Augsburg, 1984), pp. 155, 157.

34. Sacred Congregation for Divine Worship, "Circular Letter Concerning the Preparation and Celebration of the Easter Feasts," Part III, no. 40, January 16, 1988. Available at http://www.catholicliturgy.com/index.cfm/FuseAction/documentText/Index/2/SubIndex/38/Cont entIndex/323/Start/319.

35. Peter J. Elliott, *Ceremonies of the Liturgical Year According to the Modern Roman Rite* (San Francisco: Ignatius Press, 2002), pp. 208–9.

36. Ibid., pp. 210–2. For the psalms, antiphons, and readings of the Matins and Lauds of Holy Saturday, see *The Hours of the Divine Office in English and Latin*, vol. 2 (Collegeville, Minnesota: Liturgical Press, 1964), pp. 1154–73.

37. Elliott, *Ceremonies of the Liturgical Year*, p. 210.

38. A.J. MacGregor, *Fire and Light in the Western Triduum*, Alcuin Club Collection no. 71 (Minnesota: Liturgical Press, 1992), pp. 31–32.

39. Benedict XIV, *Benedicti XIV. Pont. Opt. Max. Olim Prosperi Cardinalis de Lambertinis: Opus*, vol. 10, *Institutiones Ecclesiasticas* XXIV:9 (Prati, 1844), p. 98. This translation is from Herbert Thurston, "Tenebrae," in *The Catholic Encyclopedia* (1912), available at http://www.newadvent.org/cathen/14506a.htm.

40. I first read this poem when I attended a lecture given by Richard Fragomeni at the Catholic Theological Union in Chicago many years ago.

41. John Felstiner, *Paul Celan: Poet, Survivor, Jew* (New Haven: Yale University Press, 1995), pp. 103, 101.

42. Ibid., p. 101.

43. John Felstiner, "'Clawed into Each Other': Jewish vs. Christian Memory in Paul Celan's 'Tenebrae'," *TriQuarterly* 87 (Spring/Summer 1993): 195.

44. Ibid., p. 200.

45. John Caputo, *More Radical Hermeneutics* (Bloomington: Indiana University Press, 2000), p. 237.

46. Ibid.

8. EASTER AND BEYOND

1. The story appears in Yaffa Eliach, *There Once Was a World* (Boston: Little, Brown and Co., 1998), pp. 588–9. It can also be found in a slightly different form in Eliach, *Hasidic Tales of the Holocaust* (New York: Vintage, 1982), pp. 53–55.

2. Herbert J. Thurston and Donald Attwater, eds., *Butler's Lives of the Saints*, vol. 4 (Westminster, MD: Christian Classics, 1990), p. 310.

3. Leo Tolstoy, *The Complete Works of Count Tolstoy*, vol. 12, *Fables for Children* (New York: AMS, 1968), p. 459.

4. Mother Teresa, *A Simple Path*, compiled by Lucinda Vardey (New York: Ballantine, 1995), p. 155.

5. This translation of John 20:17 is offered by Michael McGehee, "A Less Theological Reading of John 20:17," *Journal of Biblical Literature* 105, no. 2 (June 1986): 299.

6. John Caputo, *On Religion* (New York: Routledge, 2001), p. 128.

7. International Commission on English in the Liturgy, *The Roman Missal: The Sacramentary* (New York: Catholic Book Publishing, 1985), p. 171.

8. Ibid., p. 183.

9. Origen, *Commentary on the Epistle to the Romans, Books 1–5*, II.13.29, The Fathers of the Church vol. 103, trans. Thomas P. Scheck (Washington, DC: Catholic University of America Press, 2001), p. 161.

10. Gerard S. Sloyan, *The Crucifixion of Jesus* (Minneapolis: Fortress, 1995), p. 107.

11. *Sacramentary*, pp. 187–92; *Lectionary* n. 41.

12. Ibid., p. 193.

13. Ibid., p. 204.

14. Caputo, *On Religion*, p. 115.

15. Ibid., p. 116.

16. Edward Schillebeeckx, *Jesus: An Experiment in Christology*, trans. Hubert Hoskins (New York: Vintage, 1979), pp. 333–4.

17. Ibid., p. 382.

18. Ibid., p. 391.

19. Ibid., p. 539.

20. Ibid., pp. 544, 649.

21. *Sacramentary* p. 205.

22. Schilleeckx, *Jesus*, p. 643.

23. Alexander Donat, *The Holocaust Kingdom* (Washington, DC: Holocaust Library, 1999), pp. 129–30.

24. Ibid., p. 310.

25. Ibid.

26. John Caputo, *More Radical Hermeneutics* (Bloomington: Indiana University Press, 2000), p. 207.

27. Joseph A. Fitzmyer, "The Ascension of Christ and Pentecost," *Theological Studies* 45 (Spring 1984): 414–5.

28. David Van Biema, "Does Heaven Exist?" *Time*, 24 March 1997, p. 75.

29. Ibid., p. 73.

30. Pope John Paul II, General Audience, Wednesday, 21 July 1999, no. 4. Available at http://www.vatican.va/holy_father/john_paul_ii/audiences/1999/documents/hf_jp-ii_aud_21071999_en.html.

31. *Catechism of the Catholic Church*, 2nd ed. (New York: Doubleday, 2003), no. 659. Emphasis added.

32. Ibid., no. 646. The reference is to I Corinthians 15:48.

33. Laurence Hull Stookey, *Calendar: Christ's Time for the Church* (Nashville: Abingdon Press, 1996), p. 66.

34. Edward Schillebeeckx, "Ascension and Pentecost," *Worship* 35, no. 6 (May 1961): 336.

35. Ibid., p. 340.
36. Ibid., p. 342.
37. Ibid., p. 352.
38. Fitzmyer, "The Ascension of Christ and Pentecost," p. 424.
39. Ibid., p. 422.
40. "Death in a Cult: Looking Forward to Going to the Next Level," *New York Times*, 28 March 1997, sec. A, p. 21.
41. "Gateway to Madness," *New York Times*, 29 March 1997, sec. 1, p. 18.
42. Karl Rahner, "The Festival of the Future of the World," in *Theological Investigations*, vol. 7, *Further Theology of the Spiritual Life 1*, trans. David Bourke (New York: Crossroad, 1971), p. 182.
43. Ibid.
44. Ibid., p. 184.
45. Karl Rahner, "He Will Come Again," in *Theological Investigations*, vol. 7, trans. Bourke, p. 179.
46. Caputo, *More Radical Hermeneutics*, p. 237.
47. Douglas Farrow, *Ascension and Ecclesia* (Grand Rapids, Michigan: William B. Eerdmans, 1999), p. 271 n. 59.
48. Emmanuel Levinas, "Loving the Torah More Than God," in *Yosl Rakover Talks to God*, trans. Carol Brown Janeway (New York: Vintage, 1999), p. 85.

9. CONCLUSION

1. Richard L. Rubenstein, *After Auschwitz: History, Theology, and Contemporary Judaism*, 2nd ed. (Baltimore: Johns Hopkins University Press, 1992), p. 85.
2. Ibid., p. 86.
3. Ibid., pp. 91–2.
4. Ibid., p. 92.
5. Ibid., p. 84.
6. Gavin I. Langmuir, *History, Religion, and Antisemitism* (Los Angeles: University of California Press, 1990), p. 250.
7. Ibid., p. 263.
8. Ibid., p. 288.
9. Ibid., p. 295.
10. Rosemary Ruether, *Faith and Fratricide* (Minneapolis: Seabury, 1974), pp. 94–95.
11. Rubenstein, *After Auschwitz*, p. 95.
12. Consultation of the National Council of Synagogues and the Bishops' Committee for Ecumenical and Interreligious Affairs, United States Conference of Catholic Bishops, "Reflections on Covenant and Mission," 12 August 2002. This text is available via the Boston College Center for Christian-Jewish Learning at http://www.bc.edu/research/ cjl/meta-elements/texts/cjrelations/resources/documents/interreligious/ncs_usccb 120802.htm.

13. Pope John Paul II, "We Remember: A Reflection on the *Shoah*," 16 March 1998, par. v. The text is available at http://www.vatican.va/ roman_curia/pontifical_ councils/ chrstuni/documents/rc_pc_chrstuni_doc_ 16031998_shoah_en.html.

14. Ibid.

WORKS CITED

Adam, Adolf. *The Liturgical Year*. Translated by Matthew J. O'Connell. New York: Pueblo, 1981.

Aelfric, Abbot of Eynsham. *Aelfric's Lives of Saints*. Edited by Walter W. Skeat. London: Early English Text Society, 1881–1900.

Allen, John L. "Good Friday's Can of Worms." *National Catholic Reporter*, 17 March 2000.

Aquinas, Thomas. *Summa Theologica*. Vol. 1. Translated by Fathers of the English Dominican Province. New York: Benziger, 1947.

Athanasius. *On the Incarnation*. Edited and translated by Penelope Lawson. New York: Macmillan, 1946.

Augustine. *The Trinity*. Translated by Edmund Hill. New York: New City Press, 1991.

Babinksy, Ellen L. "Introduction." In Marguerite Porete. *The Mirror of Simple Souls*. Translated by Ellen L. Babinsky. The Classics of Western Spirituality. New York: Paulist Press, 1993, 5–48.

Banki, Judith Hershcopf. "Historical Memories in Conflict." In *Memory Offended: The Auschwitz Convent Controversy*. Edited by Carol Rittner and John K. Roth. New York: Praeger, 1991.

Barnstone, Willis, ed. *The Other Bible*. San Francisco: Harper & Row, 1984.

Barré, Michael L. "Psalm 116: Its Structure and Its Enigmas." *Journal of Biblical Literature* 109/1 (1990): 61–79.

Bartoszewski, Wladyslaw T. *The Convent at Auschwitz*. New York: George Braziller, 1990.

Bauer, Yehuda. *A History of the Holocaust*. New York: Franklin Watts, 2002.

Benedict XIV, Pope. *Benedicti XIV. Pont. Opt. Max. Olim Prosperi Cardinalis de Lambertinis: Opus*. Vol. 10. *Institutiones Ecclesiasticas*. Prati, 1844.

Berger, Alan L. "Interview with Elie Wiesel, 28 October 1998." In *The Continuing Agony: From the Carmelite Convent to the Crosses at Auschwitz*. Edited by Alan Berger et al. American Studies in the History of Judaism. Binghamton, New York: Global Publications, 2002, 279–85.

Berkovits, Eliezer. *Faith After the Holocaust*. New York: KTAV, 1973.

Bernstein, Alan E. *The Formation of Hell*. Ithaca: Cornell University Press, 1993.

Bettenson, Henry, ed. *Documents of the Christian Church*. 2nd ed. New York: Oxford University Press, 1963.

Betz, Otto. "Jesus and Isaiah 53." In *Jesus and the Suffering Servant*. Edited by William H. Bellinger and William R. Farmer. Harrisburg: Trinity Press International, 1998.

Bishops' Committee for Ecumenical and Interreligious Affairs, National Conference of Catholic Bishops. "Criteria for the Evaluation of Dramatizations of the Passion." 1988. http://www.bc.edu/bc_org/research/cjl/Documents/Passion%20Plays.htm.

Bonhoeffer, Dietrich. *The Cost of Discipleship*. Translated by R.H. Fuller and Irmgard Booth. New York: Macmillan, 1959.

Børresen, Kari Elisabeth. "God's Image, Man's Image? Patristic Interpretation of Gen. 1,27 and I Cor. 11,7." In *The Image of God: Gender Models in Judaeo-Christian Tradition*. Edited by Kari Elisabeth Børresen. Minneapolis: Fortress Press, 1995, 187–209.

Boyarin, Daniel. *Dying for God*. California: Stanford University Press, 1999.

Boyer, Peter J. "The Jesus War." *New Yorker*, 15 September 2003, 58–71.

Boys, Mary C., et al. "Report of the Ad Hoc Scholars Group Reviewing the Script of *The Passion*." 2003. http://www.bc.edu/research/cjl/meta-elements/texts/cjrelations/resources/reviews/Passion_adhoc_report_2May. pdf.

Braude, William G., trans. *Pesikta Rabbati: Discourses for Feasts, Fasts, and Special Sabbaths*. Vol. 2. New Haven: Yale University Press, 1968.

Broder, Jonathan. "Oberammergau Cleans Up Its Act." *The Jerusalem Report*, 8 May 2000.

Brown, Raymond E. *Biblical Exegesis and Church Doctrine*. New York: Paulist, 1985.

———. *The Death of the Messiah*. Vols. 1 and 2. New York: Doubleday, 1994.

———. *The Gospel According to John (xiii–xxi)*. Anchor Bible. New York: Doubleday, 1970.

———. *The Virginal Conception and Bodily Resurrection of Jesus*. New York: Paulist, 1973.

Bryk, Andrzej. "The Struggles for Poland." In *Polin: A Journal of Polish-Jewish Studies*. Vol. 4. Edited by Antony Polonsky. Oxford: Basil Blackwell, 1989, 370–89.

Bultmann, Rudolf. *Theology of the New Testament*. Vol. 1. New York: Charles Scribner's Sons, 1951.

Caputo, John. *More Radical Hermeneutics*. Bloomington: Indiana University Press, 2000.

———. *On Religion*. New York: Routledge, 2001.

Cargas, Harry James. *Reflections of a Post-Auschwitz Christian*. Detroit: Wayne State University Press, 1989.

Catholic Church. *Catechism of the Catholic Church*. 2nd ed. New York: Doubleday, 2003.

———. *The Church Teaches: Documents of the Church in English Translation*. St. Louis: B. Herder, 1955.

———. *The Hours of the Divine Office in English and Latin*. Vol. 2. Collegeville, Minnesota: Liturgical Press, 1964.

———. *The Missal: Compiled by Lawful Authority from the Missale Romanum*. London: Burns, Oates & Washbourne, 1928.

———. *Nostra Aetate* or "Declaration on the Relationship of the Church to Non-Christian Religions." In *The Documents of Vatican II*. Edited by Walter Abbott. New York: America Press, 1966, 660–8.

Charlesworth, James H., ed. *The Old Testament Pseudepigrapha*. Vol. 2. New York: Doubleday, 1985.

Clement of Alexandria, *Christ the Educator*. Translated by Simon P. Wood. The Fathers of the Church: A New Translation. Vol. 23. New York: Fathers of the Church, 1954.

Cohen, Roger. "Poles and Jews Feud About Crosses at Auschwitz." *New York Times*, 20 December 1998.

Confraternity of Christian Doctrine. *Lectionary for Mass*. Vol. 1. *Sundays, Solemnities, Feasts of the Lord and the Saints*. Study edition. Collegeville, Minnesota: Liturgical Press, 1998.

———. *Lectionary for Mass*. Vol. II. *Proper of Seasons for Weekdays, Year I*. Collegeville, Minnesota: Liturgical Press, 2001.

———. *Lectionary for Mass*. Vol. III. *Proper of Seasons for Weekdays, Year II*. Collegeville, Minnesota: Liturgical Press, 2001.

Connell, Martin F. "*Descensus Christi ad Inferos*: Christ's Descent to the Dead." *Theological Studies* 62 (2001): 262–82.

Cooperman, Alan. "Ideas About Christ's Death Surveyed; Growing Minority: Jews Responsible." *Washington Post*, 3 April 2004.

Consultation of the National Council of Synagogues and the Bishops' Committee for Ecumenical and Interreligious Affairs, United States Conference of Catholic Bishops. "Reflections on Covenant and Mission." August 12, 2002. http://www.bc.edu/ research/cjl/meta-elements/texts/cjre-lations/resources/documents/interreligious/ ncs_usccb120802.htm.

Crossan, John Dominic. *The Cross That Spoke*. San Francisco: Harper and Row, 1988.

———. *The Historical Jesus*. San Francisco: HarperSanFrancisco, 1991.

———. "The Passion After the Holocaust." In *A Shadow of Glory: Reading the New Testament After the Holocaust*. Edited by Tod Linafelt. New York: Routledge, 2002, 171–84.

———. *Who Killed Jesus?* San Francisco: HarperSanFrancisco, 1995.

Curtis, John Briggs. "On Job's Response to Yahweh." *Journal of Biblical Literature* 98, no. 4 (1979): 497–511.

Daisenberger, Joseph Alois. *Oberammergau Passion Play 2000*. Revised by Otto Huber and Christian Stückl. Translated by Ingrid Shafer. Benediktbeuern: Gemeinde Oberammergau, 2000.

———. *The Passion Play at Oberammergau: Official Text for 1960*. Munich: Zauner-Verlag, 1960.

Davies, P.R., and Chilton, B.D. "The Aqedah: A Revised Tradition History." *Catholic Biblical Quarterly* 40 (1978): 514–46.

"Death in a Cult: Looking Forward to Going to the Next Level." *New York Times*, 28 March 1997, sec. A, p. 21.

Delaney, Carol. *Abraham on Trial*. Princeton: Princeton University Press, 1998.

Derrida, Jacques. *The Gift of Death*. Translated by David Wills. Chicago: University of Chicago Press, 1995.

Donat, Alexander. *The Holocaust Kingdom*. Washington, DC: Holocaust Library, 1999.

Dulles, Avery. *Models of Revelation*. Maryknoll, New York: Orbis, 1992.

Durkheim, Emile. *The Elementary Forms of the Religious Life*. Translated by Joseph Ward Swain. New York: Free Press, 1915.

Dylewski, Adam. *Where the Tailor Was a Poet* . . . Translated by Wojciech Graniczewski and Ramon Shindler. Bielsko-Biala: Pascal, 2002.

Eliach, Yaffa. *Hasidic Tales of the Holocaust*. New York: Vintage, 1982.

———. *There Once Was a World*. Boston: Little, Brown and Co., 1998.

Elliott, Charles. *Sinfulness of American Slavery*. In *Eve and Adam: Jewish, Christian, and Muslim Readings on Genesis and Gender*. Edited by Kristen E. Kvam et al. Bloomington: Indiana University Press, 1999.

Elliott, Peter J. *Ceremonies of the Liturgical Year According to the Modern Roman Rite*. San Francisco: Ignatius Press, 2002.

Emerton, J.A. "How Does the Lord Regard the Death of His Saints in Psalm cxvi.15?" *Journal of Theological Studies* 34 (April 1983): 146–56.

Ephraim of Bonn, Rabbi. *Akedah*. In Shalom Spiegel. *The Last Trial*. Translated by Judah Goldin. New York: Pantheon, 1967, 143–52.

———. *Sefer Zekhirah, or The Book of Remembrance*. In *The Jews and the Crusaders: The Hebrew Chronicles of the First and Second Crusades*. Edited and translated by Shlomo Eidelberg. New Jersey: KTAV, 1977, 121–33.

Epstein, I., ed. *Hebrew-English Edition of the Babylonian Talmud*. London: Soncino, 1988.

Erhueh, Anthony O. *Vatican II: Image of God in Man*. Rome: Urbaniana University Press, 1987.

Fackenheim, Emil. *God's Presence in History*. New York: Harper and Row, 1970.

———. *To Mend the World*. New York: Schocken Books, 1982.

Farrow, Douglas. *Ascension and Ecclesia*. Grand Rapids, Michigan: William B. Eerdmans, 1999.

Felstiner, John. "'Clawed into Each Other': Jewish vs. Christian Memory in Paul Celan's 'Tenebrae.'" *TriQuarterly* 87 (Spring/Summer, 1993): 193–203.

———. *Paul Celan: Poet, Survivor, Jew*. New Haven: Yale University Press, 1995.

Fiorenza, Elisabeth Schüssler. "Redemption as Liberation: Apoc 1:5f. and 5:9f." *Catholic Biblical Quarterly* 36 (April 1974): 220–32.

Fitzmyer, Joseph A. "The Ascension of Christ and Pentecost." *Theological Studies* 45 (Spring 1984): 409–40.

Fortescue, Adrian. *The Ceremonies of the Roman Rite Described*. London: Burns, Oates and Washbourne, 1930.

Foxman, Abraham H., and Klenicki, Leon. "An Unnecessary Saint." *Jerusalem Post*, 20 October 1998.

Fredriksen, Paula. "Mad Mel: The Gospel According to Gibson." *The New Republic*, 28 July 2003–4 August 2003.

Friedman, Saul S. *The Oberammergau Passion Play: A Lance Against Civilization*. Carbondale: Southern Illinois University Press, 1984.

Friedmann, Friedrich Georg. "Not Like That! On the Beatification of Edith Stein." In *Never Forget: Christian and Jewish Perspectives on Edith Stein*. Edited by Waltraud Herbstrith. Translated by Susanne Batzdorff. Washington, DC: ICS Publications, 1998, 109–20.

Funk, Robert W., et al. *The Acts of Jesus*. San Francisco: Harper San Francisco, 1998.

"Gateway to Madness." *New York Times*, 29 March 1997.

Gilbert, Martin. *The Holocaust*. New York: Henry Holt, 1985.

Ginzberg, Louis. *The Legends of the Jews*. Vol. 1. *From the Creation to Jacob*. Baltimore: Johns Hopkins University Press, 1909, 1937.

Glatstein, Jacob. "My Father Isaac." In *Modern Poems of the Bible*. Edited by David Curzon. Philadelphia: Jewish Publication Society, 1994, 143–44.

Goebbels, Joseph. *The Goebbels Diaries 1942–1943*. Edited by Louis P. Lochner. New York: Doubleday, 1948.

Goldhagen, Daniel Jonah. *A Moral Reckoning: The Role of the Catholic Church in the Holocaust and Its Unfulfilled Duty of Repair*. New York: Alfred A. Knopf, 2002.

Good, Edwin M. *In Turns of Tempest: A Reading of Job*. Stanford, California: Stanford University Press, 1990.

Gradowski, Salmen. "Letter." In *Amidst a Nightmare of Crime: Manuscripts of Prisoners in Crematorium Squads Found at Auschwitz*. Edited by Jadwiga Bezwinska and Danuta Czech. Translated by Krystyna Michalik. New York: Howard Fertig, 1992, 75–77.

Greenberg, Irving. "Cloud of Smoke, Pillar of Fire: Judaism, Christianity, and Modernity After the Holocaust." In *Auschwitz: Beginning of a New Era?*. Edited by Eva Fleischner. New York: KTAV, 1977, 7–55.

———. *The Jewish Way*. New York: Summit, 1988.

Gross, Jan T. *Neighbors: The Destruction of the Jewish Community in Jedwabne, Poland*. New York: Penguin, 2001.

Gubkin, Liora. "As If You Were There: Knowledge and Identity in *The Devil's Arithmetic*." Presented at the 2003 Annual Meeting of the American Academy of Religion.

Gutman, Israel, ed. *Encyclopedia of the Holocaust*. Vol. 3. New York: Macmillan, 1990.

Harrington, Daniel J. "The Bible in Catholic Life." In *The Catholic Study Bible: The New American Bible*. Edited by Donald Senior. New York: Oxford, 1990, RG 16–30.

Hilberg, Raul. *The Destruction of the European Jews*. Student edition. New York: Holmes and Meier, 1985.

Hitler, Adolph. *Hitler's Secret Conversations, 1941–1944*. Translated by Norman Cameron and R.H. Stevens. New York: Signet, 1953.

Hooker, Morna D. "Did the Use of Isaiah 53 to Interpret His Mission Begin with Jesus?" In *Jesus and the Suffering Servant*. Edited by William H. Bellinger and William R. Farmer. Harrisburg: Trinity Press International, 1998.

———. *Jesus and the Servant*. London: SPCK, 1959.

Höss, Rudolf. *Autobiography of Rudolf Höss*. Translated by Constantine FitzGibbon. In Rudolf Höss et al. *KL Auschwitz Seen by the SS*. Oswiecim: Auschwitz-Birkenau State Museum, 2002, 27–101.

International Commission on English in the Liturgy. *Christian Prayer: The Liturgy of the Hours*. Boston: Daughters of Saint Paul, 1976.

———. *New Saint Joseph Sunday Missal*. New Jersey: Catholic Book Publishing, 1999.

———. *The Rites of the Catholic Church*. Vol. 1. Collegeville, Minnesota: Liturgical Press, 1990.

———. *The Roman Missal: The Sacramentary*. New York: Catholic Book Publishing, 1985.

Iverem, Esther. "'Murder of Emmett Till' Still Haunts." Posted 18 January 2003. http://www.bet.com/Entertainment/Archives/BET.com+-+_ Murder+ of+Emmett+Till_ +Still+Haunts+178.htm.

Jacobus de Voragine. *The Golden Legend*. Translated by William Granger Ryan. Vol. 1. Princeton: Princeton University Press, 1993.

John of the Cross. *Ascent of Mount Carmel*. Edited and translated by E. Allison Peers. New York: Triumph Books, 1935, 1953, 1983.

———. *Dark Night of the Soul*. Edited and translated by E. Allison Peers. New York: Image Books, 1959.

John Chrysostom. *Discourses Against Judaizing Christians*. The Fathers of the Church. Vol. 68. Translated by Paul W. Harkins. Washington, DC: The Catholic University of America Press, 1979.

———. *Chrysostom: Homilies on the Acts of the Apostles and the Epistle to the Romans*. Nicene and Post-Nicene Fathers. Vol. 11. Edited by Philip Schaff. Translated by J. Walker et al. Massachusetts: Hendrickson, 1889, 1995.

———. *Chrysostom: Homilies on the Gospel of Saint Matthew*. Nicene and Post-Nicene Fathers. Vol. 10. Edited by Philip Schaff. translated by George Prevost. Massachusetts: Hendrickson, 1888, 1994.

John Paul II, Pope. General Audience, Wednesday, 21 July 1999. http://www.vatican.va/ holy_father/john_paul_ii/audiences/1999/documents/hf_jp-ii_aud_21071999_en.html.

———. Homily, Sunday, 11 October 1998. http://www.vatican.va/ holy_father/john_paul_ii/homilies/1998/documents/hf_jp-ii_hom_11101998_stein_en.html.

———. "We Remember: A Reflection on the *Shoah*." 16 March 1998, par. II. http://www.vatican.va/roman_curia/pontifical_councils/ chrstuni/documents/rc_pc_ chrstuni_doc_16031998_shoah_en.html.

Kasher, Menahem M. *Encyclopedia of Biblical Interpretation*. Vol. 1. *Genesis*. New York: American Biblical Encyclopedia Society, 1953.

———. *Encyclopedia of Biblical Interpretation*. Vol. 8. *Exodus*. Translated by Harry Freedman. New York: American Biblical Encyclopedia Society, 1970.

Kelly, J.N.D. *Early Christian Creeds*. 3rd ed. New York: David McKay, 1972.

Klein, Emma. *The Battle for Auschwitz*. Portland, Oregon: Vallentine Mitchell, 2001.

Kleist, James, trans. *The Didache, The Epistle of Barnabas, The Epistles and the Martyrdom of St. Polycarp, The Fragments of Papias, The Epistle to Diognetus.* Ancient Christian Writers no. 6. Maryland: Newman Press, 1948.

Koester, Helmut. *Ancient Christian Gospels: Their History and Development.* Philadelphia: Trinity Press International, 1990.

Kolitz, Zvi. *Yosl Rakover Talks to God.* Translated by Carol Brown Janeway. New York: Vintage, 1999.

Korczak, Janusz. *Ghetto Diary.* New York: Holocaust Library, 1978.

Krajewski, Stanislaw. "The Controversy Over Carmel at Auschwitz: A Personal Polish-Jewish Chronology." In *Memory Offended: The Auschwitz Convent Controversy.* Edited by Carol Rittner and John K. Roth. New York: Praeger, 1991.

Langmuir, Gavin I. *History, Religion, and Antisemitism.* Los Angeles: University of California Press, 1990.

Leo XIII, Pope. *Providentissimus Deus: Encyclical of Pope Leo XIII on the Study of Holy Scripture,* 1893. http://www.vatican.va/holy_father/leo_xiii/encyclicals/documents/hf_l-xiii_enc_18111893_providentissimus-deus_en.html.

Levi, Primo. *Survival in Auschwitz.* Translated by Stuart Woolf. New York: Collier, 1959.

Levinas, Emmanuel. "Loving the Torah More Than God." In Zvi Kolitz. *Yosl Rakover Talks to God.* Translated by Carol Brown Janeway. New York: Vintage, 1999, 79–87.

Levine, Amy-Jill. "Mel Gibson, the Scribes, and the Pharisees." In *Re-Viewing the Passion.* Edited by S. Brent Plate. New York: Palgrave Macmillan, 2004.

———. "The Real Problem with 'Passion.'" 2005. http://www.beliefnet.com/story/130/story_13051_1.html.

Lifton, Betty Jean. *The King of Children: A Biography of Janusz Korczak.* New York: Farrar, Straus and Giroux, 1988.

Lifton, Robert Jay. *The Nazi Doctors.* New York: Basic Books, 1986, 2000.

Liguori, Alphonsus. "The Way of the Cross." New York: Catholic Book Publishing, 1974–69.

Linafelt, Tod. *Surviving Lamentations.* Chicago: University of Chicago Press, 2000.

Littell, Franklin. *The Crucifixion of the Jews.* Macon, Georgia: Mercer University Press, 1986.

Loewe, Ralph. "Prolegomenon." In *The Fifty-Third Chapter of Isaiah According to the Jewish Interpreters.* Vol. 2. *Translations.* Edited by S.R. Driver and A. Neubauer. New York: KTAV, 1969, 1–38.

Maccoby, Hyam. *Judas Iscariot and the Myth of Jewish Evil.* New York: Free Press, 1992.

MacCulloch, J.A. *The Harrowing of Hell.* Edinburgh: T&T Clark, 1930.

MacGregor, A.J. *Fire and Light in the Western Triduum.* Alcuin Club Collection no. 71. Minnesota: Liturgical Press, 1992.

Maimonides, Moses. "The Epistle of Martyrdom." In *Epistles of Maimonides.* Translated by Abraham Halkin. Philadelphia: Jewish Publication Society of America, 1985.

————. *The Guide for the Perplexed.* Translated by M. Friedlander. 2nd ed. New York: Dover, 1956.

Malkiel, David J. "Infanticide in Passover Iconography." *Journal of the Warburg and Courtauld Institutes* 56 (1993): 85–99.

McGehee, Michael. "A Less Theological Reading of John 20:17." *Journal of Biblical Literature* 105, no. 2 (June 1986): 299–302.

Meacham, Jon. "Who Killed Jesus?" *Newsweek*, 16 February 2004.

Meier, John P. "The Eucharist at the Last Supper: Did It Happen?" *Theology Digest* 42, no. 4 (Winter, 1995): 335–51.

————. *A Marginal Jew: Rethinking the Historical Jesus.* Vol. 1. *The Roots of the Problem and the Person.* New York: Doubleday, 1991.

"Mel Gibson's Great Passion," NewsMax Wires, 10 March 2003. http://www.newsmax. com/archives/articles/2003/3/9/14907.shtml.

Miles, Jack. *God: A Biography.* New York: Vintage, 1995.

Modras, Ronald. *The Catholic Church and Anti-Semitism: Poland, 1933–39.* Switzerland: Harwood, 1994.

Musial, Stanislaw. "The Cross at the Gravel Heap at the Oswiecim Camp." In *The Continuing Agony: From the Carmelite Convent to the Crosses at Auschwitz.* Edited by Alan L. Berger et al. American Studies in the History of Judaism. Binghamton, New York: Global Publications, 2002, 49–54.

Muszynski, Henryk. "The Cross as the Symbol of the Highest Love of Man." In *The Continuing Agony: From the Carmelite Convent to the Crosses at Auschwitz.* Edited by Alan L. Berger et al. American Studies in the History of Judaism. Binghamton, New York: Global Publications, 2002, 115–7.

Neff, David, and Struck, Jane Johnson. "'Dude, That Was Graphic,': Mel Gibson Talks About *The Passion of the Christ.*" http://www.christianitytoday.com/movies/interviews/melgibson.html.

Nelson, Richard D. "He Offered Himself: Sacrifice in Hebrews." *Interpretation* 57, no. 3 (July 2003): 251–65.

Neusner, Jacob. "Crosses in Auschwitz: Crisis and Turning." In *The Continuing Agony: From the Carmelite Convent to the Crosses at Auschwitz.* Edited by Alan L. Berger et al. American Studies in the History of Judaism. Binghamton, New York: Global Publications, 2002, 55–77.

————. *Genesis Rabbah.* Vols. 1 and 2. Brown Judaic Studies. Vol. 104. Atlanta: Scholars Press, 1985.

————. *Lamentations Rabbah: An Analytical Translation.* Atlanta: Scholars Press, 1989.

————. *Mekhilta According to Rabbi Ishmael.* Vol. 1. Atlanta: Scholars Press, 1988.

Nostra Aetate or "Declaration on the Relationship of the Church to Non-Christian Religions." In *The Documents of Vatican II.* Edited by Walter Abbott. New York: America Press. 1966.

O'Reilly, Bill. Interview with Mel Gibson. 25 February 2004. http://www.foxnews.com/story/0,2933,112436,00.html.

Origen. *Commentary on the Epistle to the Romans, Books 1–5.* The Fathers of the Church. Vol. 103. Translated by Thomas P. Scheck. Washington, DC: Catholic University of America Press, 2001.

Oshry, Ephraim. *Responsa from the Holocaust.* Translated by Y. Leiman. New York: Judaica Press, 1983.

Ozick, Cynthia. "Notes Toward a Meditation on 'Forgiveness.'" In *The Sunflower.* Edited by Simon Wiesenthal. New York: Schocken Books, 1976, 184–90.

Paffenroth, Kim. *Judas: Images of the Lost Disciple.* Louisville: Westminster John Knox, 2001.

Pagels, Elaine. *Adam, Eve, and the Serpent.* New York: Random House, 1988.

Patterson, David. "Prayers of Victims, Victims of Prayer." In *The Continuing Agony: From the Carmelite Convent to the Crosses at Auschwitz.* Edited by Alan L. Berger et al. American Studies in the History of Judaism. Binghamton, New York: Global Publications, 2002, 237–56.

Paul VI, Pope. *Dei Verbum.* http://www.vatican.va/archive/hist_councils/ii_vatican_council/documents/vat-ii_const_19651118_dei-verbum_en.html.

Piper, Franciszek. "Gas Chambers and Crematoria." In *Anatomy of the Auschwitz Death Camp.* Edited by Yisrael Gutman and Michael Berenbaum. Bloomington: Indiana University Press, 1994, 157–82.

———. "The Number of Victims." In *Auschwitz: Nazi Death Camp.* Edited by Francisek Piper and Teresa Swiebocka. Oswiecim: Auschwitz-Birkenau State Museum, 2002, 182–95.

Pius X, Pope. *Pascendi Dominici Gregis.* http://www.vatican.va/holy_father/pius_x/encyclicals/documents/hf_p-x_enc_19070908_pascendi-dominici-gregis_en.html.

Pius XII, Pope. *Divino Afflante Spiritu.* http://www.vatican.va/holy_father/pius_xii/encyclicals/documents/hf_p-xii_enc_30091943_divino-afflante-spiritu_en.html.

Poliakov, Léon. *The History of Anti-Semitism.* Vol. 1. Translated by Richard Howard. New York: Vanguard, 1965.

Porete, Marguerite. *The Mirror of Simple Souls.* Translated by Ellen L. Babinsky. The Classics of Western Spirituality. New York: Paulist Press, 1993.

Pressac, Jean-Claude, and Van Pelt, Robert-Jan. "The Machinery of Mass Murder at Auschwitz." In *Anatomy of the Auschwitz Death Camp.* Edited by Yisrael Gutman and Michael Berenbaum. Bloomington: Indiana University Press, 1994, 183–245.

Rahner, Karl. "Christian Dying." In *Theological Investigations.* Vol. 18. *God and Revelation.* Translated by Edward Quinn. New York: Crossroad, 1983, 226–56.

———. "Christianity and the Non-Christian Religions." In *Theological Investigations.* Vol. 5. *Later Writings.* Translated by Karl-H. Kruger. New York: Crossroad, 1966, 115–34.

———. "The Festival of the Future of the World." In *Theological Investigations.* Vol. 7. *Further Theology of the Spiritual Life 1.* Translated by David Bourke. New York: Crossroad, 1971.

——. "He Will Come Again." In *Theological Investigations*. Vol. 7. *Further Theology of the Spiritual Life 1*. Translated by David Bourke. New York: Crossroad, 1971.

——. "The Sin of Adam." In *Theological Investigations*. Vol. 11. *Confrontations 1*. Translated by David Bourke. New York: Crossroad, 1982, 247–62.

Rembaum, Joel E. "The Development of a Jewish Exegetical Tradition Regarding Isaiah 53." *Harvard Theological Review* 75 (July 1982): 289–311.

Ringelblum, Emmanuel. *Polish-Jewish Relations During the Second World War*. Edited by Joseph Kermish and Shmuel Krakowski. Translated by Dafna Allon et al. New York: Howard Fertig, 1976.

Rittner, Carol, and Roth, John K. "Introduction: Memory Offended." In *Memory Offended: The Auschwitz Convent Controversy*. Edited by Carol Rittner and John K. Roth. New York: Praeger, 1991.

Rosenbaum, M., and Silbermann, A.M., trans. *Pentateuch with Targum Onkelos, Haphtaroth and Rashi's Commentary*. New York: Hebrew Publishing, 1946.

Rubenstein, Richard. *After Auschwitz*. 2nd edition. Baltimore: Johns Hopkins University Press, 1966, 1992.

——. "Some Perspectives on Religious Faith After Auschwitz." In *The German Church Struggle and the Holocaust*. Edited by Franklin H. Littell and Hubert G. Locke. Detroit: Wayne State University Press, 1974, 256–68.

Rubenstein, Richard, and Roth, John K. *Approaches to Auschwitz*. Atlanta: John Knox, 1987.

Ruether, Rosemary. *Faith and Fratricide*. Minneapolis: Seabury, 1974.

Sacred Congregation for Divine Worship. "Circular Letter Concerning the Preparation and Celebration of the Easter Feasts." January 16, 1988. http://www.catholicliturgy.com/index.cfm/FuseAction/documentText/Index/2/SubIndex/38/ContentIndex/323/Start/319.

Saperstein, Marc. *Moments of Crisis in Jewish-Christian Relations*. London: SCM Press, 1989.

Schillebeeckx, Edward. "Ascension and Pentecost." *Worship* 35, no. 6 (May 1961): 336–63.

——. *The Church with a Human Face*. New York: Crossroad, 1985.

——. *Jesus: An Experiment in Christology*. Translated by Hubert Hoskins. New York: Vintage, 1979.

Sebastian, Mihail. *Journal 1935–1944*. Translated by Patrick Camiller. Chicago: Ivan R. Dee, 2000.

Sereny, Gitta. *Into That Darkness: An Examination of Conscience*. New York: Vintage, 1974.

Shapiro, James. *Oberammergau: The Troubling Story of the World's Most Famous Passion Play*. New York: Pantheon, 2000.

Sheinson, Yosef Dov. *A Survivor's Haggadah*. Edited by Saul Touster. Philadelphia: Jewish Publication Society, 2000.

Shepard, Alicia C. "A Mother's Courage." *The Washington Post*, 11 January 2003.

Shmaglevskaya, Severina. In *Trial of the Major War Criminals Before the International Military Tribunal, Nuremberg, 14 November 1945–1 October 1946*. Vol. 8. *Sixty-Third Day–Seventy-Fourth Day*, 27 February 27, 1946. http://www.yale.edu/lawweb/ avalon/imt/proc/02-27-46.htm# shmaglevskaya1.

Sloyan, Gerard S. *The Crucifixion of Jesus*. Minneapolis: Fortress, 1995.

Smolen, Kazimierz. *Auschwitz Birkenau Guide Book*. Translated by Stephen Lee. Oswiecim: State Museum in Oswiecim, 2003.

Solomon bar Simson. "The Chronicle of Solomon bar Simson." In *The Jews and the Crusaders*. Edited and translated by Shlomo Eidelberg. Hoboken: KTAV, 1996, 15–75.

Solomon ben Isaac, Rabbi (Rashi). *Rashi's Commentary on Psalms*. Edited by Mayer I. Gruber. Brill Reference Library of Judaism. Vol. 18. Boston: Brill, 2004.

Spiegel, Shalom. *The Last Trial*. Translated by Judah Goldin. New York: Pantheon, 1967.

Staniforth, Maxwell, trans. *Early Christian Writings*. New York: Penguin, 1968.

Stookey, Laurence Hull. *Calendar: Christ's Time for the Church*. Nashville: Abingdon Press, 1996.

Swidler, Leonard, and Sloyan, Gerard S. *A Commentary on the Oberammergau* Passionsspiel *in Regard to Its Images of Jews and Judaism*. New York: Anti-Defamation League of B'nai B'rith, 1978.

———. "The Passion of the Jew Jesus: Recommended Changes in the Oberammergau Passion Play After 1984." http://ecumene.org/ SHOAH/ oberammer.htm.

Szereszewska, Helena. *Memoirs from Occupied Warsaw 1940–1945*. Translated by Anna Marianska. Portland, Oregon: Valentine Mitchell, 1997.

Tagliabue, John. "Amid Convent Dispute, Cardinal Cancels U.S. Trip." *New York Times*, 10 September 1989.

Tatum, W. Barnes. *Jesus at the Movies*. California: Polebridge, 1997.

Teresa, Mother. *A Simple Path*. Compiled by Lucinda Vardey. New York: Ballantine, 1995.

Teresa of Avila. *The Collected Works of Saint Teresa of Avila*. Vol. 1. *The Book of Her Life, Spiritual Testimonies, Soliloquies*. Translated by Kieran Kavanaugh and Otilio Rodriguez. 2nd ed. Washington, DC: ICS Publications, 1987.

———. *The Interior Castle*. Translated by Kieran Kavanaugh and Otilio Rodriguez. The Classics of Western Spirituality. New York: Paulist Press, 1979.

Thomas, John Christopher. *Footwashing in John 13 and the Johannine Community*. Journal for the Study of the New Testament Supplement series 61. Sheffield, England: Sheffield Academic Press, 1991.

"300 Crosses Are Removed at Auschwitz." *New York Times*, 29 May 1999.

Thurston, Herbert. "Tenebrae." In *The Catholic Encyclopedia*, 1912. http://www.newadvent.org/cathen/14506a.htm.

Thurston, Herbert J., and Attwater, Donald, eds. *Butler's Lives of the Saints*. Vol. 4. Westminster, MD: Christian Classics, 1990.

Tolstoy, Leo. *The Complete Works of Count Tolstoy*. Vol. 12. *Fables for Children*. New York: AMS, 1968.

United States Catholic Conference. Committee on Pastoral Practices. "Penitential Practices for Today's Catholics." http://www.usccb.org/ dpp/brochure.pdf.

———. Committee on the Liturgy. "Newsletter" (February–March, 1998). http://www. usccb.org/liturgy/innews/298.shtml.

Van Biema, David, "Does Heaven Exist?" *Time*, 24 March 1997, 71–8.

West, Larry E., trans. *The Alsfeld Passion Play*. Studies in German Language and Literature. Vol. 17. Lewiston, New York: Edwin Mellen, 1997.

Westermann, Claus. *Genesis 1–11: A Commentary*. Translated by John J. Scullion. Minneapolis: Augsburg, 1984.

Wiesel, Elie. *A Jew Today*. Translated by Marion Wiesel. New York: Vintage Books, 1978.

———. *Messengers of God*. New York: Summit Books, 1976.

———. *A Passover Haggadah*. New York: Simon and Schuster, 1993.

———. "Talking and Writing and Keeping Silent." In *The German Church Struggle and the Holocaust*. Edited by Franklin H. Littell and Hubert G. Locke. Detroit: Wayne State University Press, 1974, 269–77.

Wiesenthal, Simon. *The Sunflower*. New York: Schocken Books, 1976.

Willey, Patricia Tull. *Remember the Former Things: The Recollection of Previous Texts in Second Isaiah*. SBL Dissertation Series 161. Atlanta: Scholar's Press, 1997.

Winiarz, Francis A. "We're Not Moving a Single Inch." In *Memory Offended: The Auschwitz Convent Controversy*. Edited by Carol Rittner and John K. Roth. New York: Praeger, 1991, 259–62.

Wyschogrod, Edith. *Spirit in Ashes: Hegel, Heidegger, and Man-Made Mass Death*. New Haven, Connecticut: Yale University Press, 1985.

Index

BIBLICAL PASSAGES

Old Testament

Genesis
1:1-2:2 — 161
1:26 — 142, 143, 144, 145, 150
1:27 — 142
3 — xiii, 23, 31
3:17-18 — 33
3:19 — 32
3:20 — 95
18:27 — 36
22 — 98, 99
22:1-18 — 161
22:8 — 98, 99

Exodus
12:1-8 — 92
12:3 — 98
12:11-14 — 92
12:13 — 98
14:15-15:1 — 161
19:3 — 82
19:5-6 — 82
22:8 — 41

2 Samuel
13:19 — 24

1 Kings
5:31 — 108
19:9-13 — 8

Esther
4:1 — 25

Baruch
3:9-15 — 161
3:32-4:4 — 161

Job
2:8 — 25
7:16 — 39
11:13-15 — 40
13:3 — 37
19:18 — 38
30:19 — 36
34:33 — 39
38:2-3 — 37
38:4-5 — 37
39:19 — 37
39:26 — 37
40:4 — 37
40:9 — 37
42:2-3 — 37
42:6 — 37, 38, 39, 40, 41, 43
42:7 — 40
42:8 — 43

Psalms
116 — 109, 112
116:5 — 108
116:6 — 107
116:8 — 107
116:12-13 — 106
116:15 — 106, 107, 108
116:15-16 — 106
116:17-18 — 106

Proverbs
3:15 — 107

Isaiah
10:5 — 28
40-55 — 128
50-53 — 131
50:4-7 — 54
52:13 — 129
52:13-53:12 — 127
52-53 — 130, 132
53 — 129
53:5 — 128
54:5-14 — 161
55:1-11 — 161
61:1-3ab — 80
61:1-4 — 171
61:6a — 80
61:8b-9 — 80

Jeremiah
19:1-13 — 119
27:6 — 28

Lamentations
1:22 — 131
2:22 — 131
3 — 131, 132
3:31-32 — 132
5:22 — 131

Ezekiel
27:30 — 25
36:16-17a — 161
36:18-28 — 161

Daniel
9:3-5 — 25

Joel
2:12-18 — 26
2:28 — 171

Jonah		Luke		Romans	
3:6-9	25	1:68-79	151	3:22-25	159
		4:16-21	81	4:25	120
Zechariah		4:18-19	171	6:3-11	161
11:13	119	22:3-6	51	8:32	120
		22:7-38	51	10:6-8	167
New Testament		22:39-46	51		
Matthew		22:47-53	51	1 Corinthians	
6:1-6	26	22:54-71	51	1:23-26	109
6:16-18	26	22:61-62	159	11:23	120
25:34-35	157	23:1-25	51	15:5-6	169
25:40	157	23:13	76, 136		
26:14-16	51,	23:26-49	51	2 Corinthians	
	117	24:1-12	161	4:4	145
26:17-30	51	24:16	157	4:17-18	27
26:24	123	24:26	157	5:20-6:2	26
26:36-46	51	24:31	158	6:4-5	27
26:47-56	51				
26:56	159	John		Galatians	
26:57-68	51	10:17-18	53	2:20	120
26:75	159	13:1	89		
27:1-26	51	13:1-15	113	Ephesians	
27:4	119	13:1-17:26	51	4:7-11	167
27:9-10	119	13:34	92		
27:20	76	18:1	51	Philippians	
27:24-25	65	18:1-19:42	127,	2:5-7	145
27:25	61, 153		136	2:6-11	54
27:32-56	51	18:2-12	51	2:8-9	133, 137
28:1-10	161	18:13-27	51		
28:2-15	148	18:27	159	Hebrews	
		18:28-19:16	51	4:14	167
Mark		18:36	60	4:14-16	127,
14:10-11	51	19:14	136		133
14:12-16	89	19:14-15	76	5:7-9	127, 133
14:12-25	51	19:17-37	51	9:15	134
14:24	111	19:38	159	9:26	134
14:32-42	51	20:13	158		
14:43-50	51	20:15	158	1 Peter	
14:50	159	20:17	158, 167	3:18-21	148-49
14:53-65	51			3:22	167
14:72	159	Acts			
15:1-15	51	1:9-11	166	Revelation	
15:8-11	76	1:18	117	1:5-6	81, 82
15:21-40	51	1:18-19	118	1:5-8	81
16:1-7	161	1:20	123	5:9-10	82
16:8	166	2:1-47	171		
16:19	167				

SUBJECTS

Accusing Angel, 36
'ādām, 142
Adam and Eve, 32, 33-35, 149
Akedah (binding of Isaac), 93,
  98-102, 105, 161
Akiva ben Eliezer, 94, 102-3,
  105
Alsfeld Passion Play, 124-25
Alvarez of Cordova, 156
Angel of Death, 91, 93
annihilation, mass, xiii, 2, 22,
  23, 44, 46, 47
anti-intellectualism, 63, 65
antisemitism, ix, x, xiii, 17, 19,
  51, 77, 91, 174, 178, 179
appearances, resurrection, 147,
  162, 163, 164
Aquinas, Thomas, 144
Ascension, xv, 166-71
Ash Wednesday, 23-25
  and Book of Job, 42-44
  as day of sorting, 47, 48
  liturgical ritual of, xiii, 25-31
ashes
  in Ash Wednesday ritual, 24,
    29, 48
  in Genesis 3 and Job, 31
  of Holocaust victims, 21
  in Near Eastern story and
    ritual, 24-25
  as reminder of mortal nature,
    36
  See also dust; dust and ashes
Athanasius, 134-35
atonement, 106, 130
  death of Jesus as, 134, 135,
    136, 160
  models of, 159-61
Augustine, 34, 144
Auschwitz, 1-3, 7, 8, 13-19, 22,
  23, 28-31, 44, 48, 56, 69, 77,
  86, 92, 94, 96, 97, 106, 133,
  141, 146, 147, 171, 174
  Carmelite convent near, xii, xiii,
    1-13
  cross at, xii, xiii, 13-20, 174

Auschwitz-Birkenau, 14, 15, 16,
  21, 22
authenticity paradigm, 44-46

baptism, 161-62, 163
  of the dead, 5-6
Barré, Michael, 107
Belzec, 15, 22
Benedict XIV, Pope, xiv, 152
Berkovits, Eliezer, 30, 104
biblical literalism, 63, 65
biblical scholarship, Catholic, 58,
  60, 65, 66, 67, 68, 70
birkat hamazon, 84
bishops, American
  and Christian-Jewish relations,
    4, 178
  and the passion, 67, 77
bishops, Dutch: protest against
  Nazi policies, 7
Bonhoeffer, Dietrich, 136
Borzykowski, Tuvia, 87, 88
Boyarin, Daniel, 102, 103, 104
Bradley, Mamie Till, 139
Brown, Raymond E., 71-77, 113,
  114
Bultmann, Rudolf, 129

Caiaphas, 51, 59, 63, 65, 124-25
Caputo, John, 154, 159, 161,
  162, 166, 172
Cargas, Harry James, 1
Carmelites, at Auschwitz, 1-13
Catechism of the Catholic
  Church, 5, 34-35, 67, 144,
  145, 168
Catherine of Siena, 30, 156
Catholic theology: and God's will
  in history, 30
Catholicism
  and challenges posed by Holo-
    caust, vii
  on Jews and Judaism, xv, 4-5,
    14
  and supersessionism, 3-4
  traditionalist, 70

Catholic-Jewish relations, 1, 61,
    67-68
Celan, Paul, xiv, 152, 153
Chanina, Rabbi, 103
charity, acts of. See good deeds
Chelmno, xii, 15, 22
Chrism Mass, xiii, 79, 80-86
Christians
    as new people of God, 4, 54
    as new pharaoh, 94
    treatment of Jews by, 13, 14,
        16, 44, 54, 57, 65, 68, 99,
        100, 122, 175, 177
Chrysostom, John, 14, 123-24
Clement of Alexandria, 101
cognitive dissonance, 175, 176
compassion: and Holocaust, 97
concentration camps. See under
    individual camps: Auschwitz,
    Belzec, Chelmno, Majdanek,
    Sobibor, Treblinka
Connell, Martin F., 149
conversion, 3, 4, 7, 137, 178
    posthumous, 3, 5, 6
Council of Trent, 34
covenant
    between God and Israel, 4, 28,
        82, 112, 134
    with humanity, 57, 137, 138
    new, 54, 83, 91, 109, 111, 112,
        134
"Criteria for the Evaluation of
    Dramatizations of the Pas-
    sion," 67
cross
    at Auschwitz, 1, 13-20, 172
    of Jesus, 64
    reverencing of, 137
    symbolic meaning of, 16, 19-20
Cross Gospel, 72, 74, 77
Crossan, John Dominic, 69, 71-
    77, 109-10, 112
Curtis, John Briggs, 38, 39, 43
Cyprian, 85

Daisenberger, Joseph Alois, 58
dayenu, 94-95

death
    mass, 46, 47, 48
    meaning of, xiii, 23-24
    relation to life, 45, 46
    relation to sin, 33, 34, 35
    as way to glorify God, 102
death of Jesus
    and Akedah, 101
    and animal sacrifice, 133-34,
        159-60
    interpretation of, 53, 54
    Jewish responsibility for, 55,
        73, 122, 123, 136
    and Passover, 101
    as ransom, 159-60
    and Roman authorities, 75-76,
        122
    as sacrifice, 109, 159-60
    as saving event, 105-9
Dei Verbum ("Dogmatic Consti-
    tution on Divine Revelation"),
    67
Delaney, Carol, 101
Derrida, Jacques, 28
descent to the underworld, 148-
    50
The Devil's Arithmetic, 95, 96
Didache, and Eucharist, 110, 111
discipleship, of service, 80, 81, 85
Divino Afflante Spiritu, 66, 67
Docetism, 148
Donat, Alexander, 165
"the drowned" and "the saved,"
    141
Durkheim, Emile, 25
dust, 31-44. See also ashes
dust and ashes, 36-44

Easter faith, 162, 163, 164
Easter kerygma, 53, 147, 162
Easter liturgy, 158-61
Eichmann, Adolf, 28
El'azar, Rabbi, 103
Elliott, Charles, 144
Emerton, J. A., 108
empty tomb, 147, 148, 162, 163,
    164

Ephraim, Rabbi, 94, 98, 99
Epiphanius, 149
Eucharist, 109-13
and *birkat hamazon,* 84
and footwashing, 114
and Last Supper, 110-12

Fackenheim, Emil, 28-30, 147, 150
Farrow, Douglas, 172
Felstiner, John, 153
Finkelsztajn, Menachem, 17
Fitzmyer, Joseph, 169
footwashing, 113-15
Fourth Lateran Council, 50

Gaudium et Spes, 144
Gibson, Mel, xi, 57, 68-70, 126
reaction to scholarly critique of *The Passion of the Christ,* 58, 61, 62, 63, 64, 65
Gilbert, Martin, 21
Glatstein, Jacob, 100
Goebbels, Joseph, 47
Goldhagen, Daniel Jonah, 5
Good, Edwin M., 38, 39, 40, 42, 43
good deeds, 10-12, 28
Good Friday, 127-40
Gospel of Nicodemus, 149
Gospel of Peter, 72, 74, 77
gospels: and history, 51-52, 63, 68, 71-77
grace, cheap and costly, 136
Gradowski, Salmen, 48-49
Graham, Billy, 167
Greenberg, Irving, 23, 88-89
guilt: and responsibility, 73

Himmler, Heinrich, 22
history
God acting in, 97, 98
and God's will, 30
and gospels, 51-52, 63, 68, 71-74
and Last Supper, 110-12
Hitler, Adolf, 14, 28, 47, 84
at Oberammergau, 50

Holocaust
challenges posed by, vii
and Christian supersessionism, 138
and Christians, viii, 14, 153
and compassion, 97
and faith, 12-13
as God's punishment, 17, 28, 29
and Lamentations, 131
and loss, 170
and meaning of humanity, 146
official remembrance of, 88-89
and passion stories, 76
and Passover, 93-96, 115
and Pius XII, 3
as problem of history and God's will, 28-30
and silence, 8
and symbolic value of Auschwitz, 15, 16
Holy Spirit, sending of, 171
Holy Thursday, xiii, xiv, 78-116
as festival of pain, ix, 20, 175
Holy Week, post-Auschwitz interpretation of, 1, 174, 175
Hooker, Morna D., 129
Höss, Rudolf, 22
humanity, meaning of, 146-47

Ignatius, 149
image of God: in Jewish and Christian tradition, 142-47, 150, 161
incarnation: and salvation, 134-35, 160
Irenaeus, 149
Isaac: as martyr and type of Jesus, 101, 102
Iudaioi, identification of, 60

Jacobus de Voragine, 119-20
Jesus
execution by Romans, 17, 138
humanity of, 134-35
as image of God, 145
and Isaac, 101

Jesus (continued)
  Jewishness of, 57, 175
  as new Adam, 145
  as new High Priest, 83
  and Passover, 89, 92, 93
  resurrection appearances of,
    157-58
  significance of: for Christians
    and Jews, 176
  as Suffering Servant, 129-30
  stranger as, 156, 164
  submission to God of, 133
  Jewish identity, 96, 97, 98
  Jewish-Christian relations, 1, 69,
    177-79, 178
Jews
  attitude of Christians to, viii, ix
  conversion of, 3, 4, 7, 137, 178
  European: role of Catholics in
    destruction of, vii, viii
  hatred for, vii, ix, xii, 49, 50,
    56, 59, 175
  Judas and, 118, 119, 123-25
  and Passion plays, 56, 59
  and responsibility for death of
    Jesus, x-xii, 14, 16-17, 49,
    54-55, 59, 62-63, 73, 122,
    123, 130, 136, 139, 165, 174
  salvation of, 4-5
  treatment by Christians, 13, 14,
    16, 44, 54, 57, 65, 68, 99,
    100, 122, 175, 177
Job, Book of, 36-44
John the Almsgiver, 156
John of the Cross, 9, 10, 11
John Paul II, Pope, viii, 3, 7, 14,
    15, 18, 108, 167, 178
Judas Iscariot
  in Christian tradition, 117-27
  and Jews, xiv, 118, 119, 123,
    124, 125
  and Passion story, 121-25
Judas son of Hezekiah, 17
Julian of Eclanum, 33-34
Justin Martyr, 129

Kelly, J. N. D., 149

Kiddush haShem, 102, 104, 105
Kolbe, Maximilian, 18, 19
Korczak, Janusz, 78, 79, 80, 85

Lamentations, Book of, 131-33
Langmuir, Gavin I., 176-77
Lanzmann, Claude, xi, xii
Last Supper
  and Catholic Mass, 90-91
  and Eucharist, 110-12
  and history, 110, 111, 112
  and Passover, 89
Leo XIII, Pope, 58, 65
Levi, Primo, 141, 150
Levinas, Emmanuel, 13, 172
Levine, Amy-Jill, 64
Liguori, Alphonsus, 126
Linafelt, Tod, 131-32
Littell, Franklin, 91, 138
Liturgy of the Hours, 149, 151
loss, of Jesus, 170-73

Maccoby, Hyam, 119
Maimonides, 103, 143
Maisel, Rabbi, 87, 88, 89, 90
Majdanek, 21, 22, 88, 165
Marcian of Constantinople, 156
Martin of Tours, 156
martyrdom: in Jewish and Chris-
    tian tradition, xiv, 102-4, 112
Mass of the Lord's Supper, 87-
    116
Maundy Thursday, 92. See also
  Holy Thursday
Meier, John, 110-12
memory: and liturgy, 53, 54
Mengele, Joseph, 92
Michalowski, Zvi, 155-56
Miles, Jack, 38, 39, 41
ministry, models of, 80, 82-86
Modernism, Modernists, 66, 70
Monophysites, 146
mortality: and human nature, 34,
    35, 44
Mother Teresa, 157
multiple attestation, 73, 110
Muselmänner, 141, 142, 150

Musiel, Stanislaw, 18, 19
Muszynski, Archbishop Henryk, 13, 16

Nehemiah, Rabbi, 131
Nelson, Richard D., 134
Nestorians, 146
Neusner, Jacob, 16
Nostra Aetate ("Declaration on the Relationship of the Church to Non-Christian Religions"), 4
"Notes on the Correct Way to Present the Jews and Judaism in Preaching and Catechesis of the Roman Catholic Church," 67-68
Nuremberg laws, 19

Origen, 159, 160
Oshry, Rabbi Ephraim, 103, 104
Oswiecim. See Auschwitz
Ozick, Cynthia, xi

Paffenroth, Kim, 120-21
Palm Sunday liturgy, xiii, 52-56
parousia, 163, 166, 170, 172
Pascendi Dominici Gregis, 66, 70
The Passion of the Christ, xi, 57, 68, 69, 126
  scholarly critique of, 58, 62-67
passion of Jesus, in liturgy, 52-55
Passion narrative
  as history remembered, 75, 77
  as prophecy historicized, 75-77
Passion plays, 50, 57
  and antisemitism, 50-51
  Oberammergau, 57, 58, 61, 62
  portrayal of Jews in, 50, 56, 58, 59, 60
Passover
  and the Akedah, 99, 100, 101
  in Catholic and Jewish tradition, xiii, 88-95, 98, 115
  and death of Jesus, 101, 160-61
  and Jesus, 51, 89, 92, 93

  and Last Supper, 89
  and the Passion, 160-61
  Passover lamb, 92, 98, 99, 105, 109, 112, 160-61
Patterson, David, 8-10
Pawlikowski, John, 61
Pentecost, 168, 171
Pius X, Pope, 66, 70
Pius XII, Pope, 3, 66
plan of God, 44, 90
Polycarp, 104, 149
Pontius Pilate, 50, 60, 63, 64, 73-77, 120, 123, 126, 136, 138, 159
Porete, Marguerite, 11-12
prayer, 6, 9, 10, 13, 19, 24
priesthood
  of God's people, 82, 83
  of Jesus, xiii
  Jewish and Christian, xiii, 80, 82-86
  renewal of commitment to service, 79-80, 82-83
  sacrificial, 83, 84, 85
  of service, 83, 84
  and solidarity with the oppressed, 80, 81, 86
  and supersessionism, 80, 83, 84, 85, 86, 174
Providentissimus Deus, 65, 66
purgatory, 6

Q, 72

Rahner, Karl, ix, 4-5, 20, 35, 170-72
Rakover, Yosl, 12-13
Rashi, 108, 129-30, 142
redemption: and conversion, 137
Reproaches, 137-39, 174
resurrection, 53-54, 147, 148, 166-71
revelation, views of, 70-71
reward-punishment schema, 28, 29, 31, 44
Rilke, Rainer Maria, 45
Roman authorities: and crucifixion of Jesus, 17, 122, 138

Rubenstein, Richard, 28-29, 175, 176
Ruether, Rosemary, 178

sacrifice, animal: and death of Jesus, 129, 133-34
salvation
  and incarnation, 134-35, 160
  universal, 4-5
Satan, ransom paid to, 159-60
Schillebeeckx, Edward, 84, 85, 162, 163, 164, 168
Schüssler Fiorenza, Elisabeth, 82, 85
Sebastian, Mihail, 56, 57
Sereny, Gitta, 21
silence, 8, 13, 154, 158
sin, 33-35
slavery, 92, 94, 137, 138, 144
Sloyan, Gerard, 52, 57-58, 60, 62, 68, 122, 129, 160
Sobibor, 21, 22
Solomon bar Simson, 100, 103
Solomon ben Isaac. See Rashi
sorting myth, 47, 48
Spiegel, Shalom, 98
Stangl, Franz, 22, 28, 146
Stein, Edith, 7
Stookey, Laurence Hull, 168
Suffering Servant, 127-33
supersessionism, xiv, 4, 80, 83, 84, 85, 86, 91, 106, 112, 138, 160, 174, 178
Swidler, Leonard, 57-60, 62, 68
Switon, Kazimierz, 15
Szereszewska, Helena, 17

Talmud: in Jewish community, 177, 178
Tatum, W. Barnes, 56
Tenebrae
  Celan poem, 152-53
  and Jews, xiv, 152
  liturgy, xiv, 151-54
Teresa of Avila, 9, 11
Tertullian, 149
Theodore of Mopsuestia, 33-34

Thomas, John Christopher, 114-15
Till, Emmett, 139
Tolstoy, Leo, 156
Torah, 12, 13, 33
Treblinka, 15, 21, 22, 28, 79, 87, 88, 146
triumphalism, xv, 14, 90, 174

undecidability, 154, 159, 166, 172
Urban II, Pope, 24

Vatican, and World War II, viii
Vatican Council II
  and historical-critical scholarship, 65
  on Jews, 60

Warsaw Ghetto, 12, 78, 79, 87, 88, 89, 165
Way of the Cross, 125-26
"We Remember: A Reflection on the Shoah," 14, 178
Weiss, Avraham, 14-15
Wiesel, Elie, 97, 98, 104
  and Holocaust as Christian problem, viii, 115
  and human experience of faith, 30
  interpretation of Job by, 40-43
  on sacrifice and salvation, 101, 102, 112
  on speaking about the Holocaust, 8
Wiesenthal, Simon, x, xi
will of God, 4, 28-30, 53, 71, 73, 81, 104, 133, 166, 175
Willey, Patricia Tull, 131
Wirth, Christian, 146
Word of God
  Jesus as, 135
  Torah as: in Judaism, 13
Wyschogrod, Edith, xiii, 44-47

yāqār, 107-8